IMAGES
of America

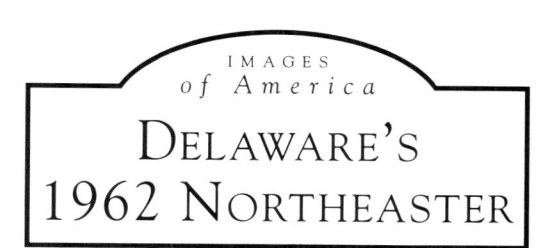

DELAWARE'S
1962 NORTHEASTER

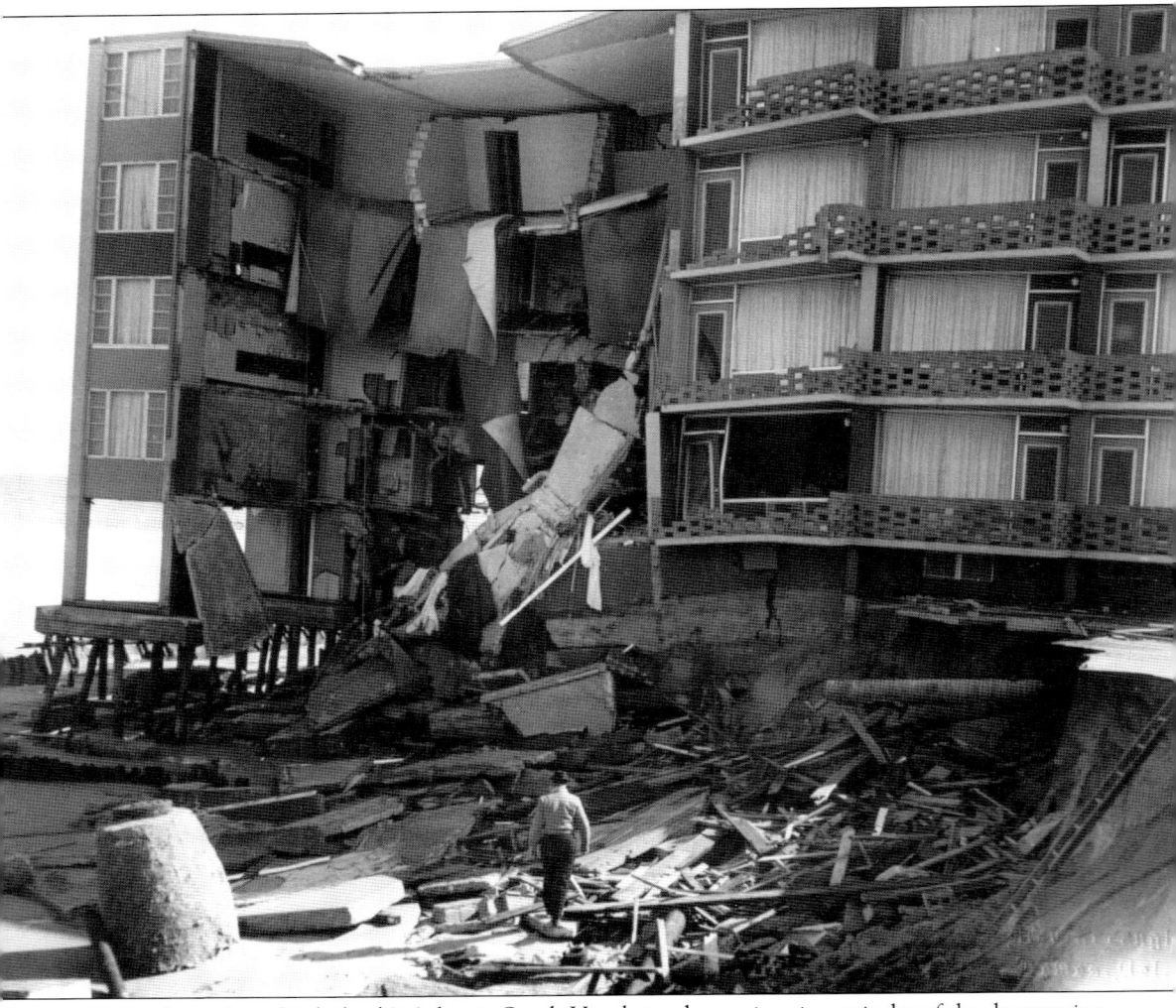

Ruined remains of Rehoboth's Atlantic Sands Hotel stand as an iconic reminder of the devastating force of the storm's winds, waves, and tides. The scale of wreckage and destruction is clearly illustrated not only by the person inspecting the damage, but also by the ladder used to descend from street level to the beach (bottom right) and by the manhole cover (bottom left). (Courtesy Colonel McGarraugh via Marna Cupp.)

ON THE COVER: In early March 1962, a powerful northeaster relentlessly battered Delaware's coast over the course of three days and five high tide cycles. Although this photograph was taken in the storm's aftermath, it clearly illustrates the dramatic impact of storm surge and 20–30 foot waves on Rehoboth's boardwalk and beachfront businesses. (Courtesy Norman Rossiter.)

IMAGES of America
DELAWARE'S 1962 NORTHEASTER

Wendy Carey, Tony Pratt,
and Kimberly McKenna

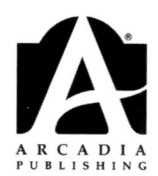

ARCADIA
PUBLISHING

Copyright © 2014 by Wendy Carey, Tony Pratt, and Kimberly McKenna
ISBN 978-1-4671-2262-7

Published by Arcadia Publishing
Charleston, South Carolina

Printed in the United States of America

Library of Congress Control Number: 2014939831

For all general information, please contact Arcadia Publishing:
Telephone 843-853-2070
Fax 843-853-0044
E-mail sales@arcadiapublishing.com
For customer service and orders:
Toll-Free 1-888-313-2665

Visit us on the Internet at www.arcadiapublishing.com

To all who endured the devastation, responded, and rebuilt the Delaware coast, and to those who continue working towards a more sustainable and resilient Delaware.

Contents

Acknowledgments ... 6

Introduction ... 7

1. The Delaware Coast before the Storm ... 9
2. Storm Clouds on the Horizon ... 17
3. Coastal Floods and Fury ... 25
4. Widespread Wreckage ... 57
5. Changing the Face of the Coast ... 87
6. Response, Recovery, and Resiliency ... 99
7. Lasting Risks and Vulnerabilities ... 119

Bibliography ... 127

Acknowledgments

The authors wish to provide a special expression of gratitude to all the Delaware residents who shared their photographs and memories with state and local historical societies. These recollections and images reflect not only the hardships endured during the storm, but also the enduring resiliency of the response at an individual, community, and statewide level. Randy Goss and the Delaware Public Archives provided valuable guidance and information regarding the state's extensive collection of 1962 storm history. Many other individuals, communities, and organizations were also very generous and cooperative in sharing their experiences and photographs and are listed as follows: Marna Cupp for the Colonel McGarraugh photographs; Norman Rossiter, the Rossiter family, and Richard Travers; Michael DiPaolo, Lewes Historical Society, City of Lewes; Nancy Alexander and Joshua Smith, Rehoboth Beach Museum, City of Rehoboth Beach; Barbara Dougherty, Town of Dewey Beach; Cliff Graviet, Town of Bethany Beach; Mary Suazo, South Bethany Historical Society, Town of South Bethany; and Mary Pat Kyle, Town of Fenwick Island. Much of the detailed chronology of the storm as it unfolded, as well as specific quotations from those with firsthand experience of the event, response, and recovery were obtained from March 1962 newspaper accounts and reports.

We also wish to acknowledge the general assistance of Lisa Dorey, Delaware Sea Grant College Program, as well as review comments provided by Katy O'Connell and Teresa Messmore, Delaware Sea Grant Environmental Public Education Office. Delaware's Department of Natural Resources and Environmental Control (DNREC) provided extensive resources, materials, and knowledge about the Delaware coast before, during, and after the storm. Appreciation is also extended to the University of Delaware Sea Grant College program for support of initiatives such as this that focus on providing assistance to communities throughout Delaware as they tackle common problems and become engaged in effective adaptation and hazard mitigation planning, action, and activities.

Introduction

Delaware's 1962 Northeaster, the state's coastal storm of record, struck from March 6 to 8, 1962. Never again have storm tides reached such high levels, and no storm since 1962 has resulted in as much destruction to life and property along Delaware Bay, the Inland Bays, or Delaware's Atlantic coast.

Also known as "The Ash Wednesday Storm," "The Great Atlantic Coast Storm," and "The Great Storm of March," this northeaster hit with little warning and without historic precedent. Lasting through five high tides and generating waves as high as 20 to 40 feet, this formidable force of nature pushed the Atlantic Ocean onto the Delaware coast with a fury. The onslaught of waves and tidal action weakened and undermined even the most permanent shoreline structures, resulting in structural damage and collapse.

Over 50 years ago, development along the Delaware coast was relatively sparse by today's standards. Beachfront cottages, many at ground level on concrete block foundations, were built without the expectancy of huge waves washing completely over barrier beaches. The unusually high wind-driven tides carried the breaking waves inland to reach buildings and structures that ordinarily would have been beyond the reach of the surf. Boardwalks, houses, and other structures were destroyed on sites where they had been safe for many decades.

Prior to March 1962, few individuals could have imagined the extent of damage and destruction resulting from flooding that caused the undermining and toppling of shorefront properties and public facilities. In Delaware alone, private and public property damage estimates exceeded $70 million (equivalent to approximately $547 million in 2014), personal property losses were estimated at $20 million (equivalent to approximately $156 million in 2014), and additional damages were incurred by the agricultural industry and others through disruption of electrical service and normal activities.

As storm waves swept over the beach and dunes, sand was moved from the oceanfront beach to the back bays. Huge waves eroded the beaches, pounded the shore, and flattened the dunes, continuously battering coastal areas for three days. Sand that had been held in beach and dune systems surged landward with the encroaching storm surf. The storm washed vast quantities of sand inland, depositing it on highways and in and around homes. One of the first major efforts after the storm was to remove sand from roadways and yards so that normal functions could be resumed.

What is remembered most about this storm is the tragic loss of life, the destruction of homes and businesses, and roadways buried under tons of sand. The most catastrophic damage resulted from the sea breaking over the dunes and through the barrier beach, completely obliterating everything in its path—homes, utilities, roads, and vehicles. As the beaches eroded, rows of houses were undermined and collapsed. The high tides and continuous pounding of the waves caused extensive flooding in communities, with water levels rising three to six feet above street level.

Many communities along the Kent and Sussex shores of Delaware Bay from Pickering Beach to Lewes reported floodwater depths exceeding four and a half feet. Damages to beaches and dunes were extensive in these areas, and homes were washed away. Communities fronting the Inland Bays' shorelines suffered similar damages. Oak Orchard recorded two to three feet of floodwaters with waves up to four feet rolling across Rehoboth Bay.

Along the Atlantic coast, boardwalks in Bethany Beach and Rehoboth Beach were pulverized. Buildings that had fronted on the sea for over half a century were demolished. A total of 1,932 homes sustained damage from widespread tidal flooding in Dewey Beach, Bethany Beach, South Bethany, and Fenwick Island. Wave action destroyed 28 of 29 oceanfront homes in Bethany, as well as every oceanfront home in South Bethany.

The ocean swept straight through to the bay in Dewey, South Bethany, and Fenwick, and the undeveloped land in between suffered similar fates. Ocean waves carried sand and debris with them as they traveled down the streets and through yards. The coastal highway, Route 14, was rendered impassable because of flooding, breaching, and deposited sand.

The cost of recovery was unlike anything the state had experienced before. Private property loss, much of it uninsured (there was no federal flood insurance at the time), and public infrastructure costs were at a record high. Additional costs of the storm included casualties suffered by power companies, telephone and telegraph companies, gas companies, water and sewage treatment companies, and the costs of debris removal, combating health hazards, evacuation and relief to flood victims, losses to oyster grounds and clam beds, and policing to prevent looting.

This slow-moving, late-winter coastal storm was unusual in its development, composition, and behavior. Two low-pressure systems formed off the East Coast, held in place by a high-pressure system that was stationary over eastern Canada. The high-pressure system stalled the forward movement of the coastal storm, resulting in the generation of record-setting winds, waves, and tides. The funneling of wind between the Canadian high and the East Coast low produced northeast winds that blew across 1,000 miles of ocean before striking the Atlantic seaboard. Estimates of deep-water waves off the Delaware coast were reported to be 40 feet in height, and breaking waves along the coast in Delaware's surf zone reached heights estimated between 20 and 30 feet.

Steady winds of gale force (35–45 miles per hour) from the northeast, with gusts up to 70 miles per hour, resulted in a continuously elevated tidal water level (storm surge) of three to five feet above normal. The magnitude of the waves and tides produced by this rare meteorological event was further amplified because these tides were exceptionally high lunar (or spring) tides. In fact, the high tide on March 6, 1962, remains the highest ever recorded at Breakwater Harbor at the mouth of Delaware Bay.

Exceptionally high tides accompanying the storm occurred for four to five successive high tides, raising spring tides to record levels. The combination of high winds, waves, and tides created enormous seas, which pounded savagely at Delaware's shore, changing the face of the coastline.

What if a similar storm were to strike today? Would the state have the same problems now as it did then? The answer is "yes" in some respects and "no" in others. Probably the biggest concern is the increase in development and population along our coastline—more structures and people are at risk.

Although there are more housing units along the Delaware coast now compared to 1962, it is important to remember that knowledge of coastal processes (erosion and storm impacts), building construction practices, and building code implementation have all improved greatly during the last half century, as has the ability to predict storms many more days out. For example, minimum base flood elevation requirements have been established, homes are no longer built on concrete block or slab foundations in flood zones, and federal and state investments have been made towards storm damage reduction projects.

The population along the coast has increased, but today's residents are much more aware of associated risks and are better prepared for storms of this magnitude. Storm warning systems are far better than those of 1962, and structures are built to be much more resistant to storms.

Coastal storms will always pose a threat to Delaware's communities. The keys to safety are improved development and zoning and construction practices, along with a sensible response by the public to warnings when they are issued. Risk can be minimized through increased awareness, preparation, and preparedness.

One

THE DELAWARE COAST BEFORE THE STORM

Why is society so attracted to the coast? Do the open vistas, sound of crashing waves, soft sand, and relaxing vibe fulfill some deep human need? And what is it about the ocean that inspires humanity to think beyond the present day to preserving the environment for future generations.

Summer visitors to Delaware's shoreline might believe that the coast is stable and unchanging, but in reality Delaware's beaches, dunes, and adjacent ecosystems are actually dynamic features, shifting constantly in response to winds, waves, and currents. Storms can have a profound effect on those natural environments and within a few days, even within hours, vast amounts of sand can be moved—taking away the wide sandy beach of the summer and replacing it with eroded dunes and narrowed beaches.

Delaware's Atlantic and Bay shorelines have been shaped by coastal storms and sea-level rise long before human occupation and the establishment of the shore as a tourist destination. During the last ice age (about 15,000 years ago), the shoreline was more than 100 miles east of today's position and more than 340 feet below present sea level. Delaware's resilient coastal systems have migrated landward and upward to keep pace with the rising sea. This is why marsh deposits or ancient tree stumps are found on beaches today as former coastal systems are exposed and eroded. And they are geologically young features, having formed about 2,000 to 5,000 years ago.

Prehistoric storm events were important to the evolution of the shoreline. They eroded the headlands, creating and closing new breaches and inlets that brought sediment to build up the back barriers and marshes. The coast today displays the scars from some of the past storms by displaying irregular splay and overwash fan patterns along a generally smooth shoreline. The shoreline's landward migration is a natural response to storms. Longtime residents are well aware of a storm's impact, either by having lived through major events or hearing about them from news reports or firsthand accounts. Storms are a way of life in coastal Delaware—sometimes feared but always respected.

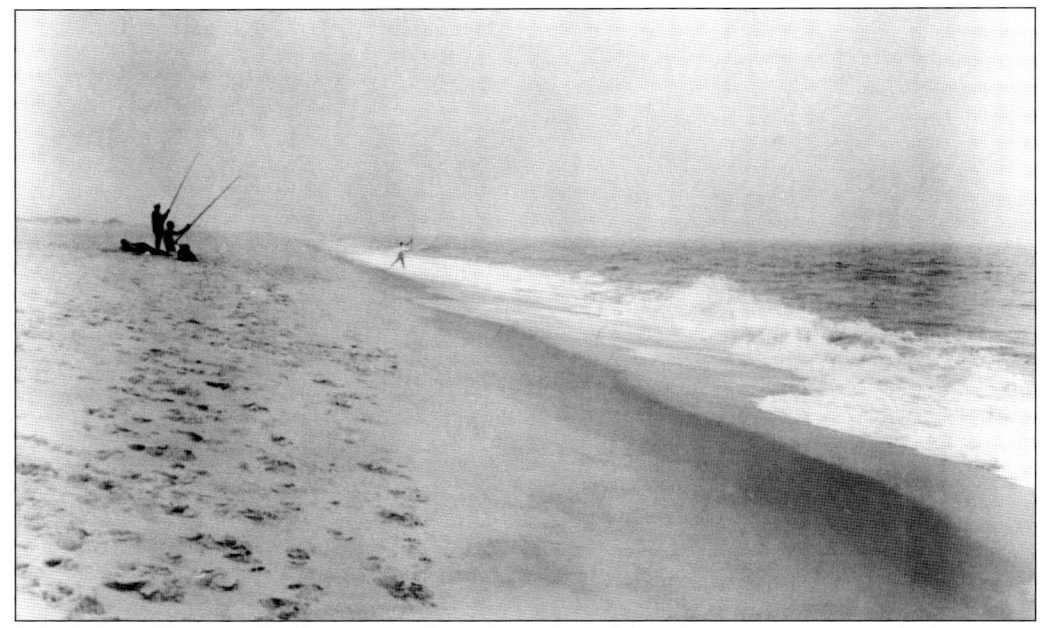

This July 1956 view of Delaware Seashore State Park (above) is representative of what many consider to be normal beach conditions along the coast. Waves, storm-driven or not, play an important role in changing the coastal landscape by continuously moving water and sand along the shore or back and forth between the coast and surf zone. In Delaware, waves are primarily the result of wind blowing over the water, with faster winds creating higher waves and greater impacts to the shoreline. Waves from heavy surf can cut into the beach face, creating erosional scarps, as is seen in the March 1960 photograph (below). With calm wave conditions, these areas can repair naturally over time. But sometimes the event is so severe that there is not enough sand for the beaches and dunes to bounce back, making human intervention necessary. (Both, courtesy Delaware DNREC.)

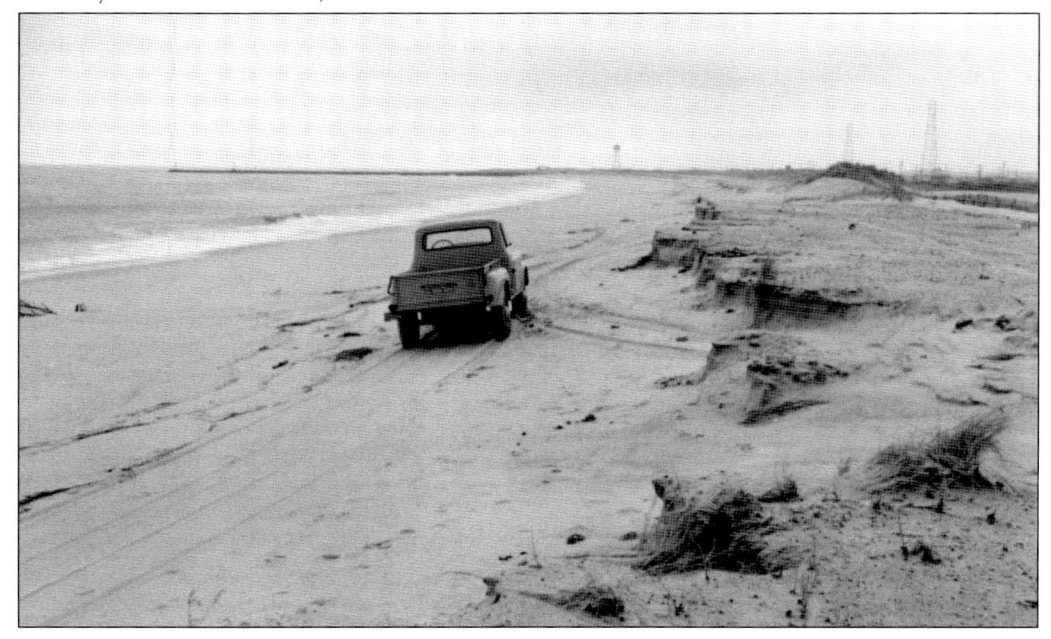

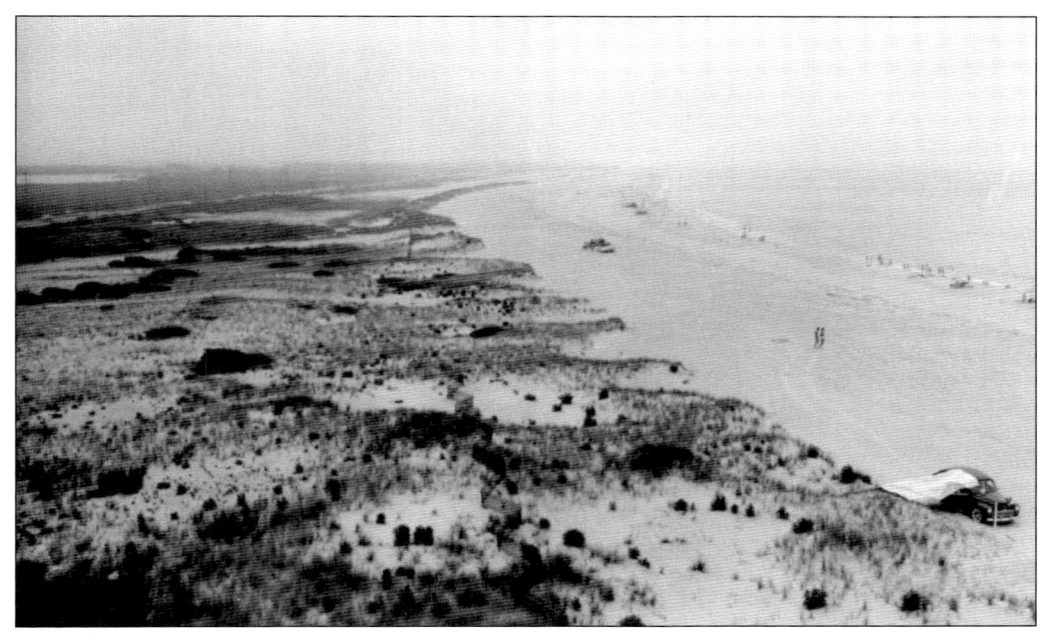

Natural dunes and enhancements such as dune fencing help trap sand that blows from the beach. Sand dunes are nature's buffer during storms. They protect landward structures and provide sediment to the beach during periods of high tides and waves. Some visitors at Delaware Seashore State Park on July 4, 1958, braved driving on the soft sandy beach or along the edge of the dunes. (Courtesy Delaware DNREC.)

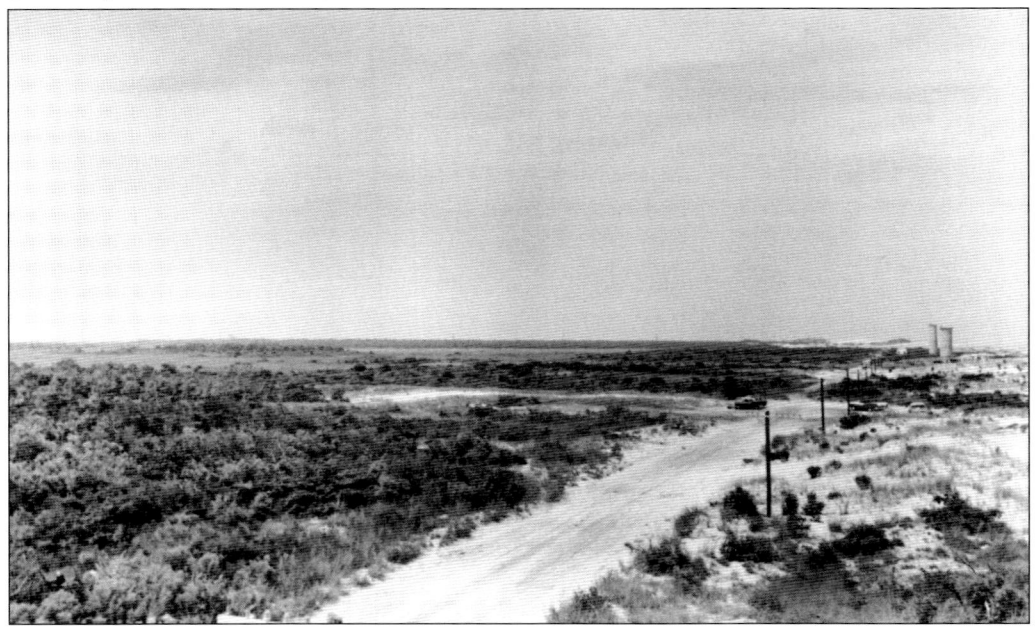

The World War II watchtowers near Gordon Pond were located behind sparse dunes in August 1960. This area of the Cape Henlopen spit complex has the highest erosion rate of the Delaware Atlantic coast. The Great Dune (northwest of the watchtowers) is a shore-perpendicular sand dune that formed as a result of deforestation for construction of the Lewes Harbor inner breakwater between 1829 and 1831. (Courtesy Delaware DNREC.)

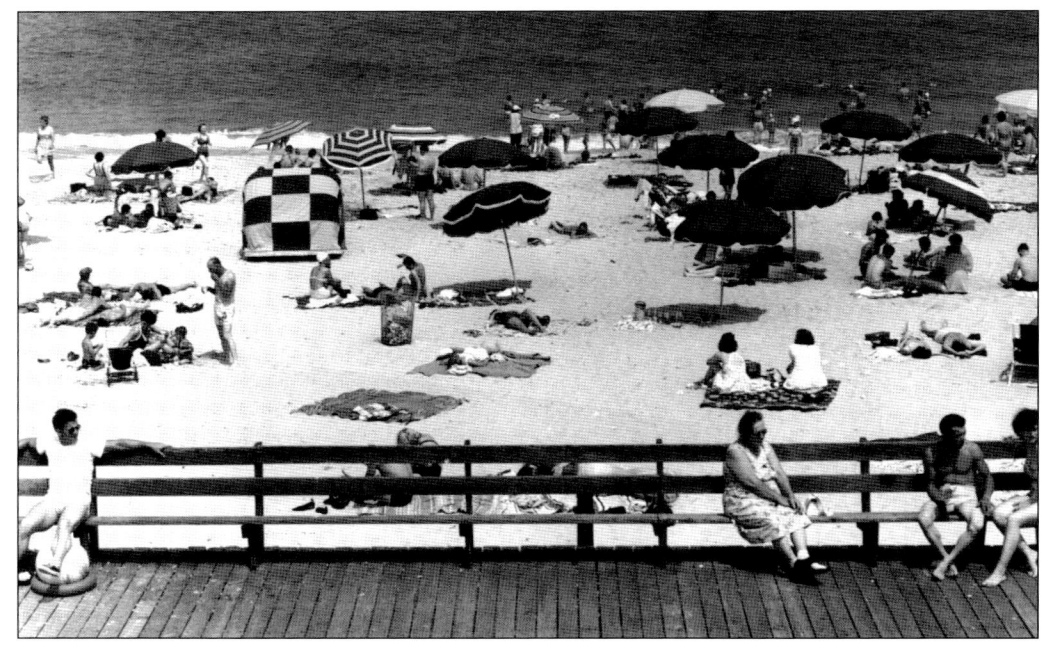

The communities of Rehoboth Beach (above) and Bethany Beach (below) were originally established as Christian summer retreats around the end of the 19th century, though visits to the Delaware shoreline increased following World War II. As the communities along the shoreline developed, dunes were not thought of as providing shore protection and typically were leveled seaward of the boardwalk to expand the narrow beaches and make more room for sunbathers. A warm June day in 1950 brought crowds to the beach in Rehoboth and people-watchers to the boardwalk while swimmers braved the early-summer water temperatures. The shore-perpendicular groins at Bethany Beach (seen here on July 4, 1959) were constructed in the mid- to late 1930s for the purpose of trapping sand and keeping the beach intact. (Above, courtesy Delaware Public Archives; below, courtesy Delaware DNREC.)

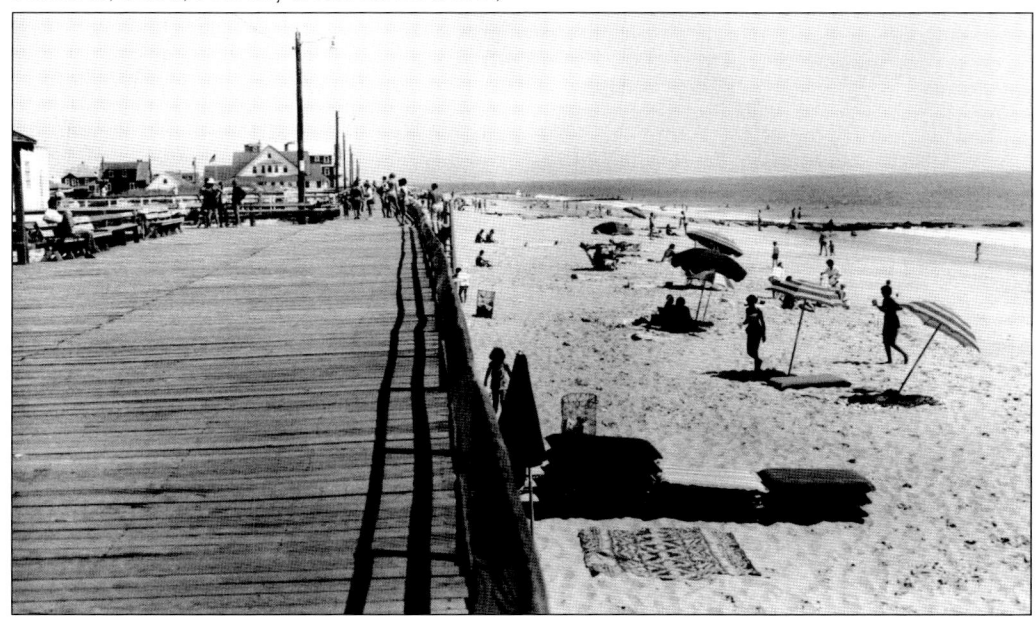

As seen in Broadkill Beach (June 1957), groins (shore-perpendicular structures that are often called jetties) were constructed to deflect waves and trap sand to build up or stabilize the dynamic beach. At that time, groins were usually not designed with detailed information on waves, currents, or sediment budget. They may actually cause erosion on adjacent beaches by not allowing enough sand to be carried along the shoreline. (Courtesy Delaware DNREC.)

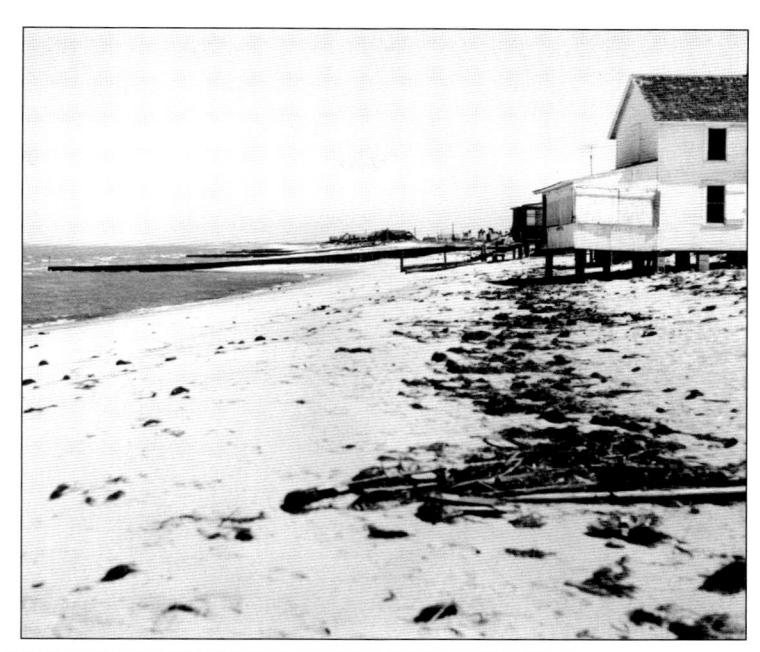

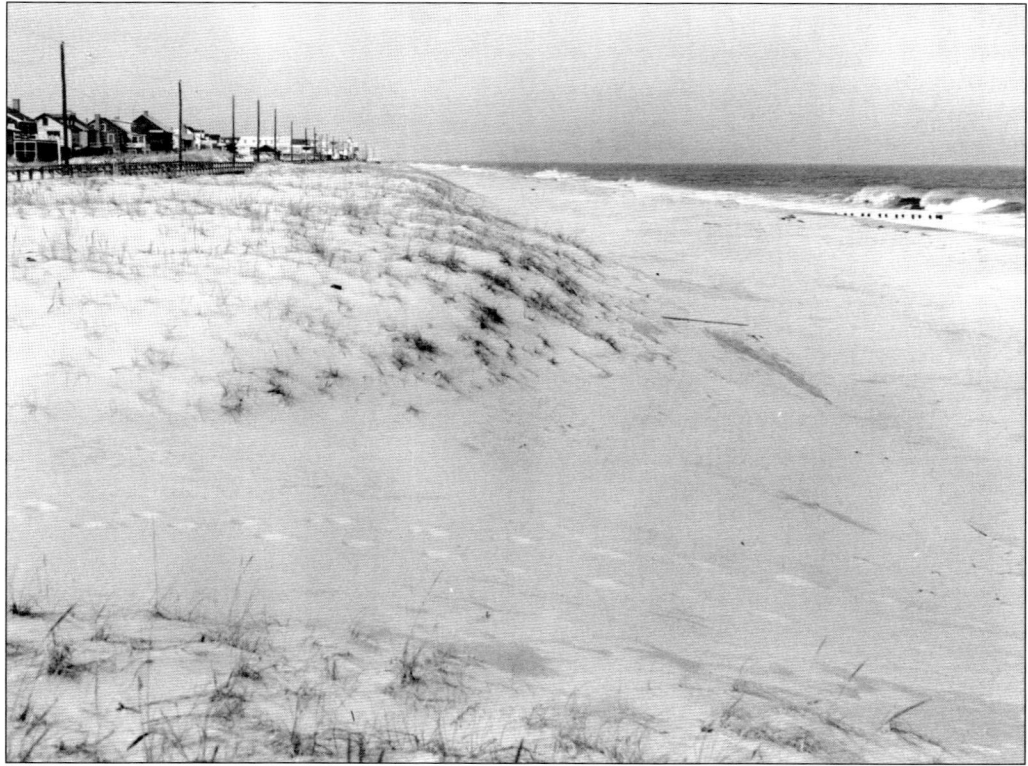

This photograph shows a winter beach in Rehoboth (February 15, 1962) just a few weeks before the storm. Note the low dune profile, sparse vegetation, and a relatively narrow, dry beach. The low area between the dunes was used for pedestrian beach access; less than three weeks later, however, it became the weak spot for channeling the storm's waves and surge from the ocean to homes that lined the shoreline. (Courtesy Delaware DNREC.)

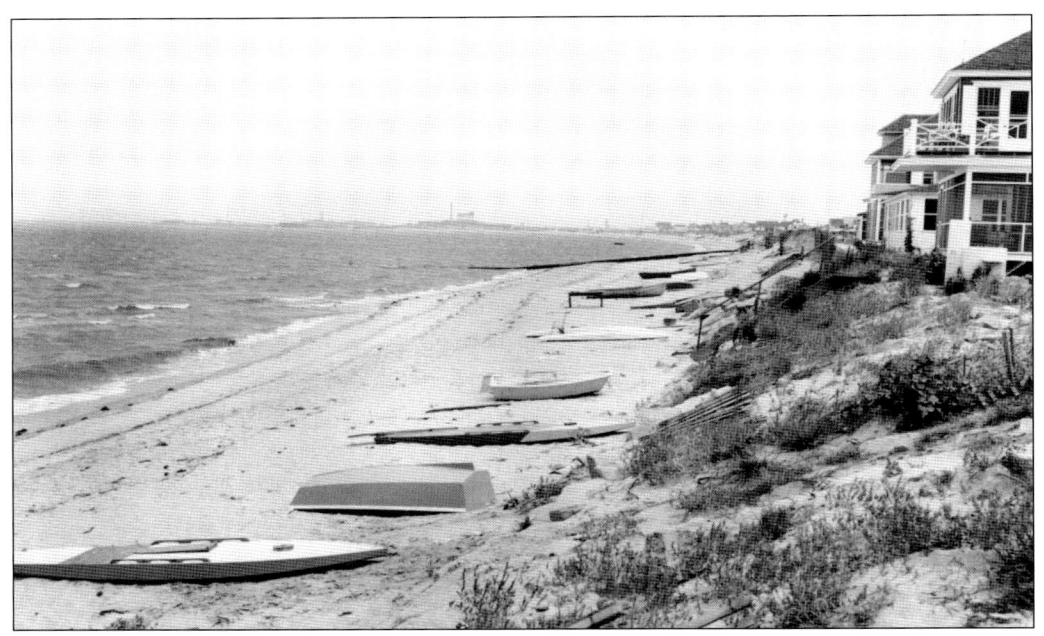

Narrow beaches and limited-sized dunes are typical features of bay (or estuarine) beaches. While shielded from the Atlantic Ocean by Cape Henlopen, Lewes Beach (seen here on August 2, 1956) is vulnerable to northeast storms, which can generate large waves on Delaware Bay. This area also suffers from long-term shoreline retreat that is influenced by Roosevelt Inlet and the breakwater in Breakwater Harbor. (Courtesy Delaware DNREC.)

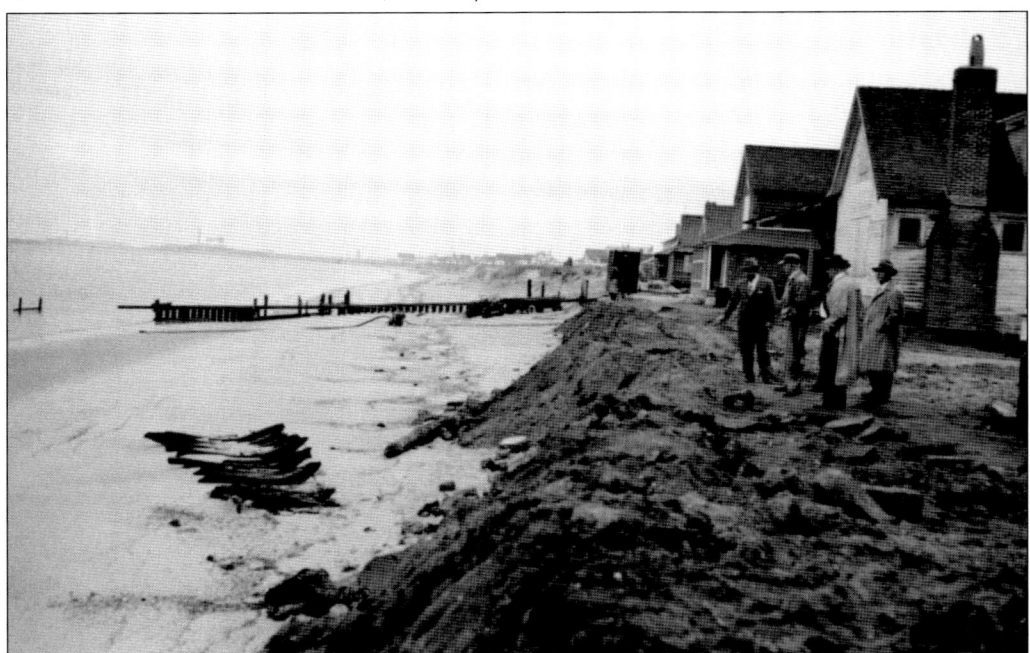

Storms are a way of life along coastal Delaware. Two months after the above photograph was taken, a storm removed sand from the beach at Lewes, lowered the beach elevation, and eroded the limited dune system. Occasionally, rapid response actions, such as bringing in fill, are used to protect the homes from further damages. (Courtesy Delaware DNREC.)

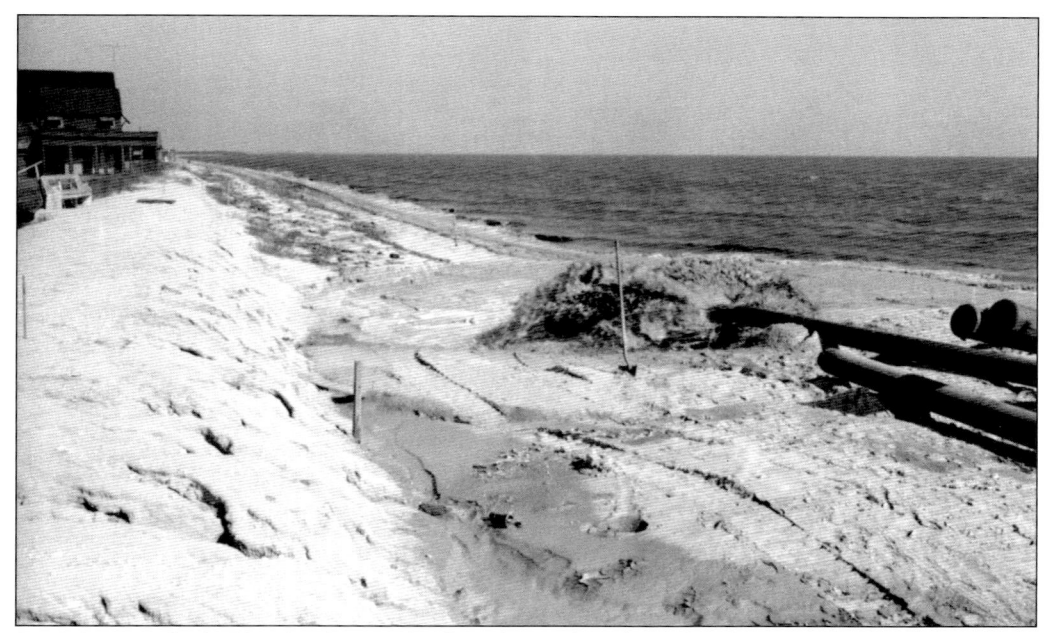

In 1961, a total of 165,000 cubic yards of sand was placed on Slaughter Beach by dredging from an offshore sand source. Federal, state, and local managers prefer beach nourishment for shoreline protection and fighting erosion because this method adds sand to the beach-dune system whereas a structure such as a rock revetment or shore-perpendicular groin (jetty) does not add sand to the eroding beach system. (Courtesy Delaware DNREC.)

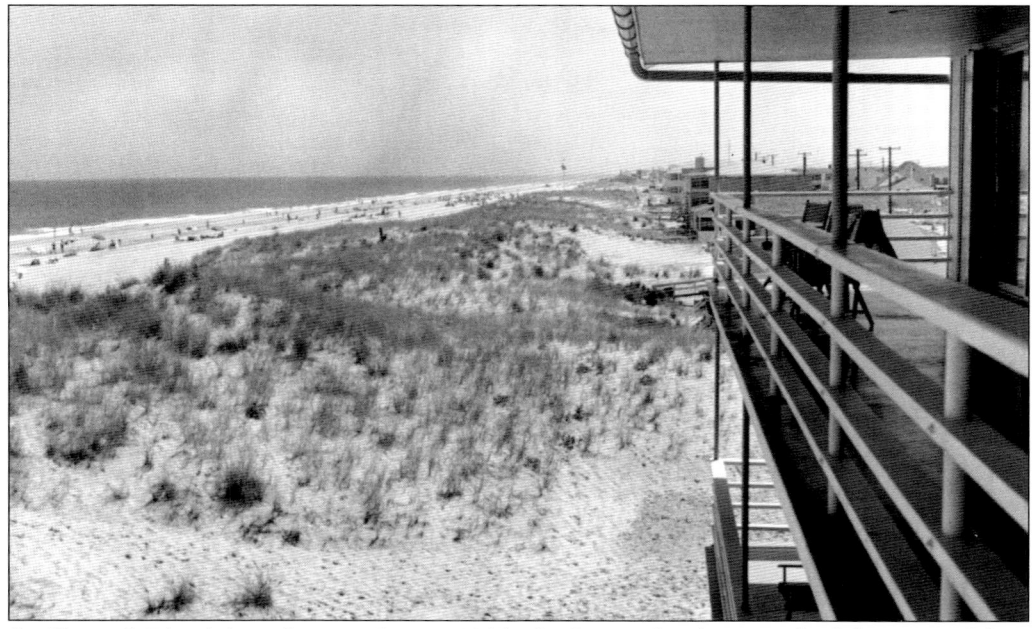

On Fenwick Island (seen here in August 1961), the Pepper family created subdivisions of their lands that kept the lots landward of the dunes and the dunes remained state property. Was this good planning or dumb luck? This alternative provided space between structures and storm waves and allowed the dunes to grow over time, which, in turn, provided additional protection and expanded the habitat for flora and fauna to thrive. (Courtesy Delaware DNREC.)

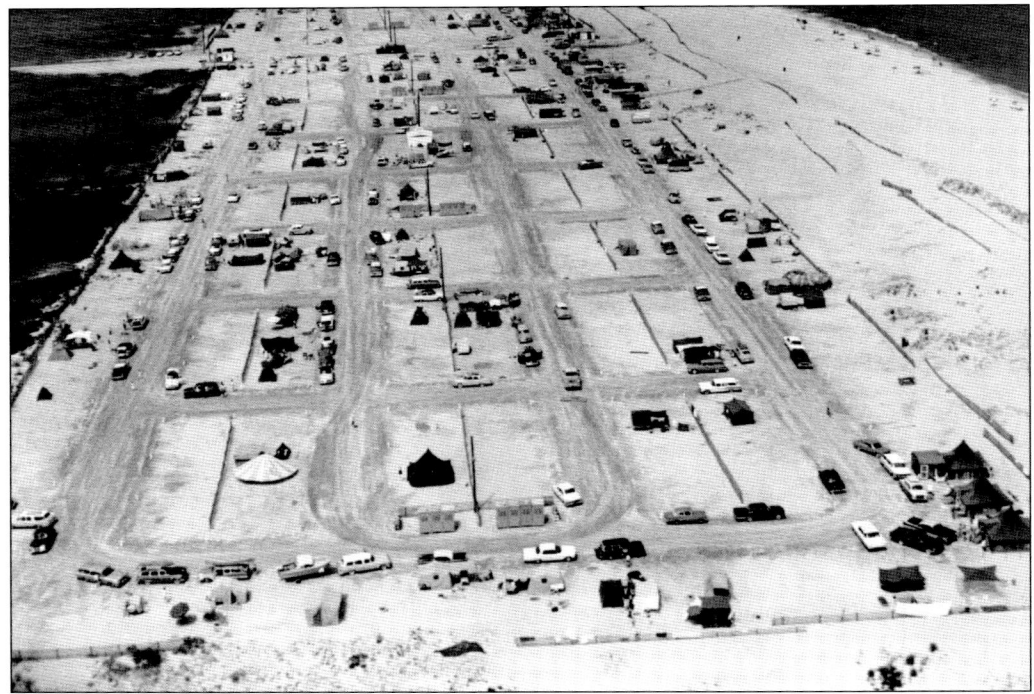

Campsites at Key Box Road (above on September 4, 1961) in Delaware Seashore State Park provided popular short-term vacation spots for beach visitors. This area was managed as a campground and not much thought was given to dune protection. Note the absence of a protective dune. Certain areas consisting of well-packed, fine-grained sand along the bayside of the park (below on July 17, 1956) offered easy access to Rehoboth Bay for fishing and water-based activities. These sandy areas are common along the backside of the barrier and were created by either former tidal inlets or as a result of storms where elevated waves and tides carried the sands across the barrier beach and deposited them into the bay. (Both, courtesy Delaware DNREC.)

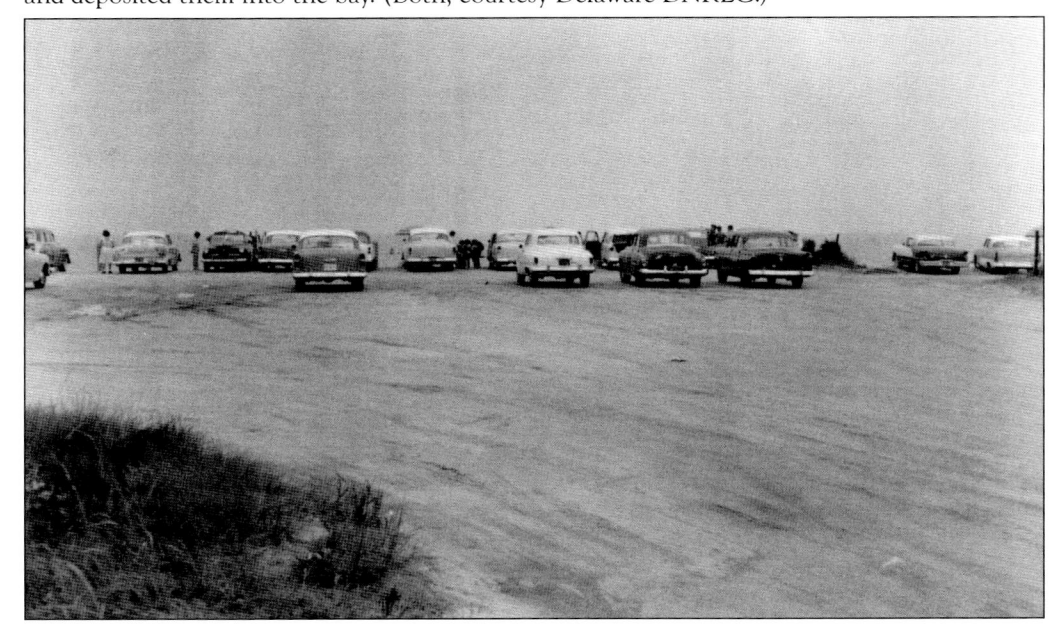

Two

Storm Clouds on the Horizon

The years following World War II were full of great prosperity, national economic growth, expanding families, greater use of personal automobiles, and the move toward family vacations. The result was the beginning of a growth explosion in resort communities along the coast. Towns had been established many years earlier, but a large uptick in development began shortly after the war ended. Large plats of land were subdivided into building lots, and towns from Rehoboth to Ocean City, Maryland, began to grow. Beach vacations offered just what young families in the 1950s were seeking—warm sun; cool, clean ocean water to bathe in; and an escape from the city and the hectic pace of the rapidly expanding corporate life of urban post–World War II America.

Life on the coast seemed idyllic. Calm and restful summer months at the beach allowed one to escape from the increasingly fast pace of work during the remainder of the year. For many families, beach vacations became the focal point of the year. Building lots were created on land that only a few decades earlier the State of Delaware was barely able to transfer into private ownership due to the low expectation of a return on the investment. But in the 1950s, houses were built in response to the growing demand for a vacation spot. The developing beach-based tourism industry translated into jobs and increasing property values that are strong and expanding even today. But there was little experience about how to build safely on a storm-prone coast.

On the weekend before the Great Storm, visitors to and residents of Delaware beach towns were likely looking at properties to purchase, enjoying a meal at a local restaurant, watching television, or taking in a movie. While families were enjoying the coast, an early-March storm was developing.

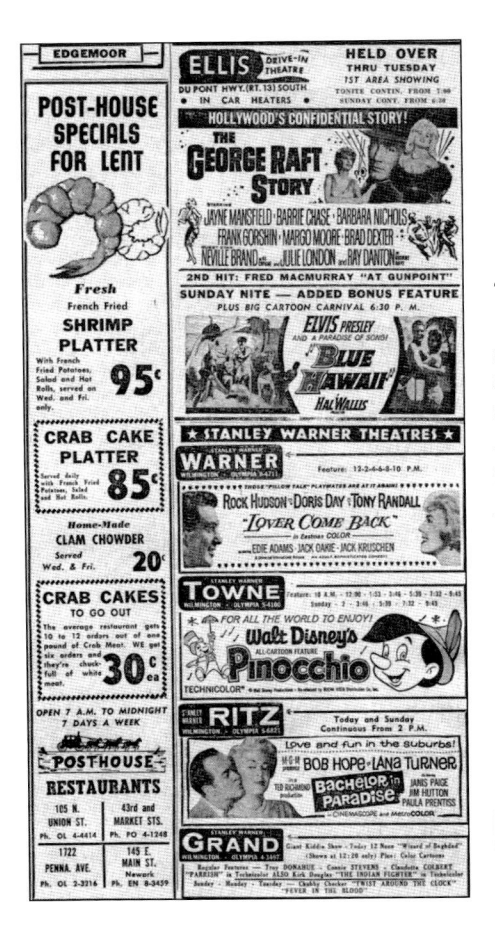

To set the stage for what life was like in March 1962, it is interesting to recall what things cost and what Delawareans were watching at the movies or on television. Technologies, economies, and daily lives were very different in 1962. The Ash Wednesday Storm struck the Delaware coast during a Tuesday through Thursday time frame. If a tourist was out on the town the weekend before the storm, his dinner and a movie date might have included a shrimp platter for 95¢ and watching *Blue Hawaii*, starring Elvis Presley, at the drive-in theater. Staying in on Saturday night, a television choice at 8:00 would have been *Hootenanny*, *Joey Bishop*, or *The Defenders*. People may have been excited to learn that Wilt Chamberlain of the Philadelphia Warriors scored a record-setting 100 points in a single game. (Both, courtesy Delaware Public Archives.)

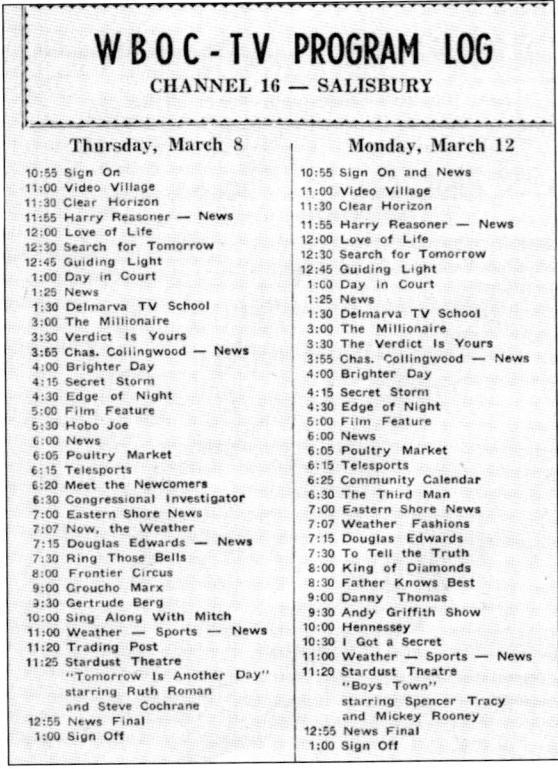

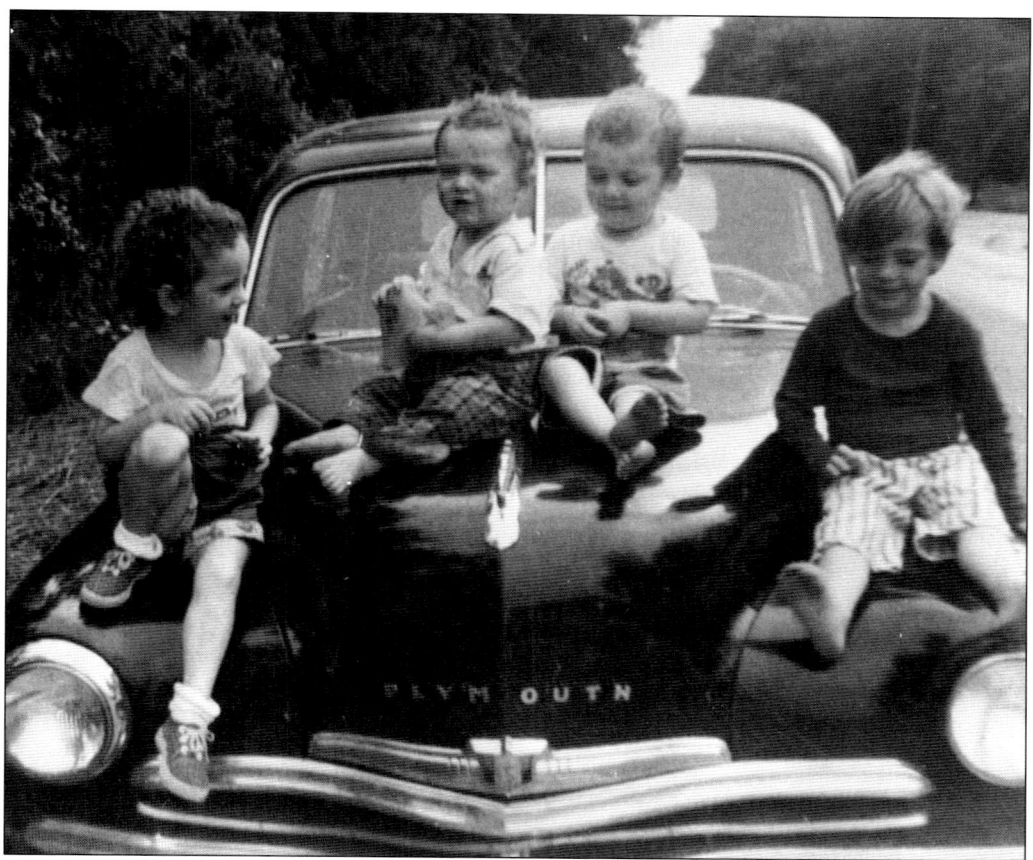

The world was different, too, in March 1962. Headlines in Delaware daily newspapers highlighted tension between President Kennedy and Soviet leader Krushchev over the atomic arms race and a proposed test ban treaty. Two Communist Party "American Red" officials were arrested for not registering the party with the government under the Subversive Activities Control Act. Freedom Riders were expected to make stops at three eastern shore communities. In their own way, social and economic realities alike were equally challenging in 1962. Delawareans in the market for a new car could have purchased a Plymouth Belvedere for $2,342. A four-bedroom oceanfront beach house in Rehoboth would have cost $16,250, and a waterfront lot in Fenwick's Paradise Shores was available for $1,550. (Both, courtesy Delaware Public Archives.)

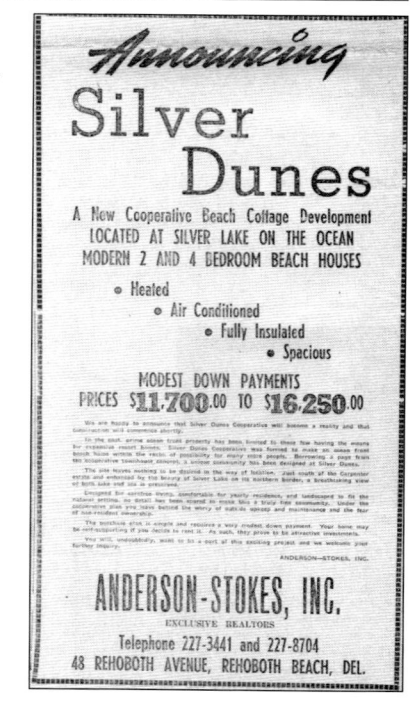

The Almanac Corner

Tuesday, March 6, 1962

h day of Winter *65th day of the Year*

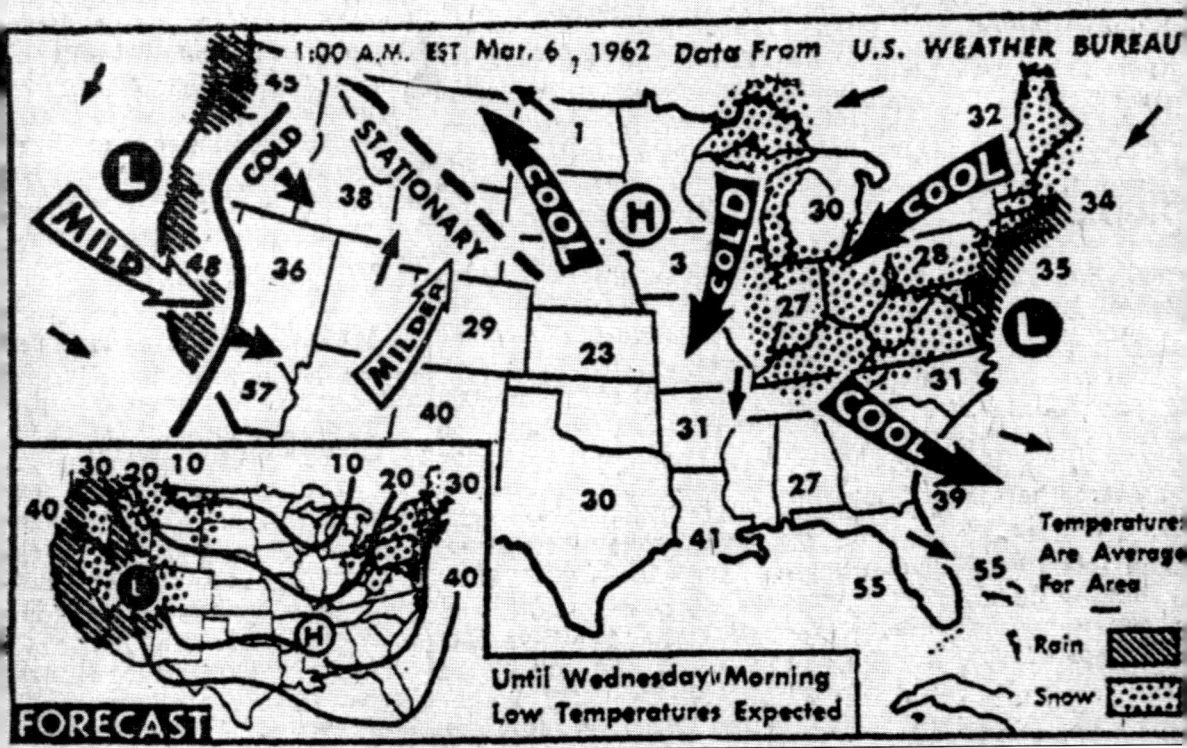

In 1962, meteorologists did not have satellites or sophisticated weather models to help them prepare their weather forecasts. So coming out of the first weekend in March 1962, it looked like a low-pressure system would enter the Atlantic Ocean off the United States' southeastern seaboard, become a more intense storm—a coastal northeaster, and then move out to sea. This is what the forecast map for March 6 looked like. The written forecast seemed only a little more serious: "Strong winds with snow accumulating a few inches but tapering off tonight, lows 26 to 32 east, and low- or middle-20s west portion. Wednesday, cloudy windy and cold, highs in the 30s. Delaware Bay forecast: Small craft warnings are displayed. Northeast to north winds 25 to 35 knots tonight. Northerly winds 20 to 35 knots Wednesday. Snow tonight. Mostly cloudy Wednesday. Visibility two miles to zero in snow improving to ten miles." (Courtesy Delaware Public Archives.)

The Almanac Corner

Wednesday, March 7, 1962

th day of Winter   *66th day of the*

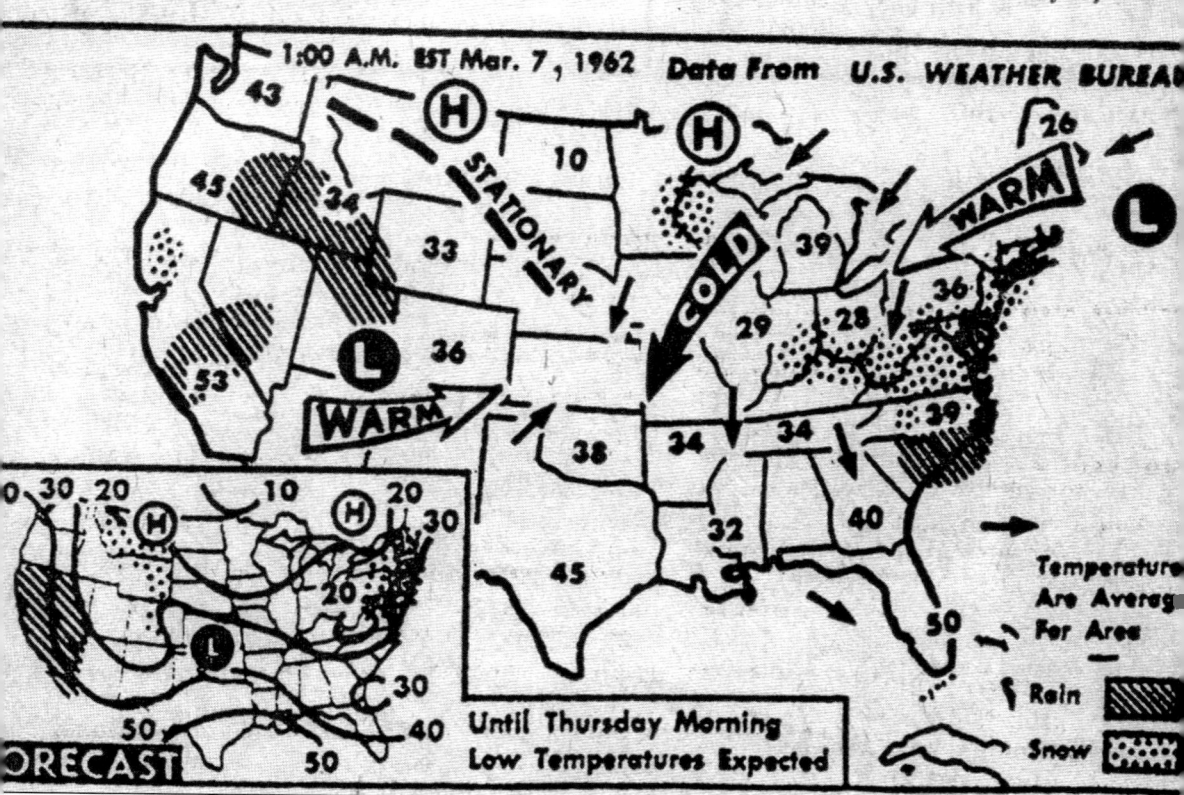

The March 7 newspaper weather map would lead one to believe that the storm was about over and that things would be calming down as the storm moved north off the Canadian coast. The morning forecast called for cloudy, windy, and cold conditions with the chance of occasional light snow. Gale warnings were posted along the coast, and tides were predicted to be two to five feet above normal with flooding of low-lying coastal areas at the times of high tide. Partial clearing was expected by nightfall, with partly cloudy and slightly warm conditions expected for Thursday. However, this forecast was far from reality. The storm center did not move north as predicted, rather it remained stationary off the mid-Atlantic coast, sending winds ashore that were sustained at 35–45 miles per hour with gusts to 70, huge waves, and the highest storm surge tide ever recorded in Delaware. Even on March 6, the first day of the three-day storm, the coastal beach and dune defenses began to unravel. (Courtesy Delaware Public Archives.)

SYNOPTIC WEATHER MAP FOR 0700 E.S.T., MARCH 7, 1962.

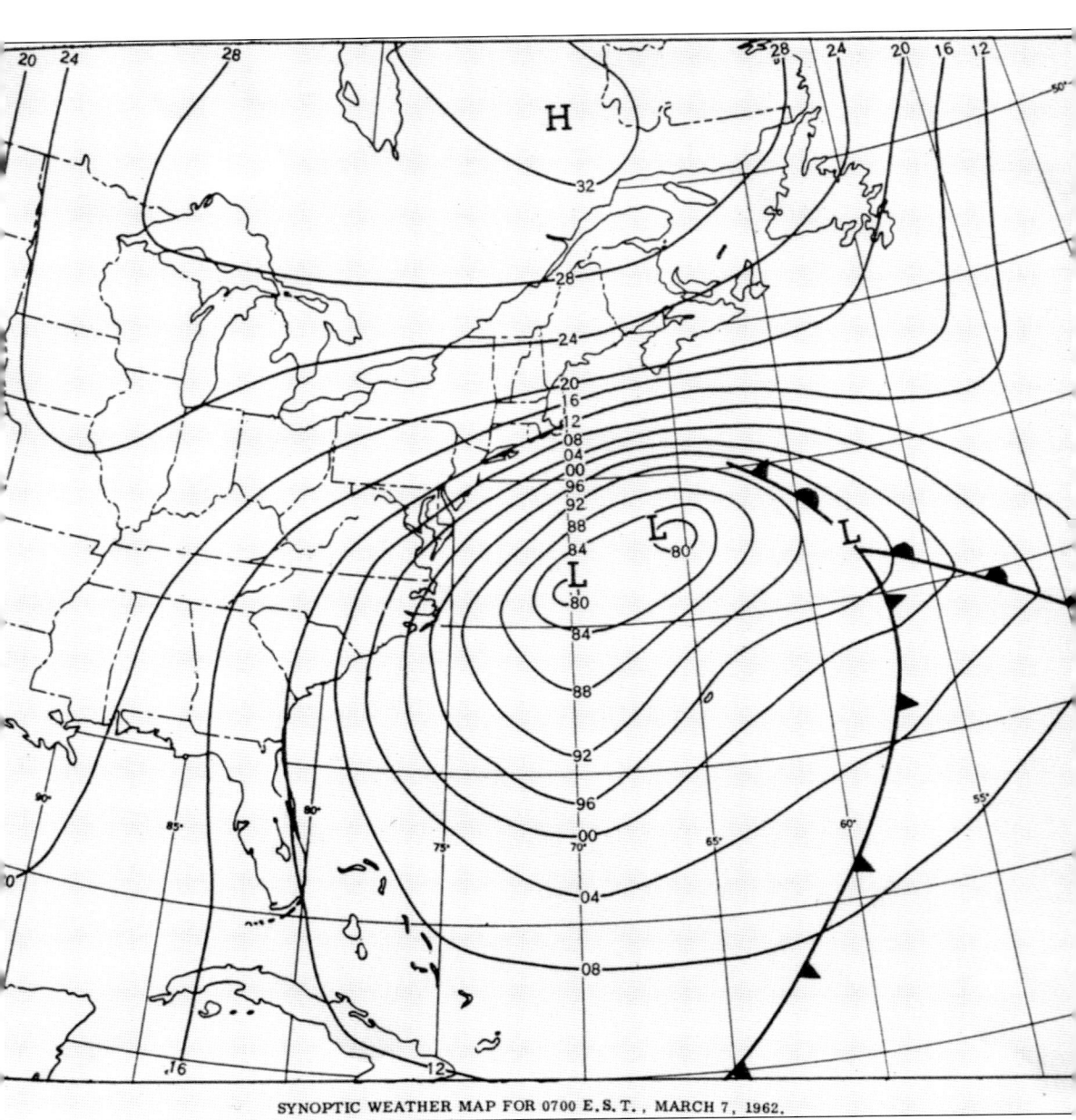

Some very unusual conditions developed that made this storm extraordinarily destructive. What were routine weather forecasts for a routine winter storm did not predict in advance that the storm would be blocked by a high-pressure system located to the north over Canada. The storm stalled off the Delaware coast with wind howling from the northeast across 1,000 miles of the North Atlantic. This long stretch of wind over the ocean is what produced such huge waves and tides over the three days. This weather map is far more serious in its look and information provided than the maps on the previous pages. The closely spaced isobar lines circling the center of the low indicate that wind is fierce in this storm. The storm also coincided with spring tides, the abnormally high tides caused by a monthly alignment of the sun and the moon. (Courtesy US Department of Commerce.)

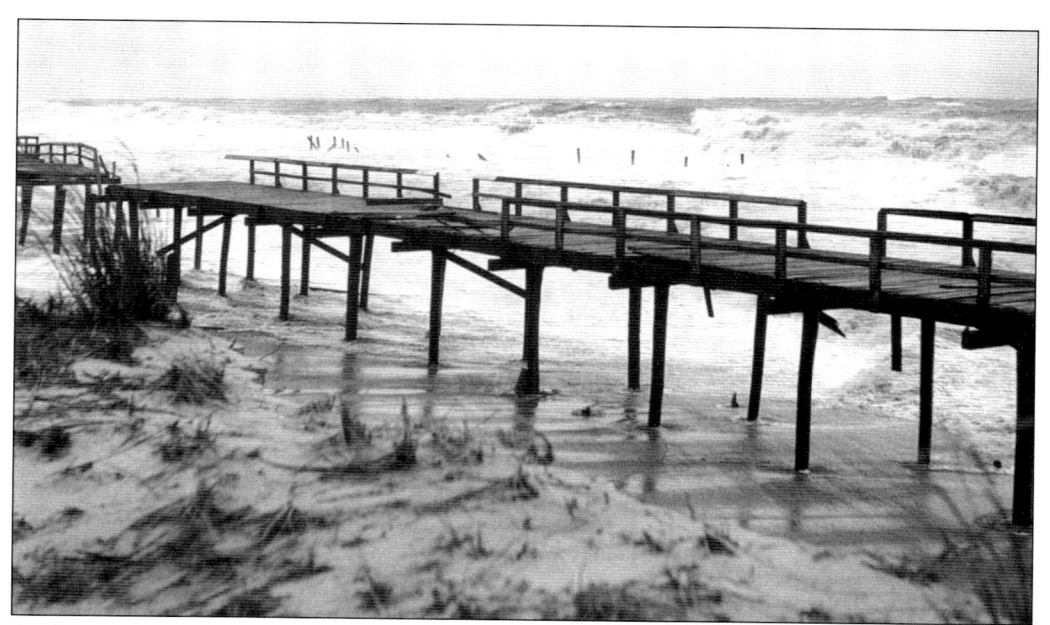

As the storm began to crank up, there were early signs that things were getting bad. Foreshadowing what was to come in the next couple of high tides, these photographs, taken on March 6, show the beginning of the worsening event. Above, the Rehoboth boardwalk is awash in the storm and begins to break apart under the constant beating by the storm waves. At this point, there was little to do but watch as waves pounded the coast hour after hour. The photograph below shows that the north end of the Rehoboth boardwalk and the parking lot were beginning to fall into the sea. Note that the Henlopen Hotel's dining room and cocktail lounge were still standing on March 6. (Above, courtesy Lewes Historical Society; below, Delaware DNREC.)

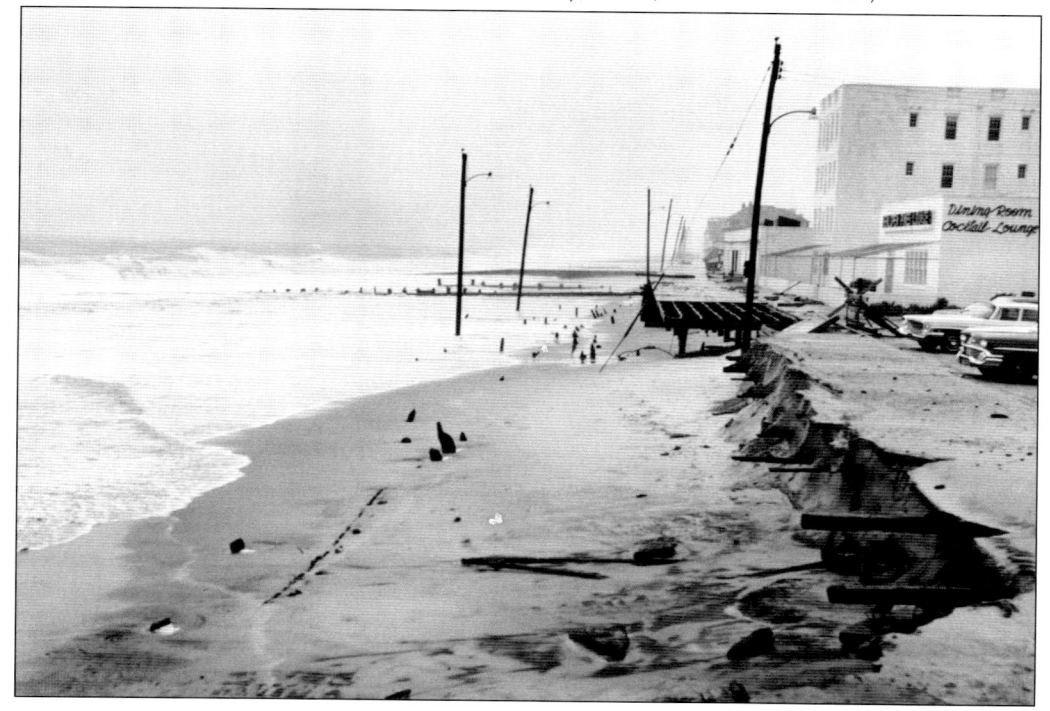

23

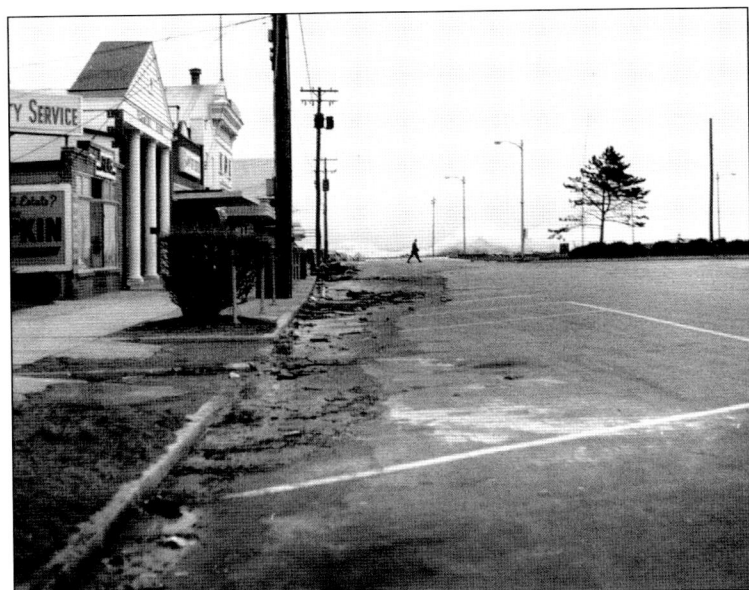

At the east end of Rehoboth Avenue, waves smacked up against a section of boardwalk, sending spray high into the air. A debris line and water marks can be seen along the curb as ocean water began to overtop the boardwalk and flow down Rehoboth Avenue. (Courtesy Lewes Historical Society.)

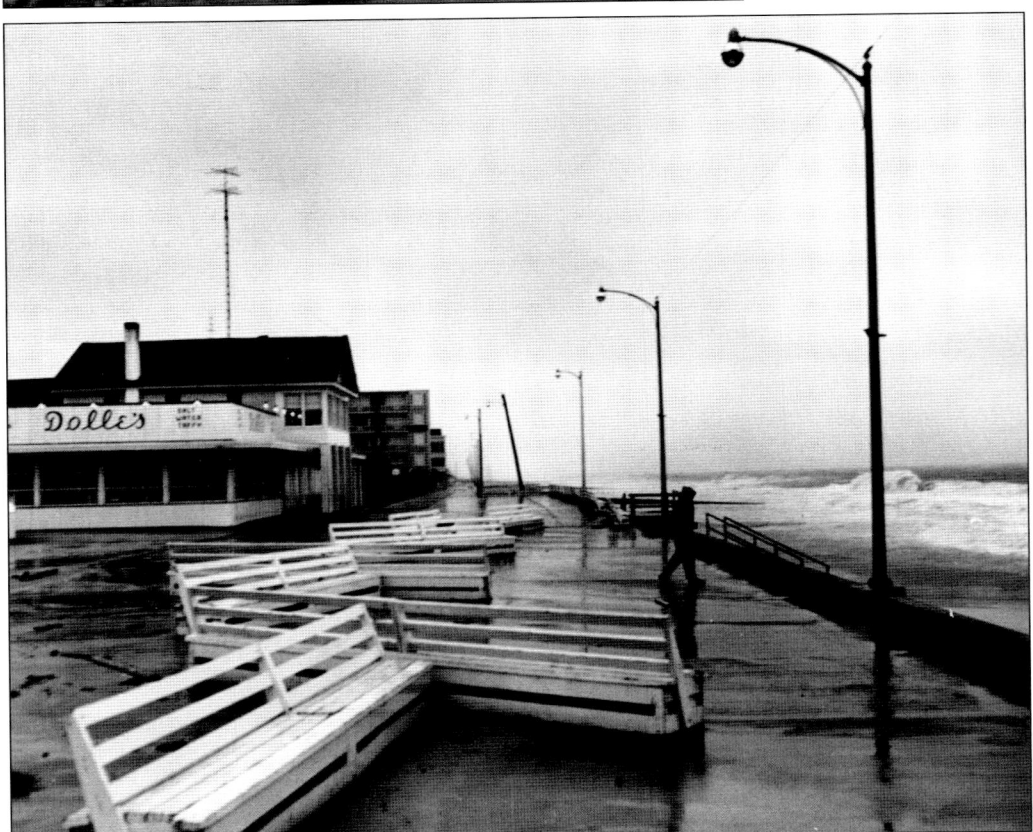

The concrete portion of the boardwalk was still intact in this March 6 photograph, and Dolle's was still standing, but this may have been the last photograph taken before their demise. Note the light pole in the mid-background that was leaning over the boardwalk, clear evidence that things were beginning to fall apart. (Courtesy Delaware Public Archives.)

Three

COASTAL FLOODS AND FURY

The 1962 storm had devastating impacts to most of Delaware—from Wilmington and neighboring towns along the Delaware River, through Kent and Sussex County beach communities, to the Inland Bays and inland areas. On March 6, gale-force winds and heavy snowfall blew through New Castle County, resulting in widespread electrical failures, downed trees, and heavy damage. In Wilmington, peak wind gusts were reported to be 51 miles per hour; a tractor-trailer overturned on the Delaware Memorial Bridge, and schools were closed due to power outages and damaged classroom windows. Lashing winds and high tides resulted in the evacuation of Kitts Hummock, Bowers, Pickering, and Woodland Beaches. *Evening Journal* accounts included eyewitness reports that "water covered most of the beach areas and was lapping at the front doors of many homes."

By March 7, after another night of battering rain, winds, waves and tides, access to nearly all of Delaware's coastal communities was cut off by waters four to five feet higher than normal. Wind-driven waves battered the shoreline as rising tides washed away beaches and roads, overturned homes in the surf, destroyed boardwalks, and demolished beachfront businesses. Fire companies, police, and National Guard units continued evacuation efforts, hauling dozens of people out of waterfront communities. Rescue and emergency workers soon realized that things were getting worse by the hour—the increasing momentum of waves and tides was engulfing and overwhelming the coastal areas of Delaware from Woodland Beach to Fenwick Island.

High tides had receded somewhat by March 8, but gale warnings were still up, as were alerts of continued flooding tides. Preliminary reports of damage soon made it clear that all parts of Delaware's shoreline—Delaware Bay, Atlantic Coast, and Inland Bays alike—suffered extreme damage and extensive devastation. Boardwalks were demolished, rows of oceanfront homes were swept away by the storm, and waves, tides, and winds damaged buildings located even blocks from the beach. Streets and highways were flooded, power lines were down, and toxic materials mixed with floodwaters, making it difficult, dangerous, and almost impossible to assess the destruction.

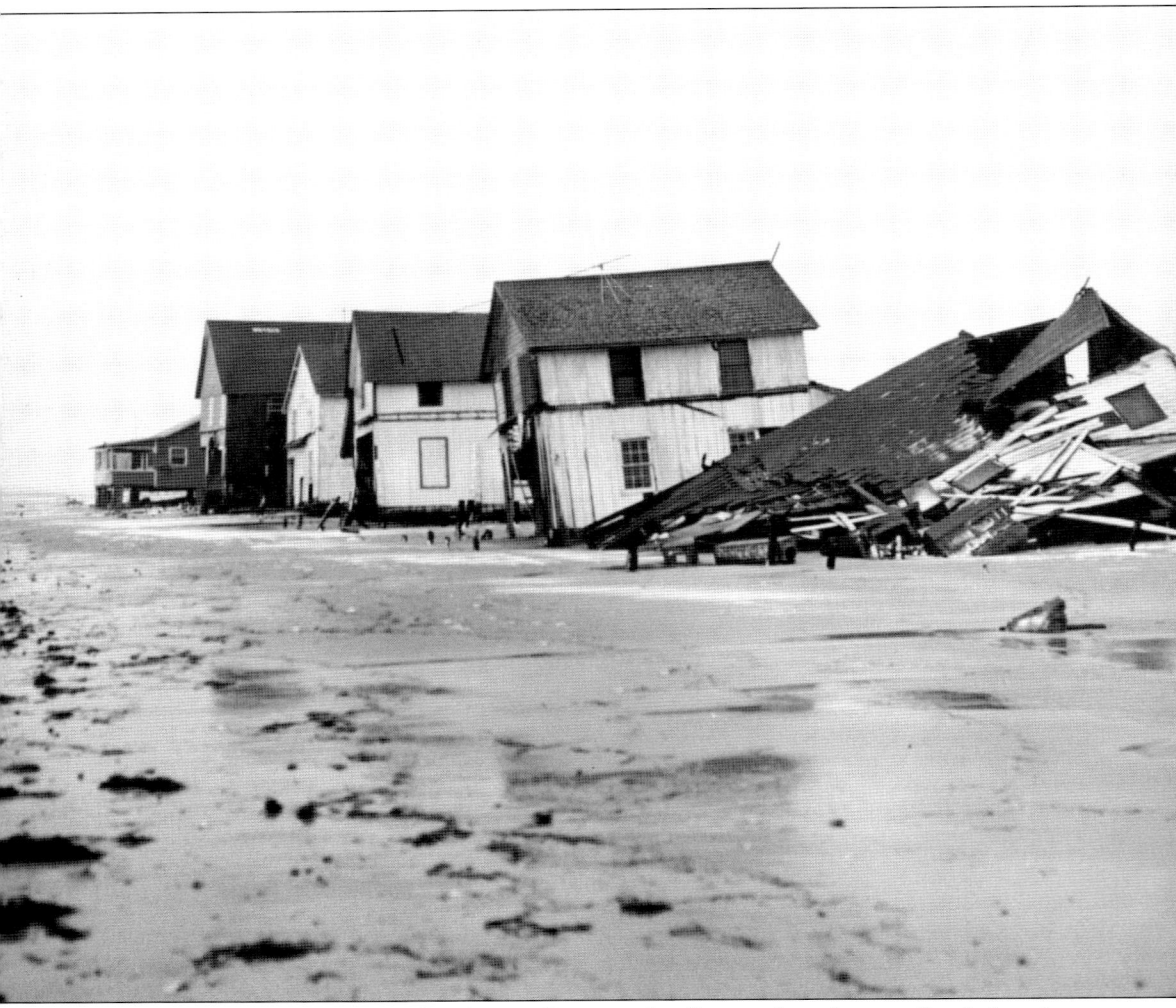

Along the Delaware River and Delaware Bay, nearly all coastal roads were flooded and some were partially washed away. Flooding tides reached inland for several miles along much of the coast. Low-lying areas in Wilmington and New Castle County reported that many roadways were under water and debris was mounting in the vicinity of the Marine Terminal. In the city of New Castle, water was two feet deep, and much of Delaware City was under water. The *Evening Journal*'s narrative of the storm included a vivid description of the community's roads, noting "chunks of ice floating down the main streets along with railroad ties, telephone poles, furniture, and other debris." Three homes in Delaware City were evacuated, and large portions of adjacent land areas, including the vicinity of the Governor Bacon Health Center, were covered with water. Extensive flooding prompted evacuation orders for all Delaware Bay beaches—from Port Mahon to Lewes. By March 7, police, firemen, and National Guard units reportedly had evacuated approximately 175 residents, chiefly from Kitts Hummock and Bowers Beach. (Courtesy Delaware Public Archives.)

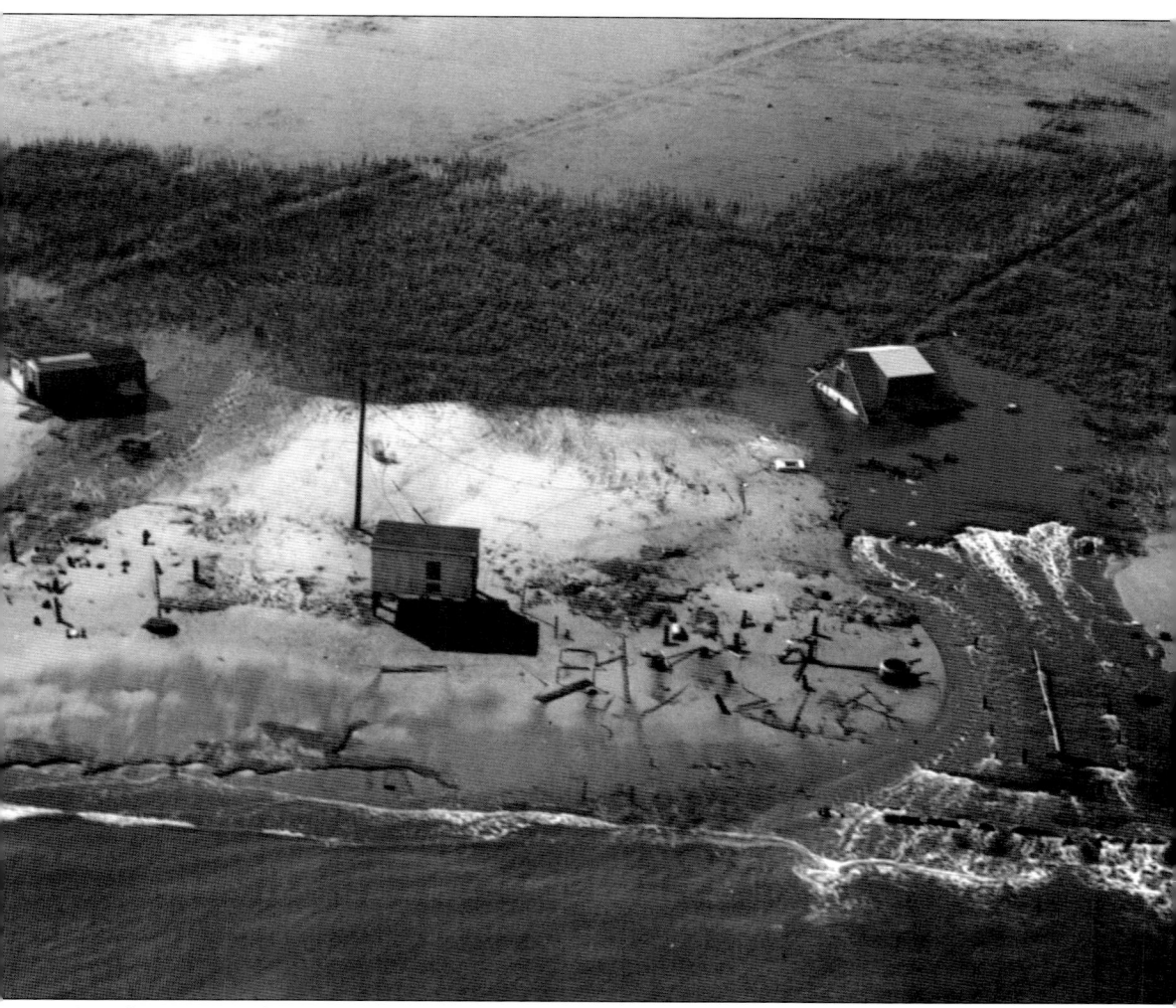

As tides continued to rise, all beach roads were under water, making it dangerous and impossible to navigate the flooded and collapsing roadbeds in anything other than a large truck or rescue vehicle. An unspeakable tragedy occurred when the Waters family lost six children to wind-driven waves and rising waters near Bowers Beach. The Waters family lived adjacent to Delaware Bay, only 20 feet from the St. Jones River. On March 6, John A. Waters awoke to find high water sweeping across the marsh, and without warning, the waves and tides rose so high that the family suddenly realized they had to evacuate. By the time Waters was able to get six of his eight children into the car, he saw there was no chance to drive away safely. The car was quickly surrounded by four feet of water and six-foot breaking waves. Five children drowned in the vehicle as it was carried away, and a seven year old was swept away by raging waves. Only the parents, two children, and a grandmother were able to escape. (Courtesy Delaware Public Archives.)

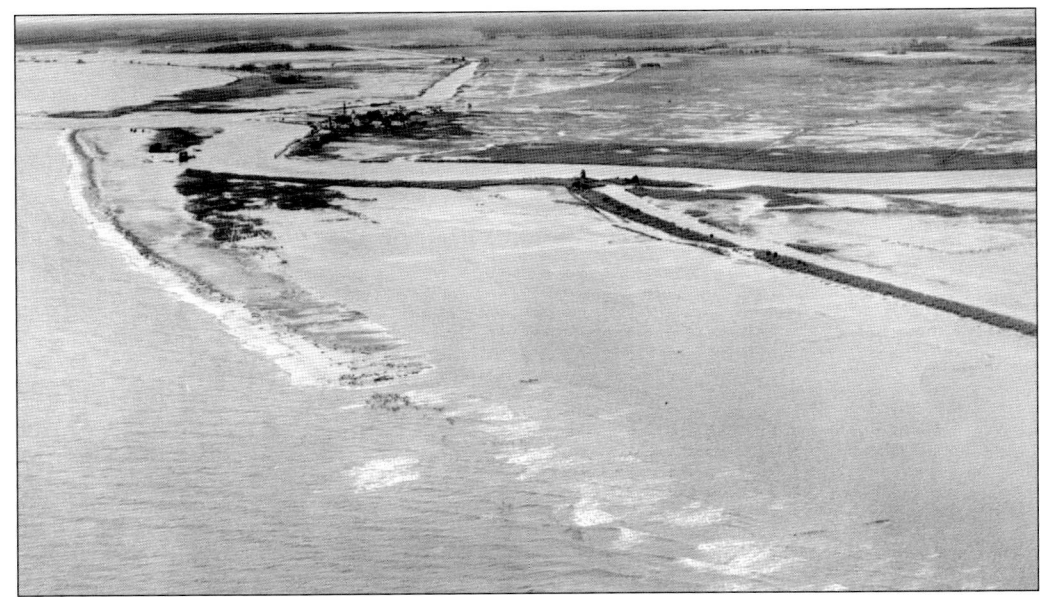

It is not difficult to sense the feeling of frightened isolation that Delaware Bay residents would have experienced on March 6 and 7. Tide heights in the bay quickly rose to unprecedented levels, flooding adjacent marshes and overtopping low, narrow, sandy beaches. Along most of the bay front it was difficult or impossible to discern the shoreline location until tides receded. These two photographs were taken on March 22, almost two weeks after the peak of the storm. Above is a view of the area north of Slaughter Beach; the image below shows the vicinity of Bowers Beach and the St. Jones River. Note the isolated structures at the edge of the river and the fishing boat stranded on the marsh surface. Many Delaware Bay homes were reportedly found up to a mile or more into the marsh. (Both, courtesy Delaware DNREC.)

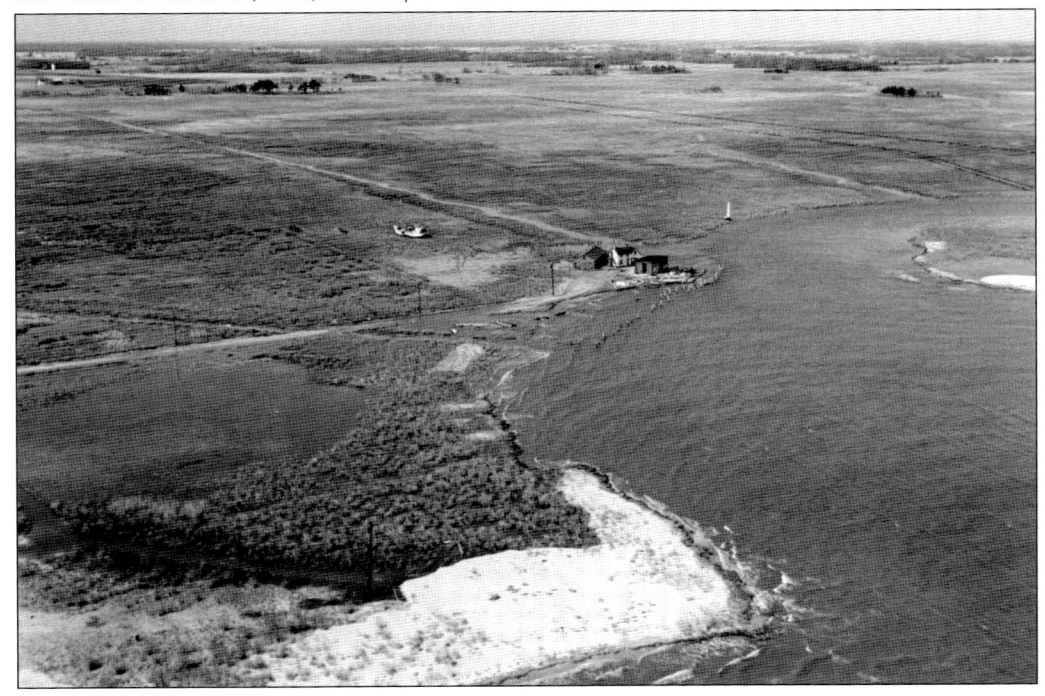

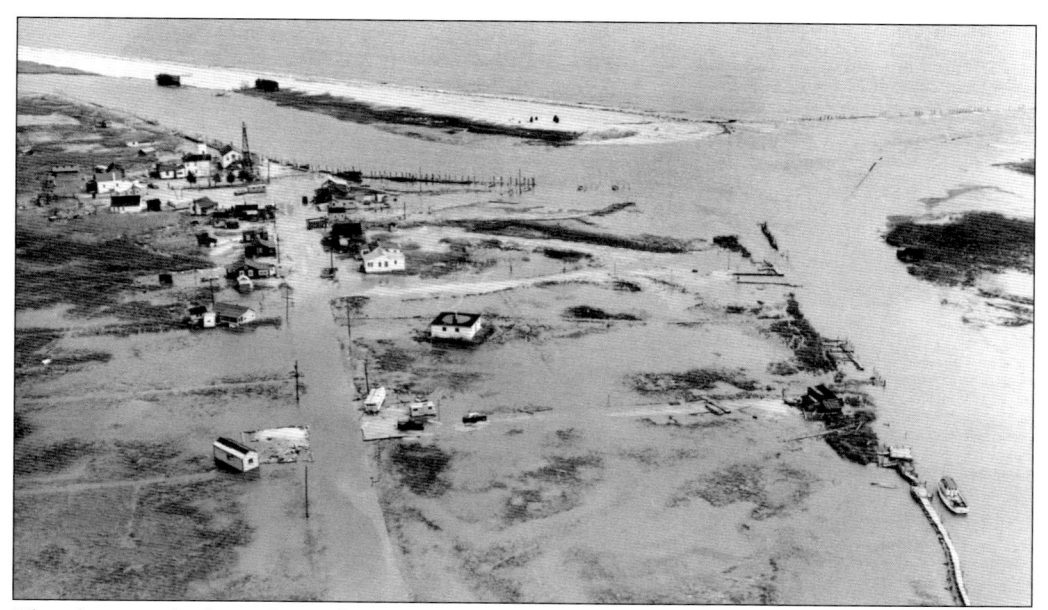

The photograph above shows flooding in the vicinity of the Mispillion River Inlet. In Slaughter Beach (below), 34 homes were destroyed—reportedly either driven from their foundations by winds and waves, or shattered by winds of up to 60 miles per hour. Many homes were splintered into pieces from the force of flooding tides and battering waves. Roadways and marshland surrounding the area were under water. On March 7, National Guardsmen conducted an unsuccessful search throughout the flooded Slaughter Beach area for the missing wife of Dover Air Force Base major Richard D. O'Brien. Major O'Brien had last seen his wife on the evening of March 6 when he reported for duty. On Wednesday morning, he returned to the beach to find his home destroyed and no trace of his wife. (Above, courtesy Delaware DNREC; below, courtesy Delaware Public Archives.)

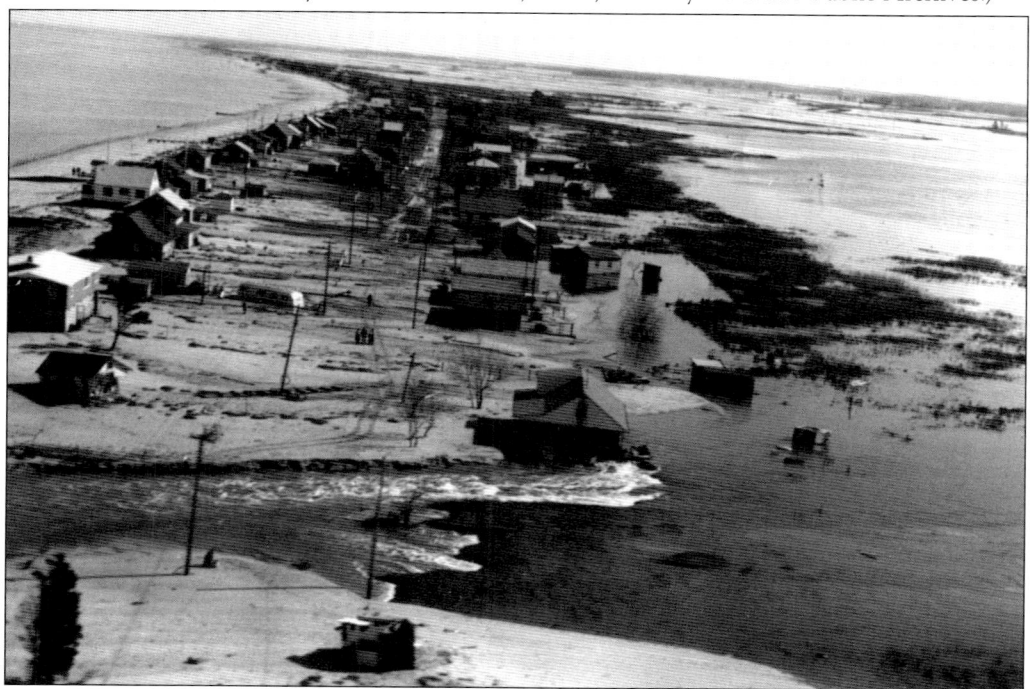

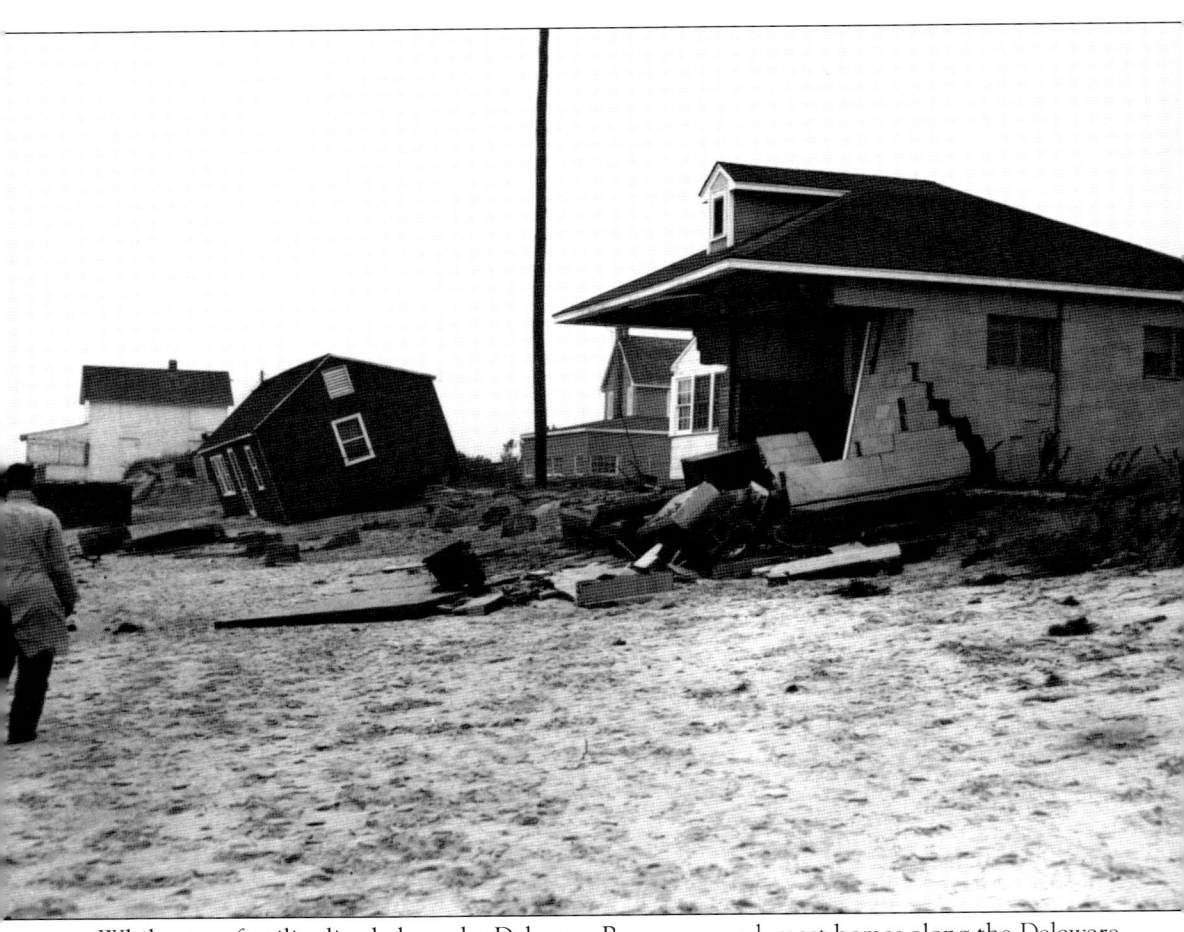

While some families lived along the Delaware Bay year-round, most homes along the Delaware Bay in 1962 were cottages used for hunting, fishing, and summer vacations. In Bowers Beach, only 10 of the town's 150 homes escaped damage. Community officials were concerned that many of the part-time residents whose homes were destroyed would not return because they had nothing to come back to. This would result in loss of tax revenue on the destroyed homes and could have significant impacts on the community's future. Many of the devastated structures were built on concrete block foundations that were undermined as waves and tides eroded the sand surface. As seen above, the community of Broadkill Beach was also hard hit by the ravaging waves. (Courtesy Delaware Public Archives.)

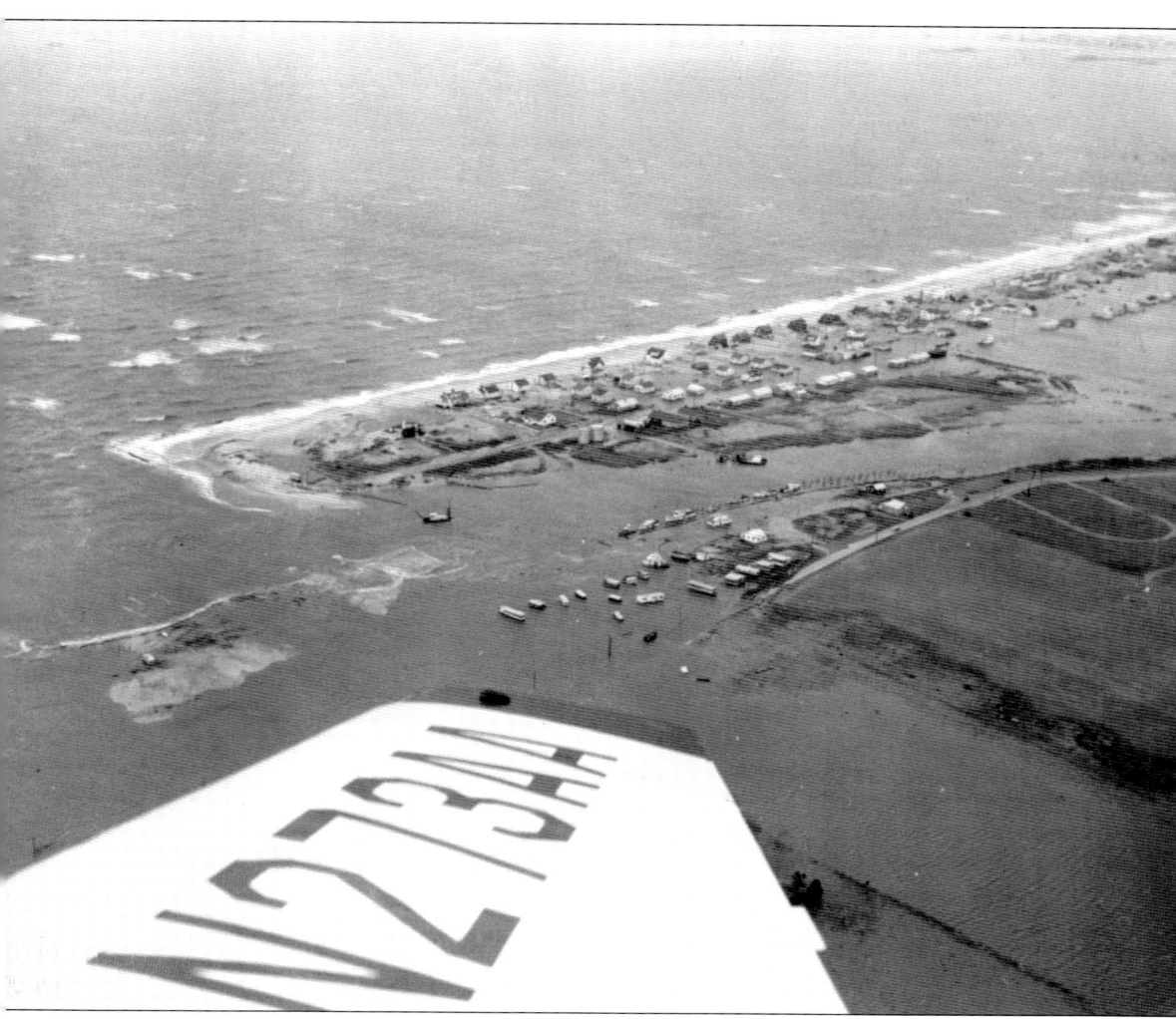

In the city of Lewes, tides were reported to be five feet above normal and all homes on Lewes Beach were flooded. Bay Avenue was covered with three to six feet of water, and about four and a half feet of water stood on Savannah Road, which connects the beach to the rest of the town. Damaging waves reportedly wrecked at least one house, and water broke over the dunes and ran from the bay to the Lewes-Rehoboth Canal. Homes in low-lying sections of Lewes Beach suffered flood, mud, and wind damage. The *Delaware State News* reported an eyewitness description of the flooding: "For a while there was no Lewes Beach . . . the Delaware Bay came right up to the canal. All you could see was water, water, water." Residents claim that the storm was the worst disaster to hit the area in over 30 years. At the height of the storm, many vowed never to return, and many talked about selling and moving off the beach for good. (Courtesy Colonel McGarraugh via Marna Cupp.)

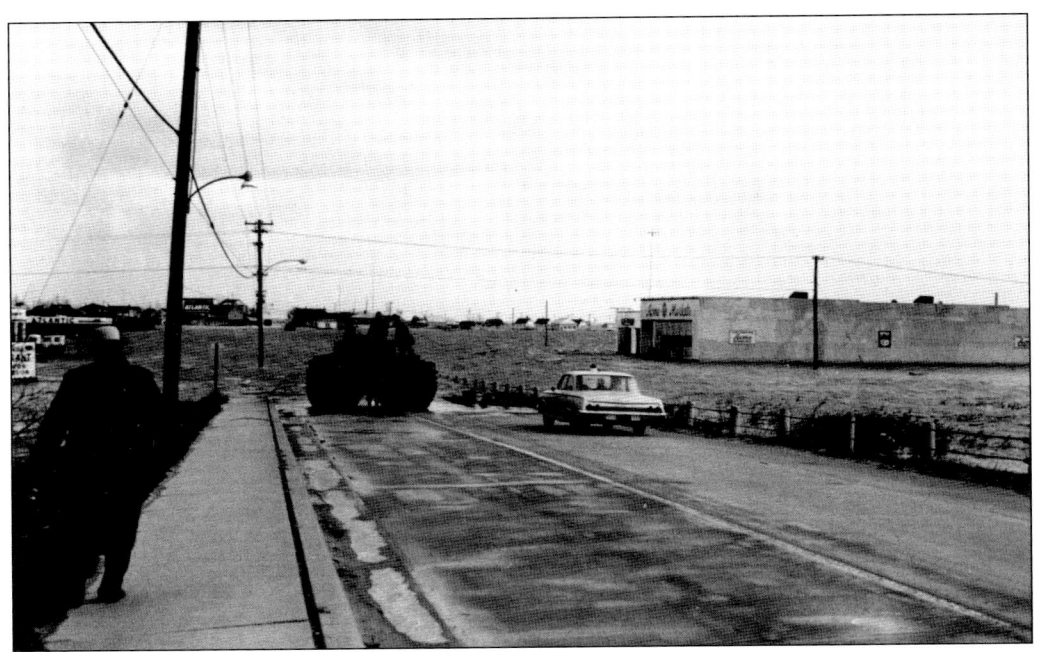

The Savannah Road Bridge over the Lewes-Rehoboth Canal was closed to all traffic except emergency vehicles. With Savannah Road flooded and the bridge closed, access to and from Lewes Beach was completely cut off. Fortunately, most of Lewes Beach had been evacuated the previous night. The National Guard picked up people in tanks, relayed them to trucks, and transferred them to higher ground. At least 50 people were given refuge at the Lewes Fire Hall. While most residents of Lewes Beach agreed to the evacuation, a few refused to leave their homes. The photograph above shows floodwaters covering Savannah Road at the base of the bridge. The photograph below shows a view of the same area from the public docks, looking across the canal. (Above, courtesy Colonel McGarraugh via Marna Cupp; below, courtesy Lewes Historical Society.)

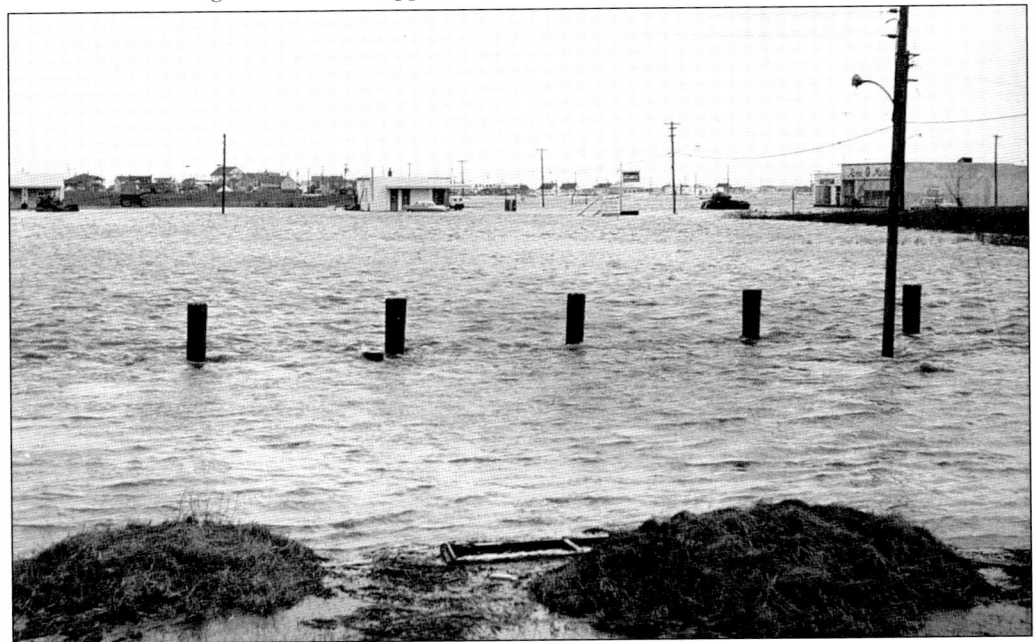

This view of Lewes shows that nearly all of Lewes Beach was submerged (the canal bridge can be seen in the middle of the picture). On the other side of the canal, even the higher sections of town were impacted. It was the first time that the canal flooded portions of Pilottown Road, and the newly constructed Little League field was under water. (Courtesy Colonel McGarraugh via Marna Cupp.)

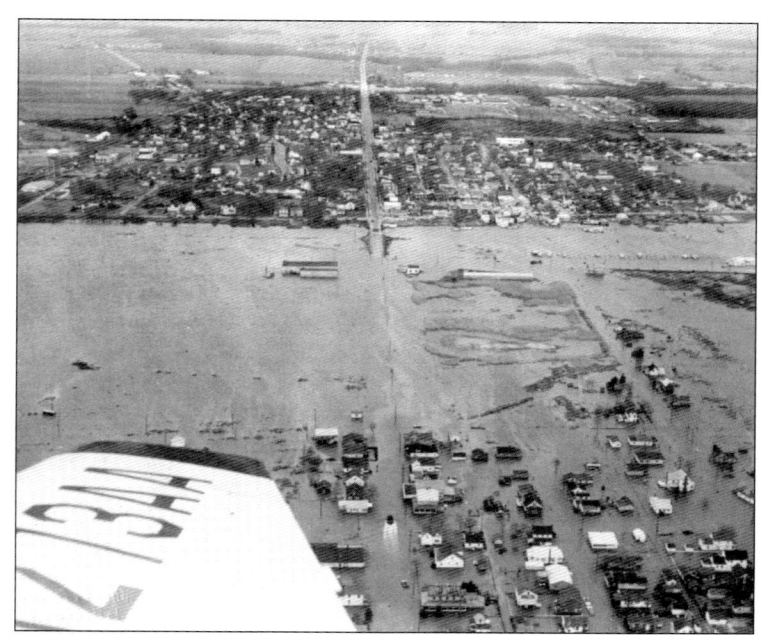

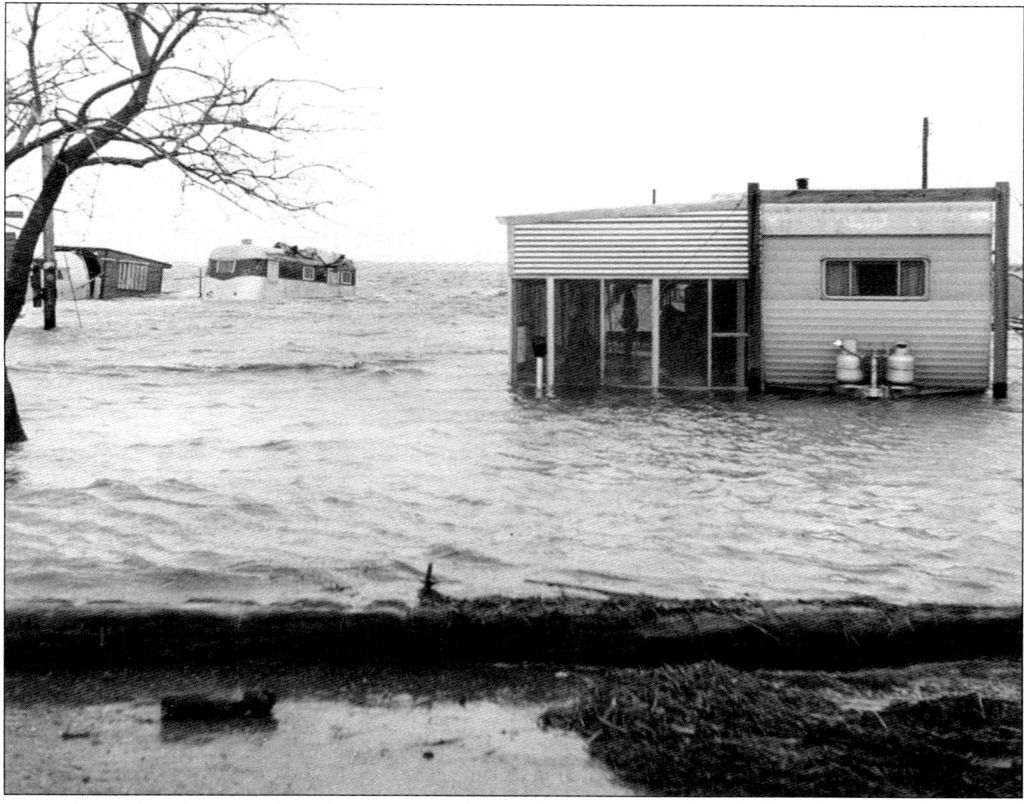

A trailer park at Roosevelt Inlet was completely flooded, and all its occupants were evacuated. The last person out of the park was a woman identified as Virginia Taylor, who was evacuated by a rescue crew even as five feet of water surrounded her trailer. Other trailers reportedly floated around the park like houseboats. (Courtesy Lewes Historical Society.)

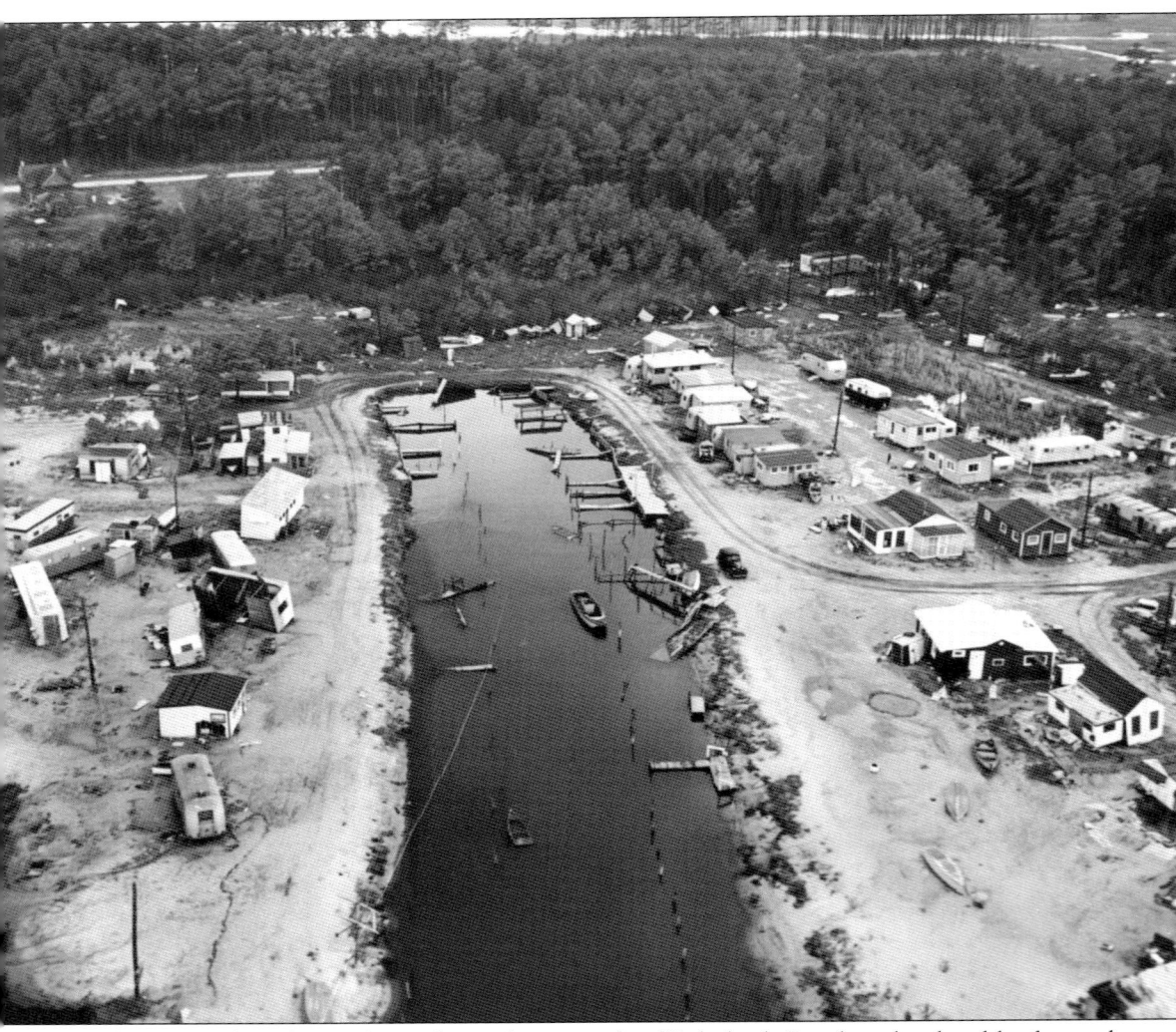

The town of Henlopen Acres, located just north of Rehoboth Beach, is bordered by forested uplands, the Lewes-Rehoboth Canal, and the Atlantic Ocean. Its proximity to tidal waters made it extremely vulnerable to the effects of storm surge and inundation from adjacent waterways. Barely recognizable in this March 13 photograph, the area surrounding Henlopen Acres' marina was significantly impacted by floodwaters and tidal currents. Trailers were toppled, docks were destroyed, and boats were carried into adjacent wooded areas. (Courtesy Delaware DNREC.)

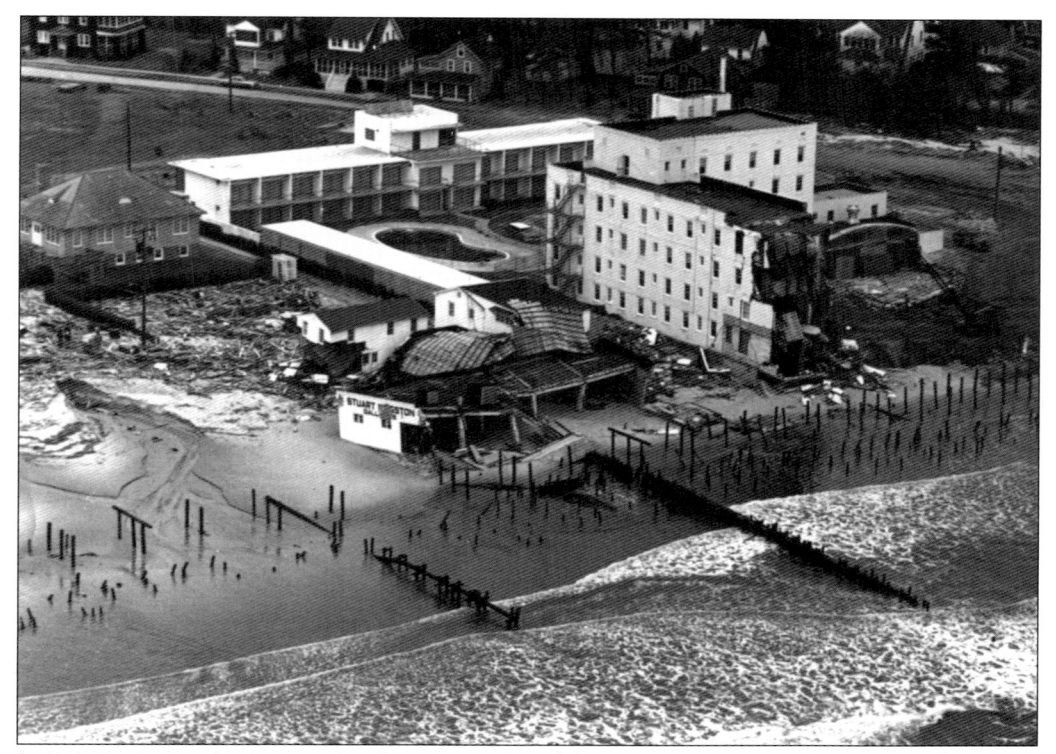

In Rehoboth Beach, the boardwalk and most beachfront structures were damaged or destroyed. These photographs show how devastating the impacts were: landmarks were wrecked, buildings were smashed, and lives and businesses were shattered and ruined. Included in the above photograph is what remained of the north end of the boardwalk and the Henlopen Hotel. Stuart Kingston Galleries (below), located just south of the Henlopen Hotel, collapsed overnight on March 6. Similar scenes of destruction were repeated along the entire length of boardwalk. The *Wilmington Morning News* quoted one eyewitness as saying, "The boardwalk and concession stands were piled up like so much cordwood along First Street." (Both, courtesy Delaware Public Archives.)

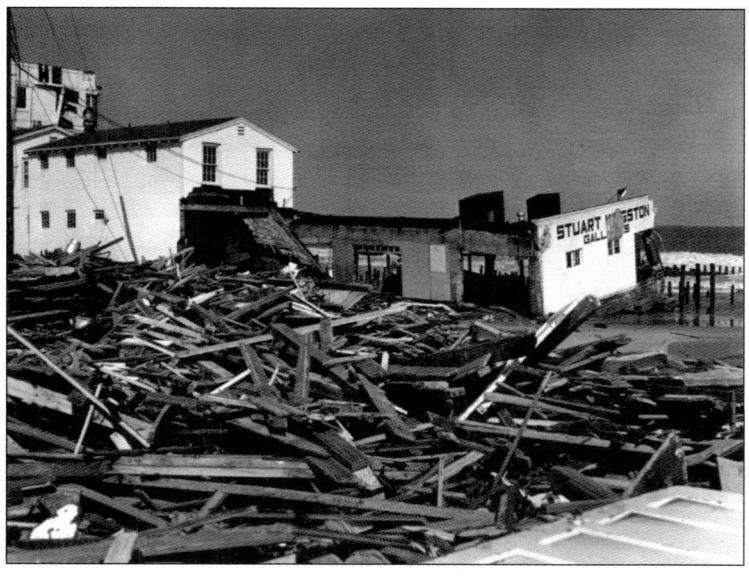

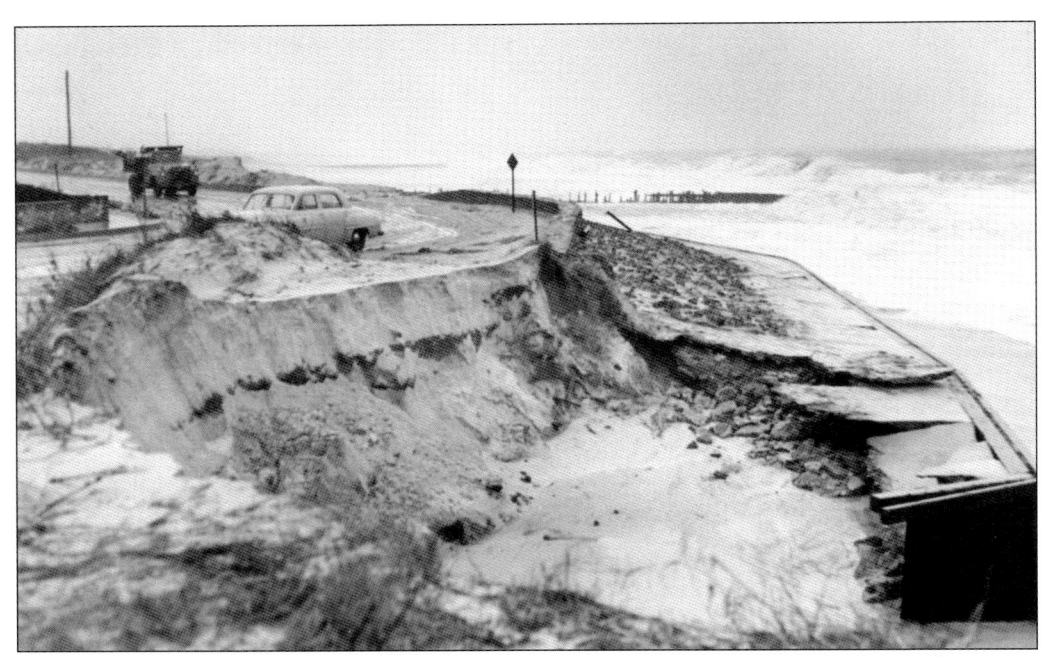

Tide and wave heights increased over time as the storm intensified and lingered over the course of three days and five high tide cycles. On March 6, eroding waves threatened to undermine Surf Avenue, located just north of the Henlopen Hotel (above). Just one day later, Surf Avenue and its seawall were washed away. Many homes were swept out to sea, and others were ravaged by sand and surf. After being battered by storm waves through several high tides, the Grier House, located just beyond the view in photograph above, collapsed and was damaged beyond repair (below). (Above, courtesy Delaware DNREC; below, courtesy Delaware Public Archives.)

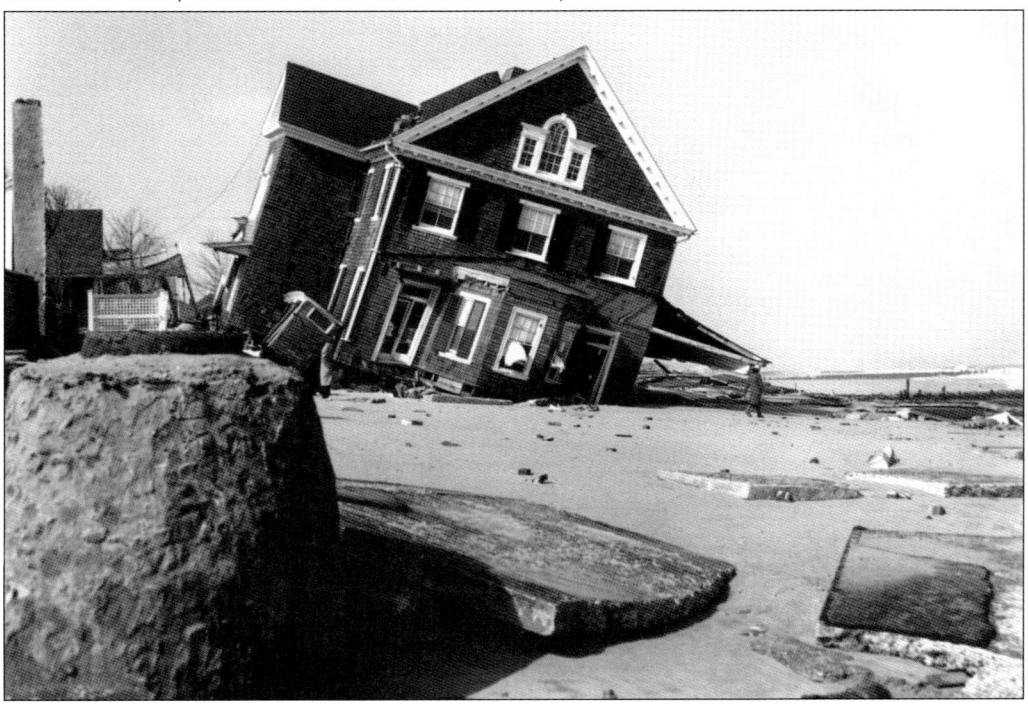

The oceanfront Atlantic Sands Hotel, built at a cost of approximately $1 million, had been open for only two seasons in 1962 when it was partially destroyed. The entire front section was torn away, and the swimming pool collapsed into the sea. (Courtesy Delaware Public Archives.)

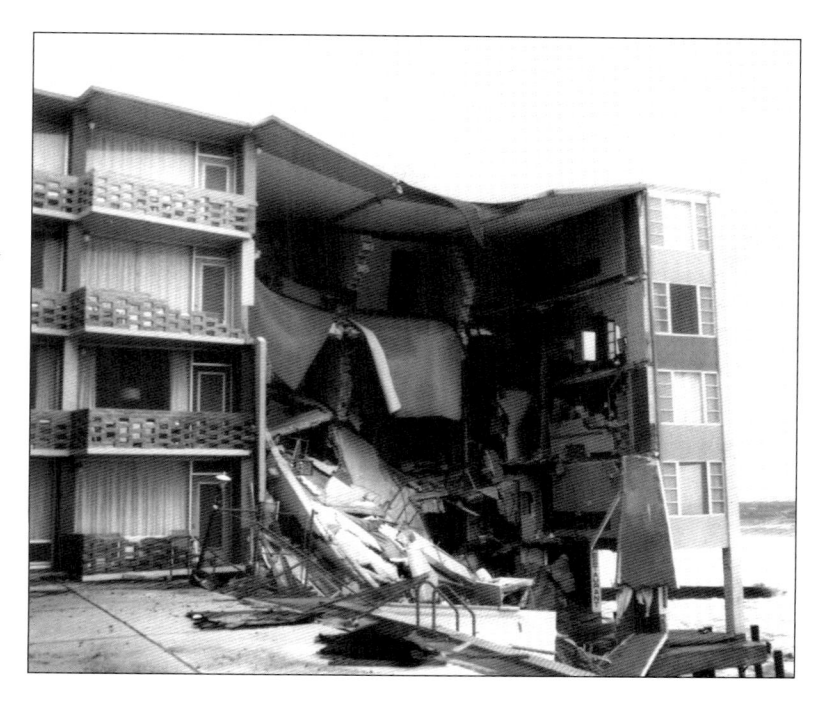

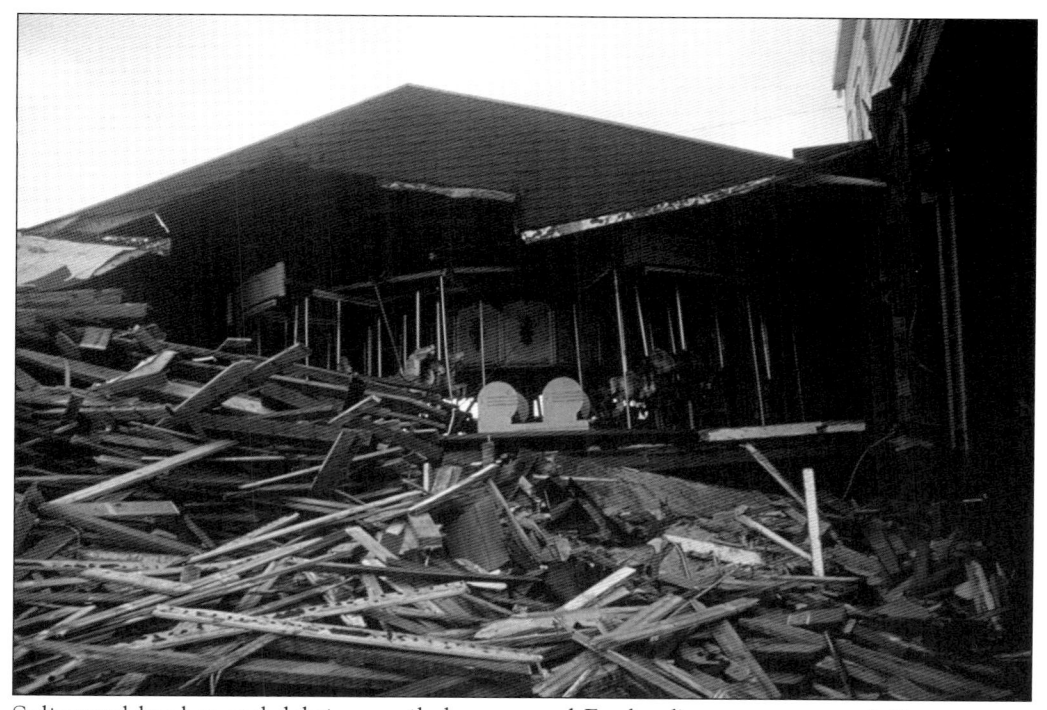

Splintered lumber and debris are piled up around Funland's merry-go-round. Bumper cars were reportedly carried blocks away by the rushing waters and waves. (Courtesy Lewes Historical Society.)

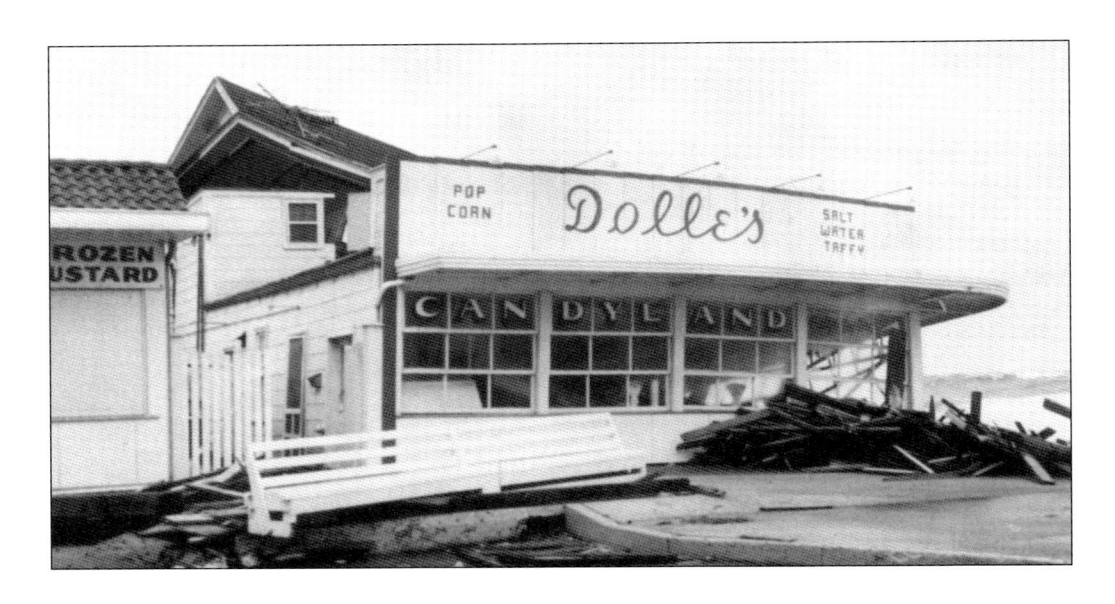

Dolle's, a saltwater taffy and popcorn store and a true Rehoboth icon for over 50 years, fell into the sea as it was hammered by waves that undermined its foundation. The above photograph was taken on March 7 and show results of the relentless impact of pounding waves. Dolle's entire front section collapsed into raging ocean waters. The building actually split apart as waves undercut the structural support. The tip of the tilting second-floor apartment can be seen as it begins to slide into the sea. In the aftermath of the storm, a local reporter from the *Delaware Coast Press* stated, "Not a single business establishment on the boardwalk was able to withstand the storm's blasting fury." (Above, courtesy *Delaware State News*; below, Delaware Public Archives.)

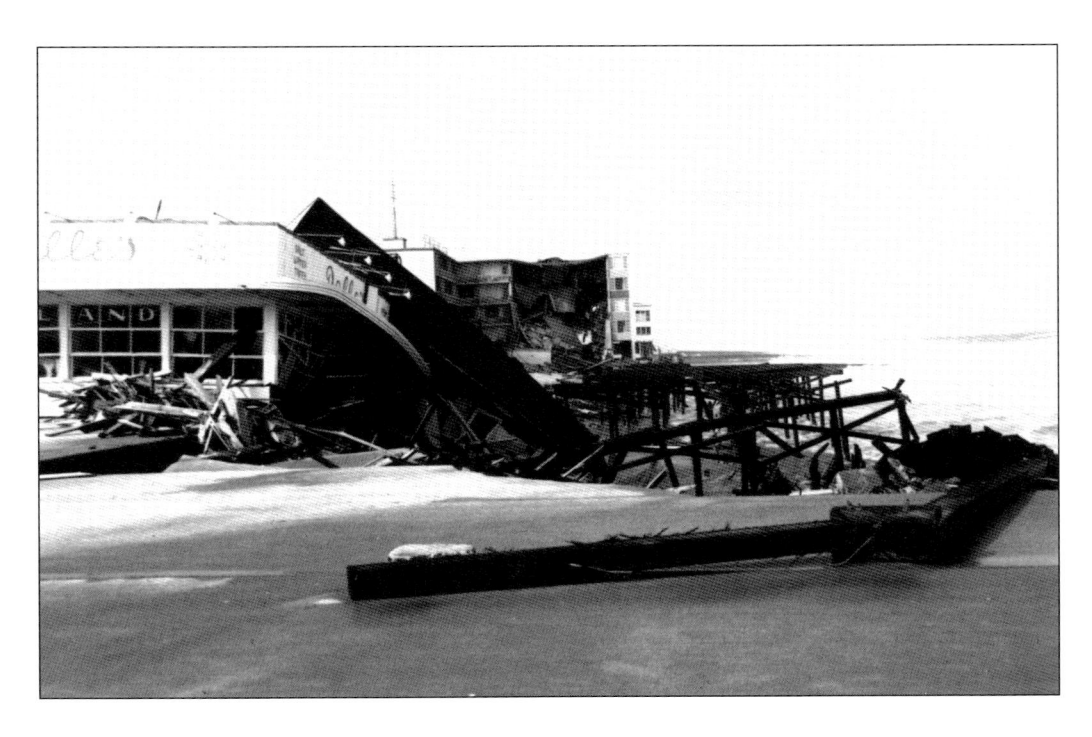

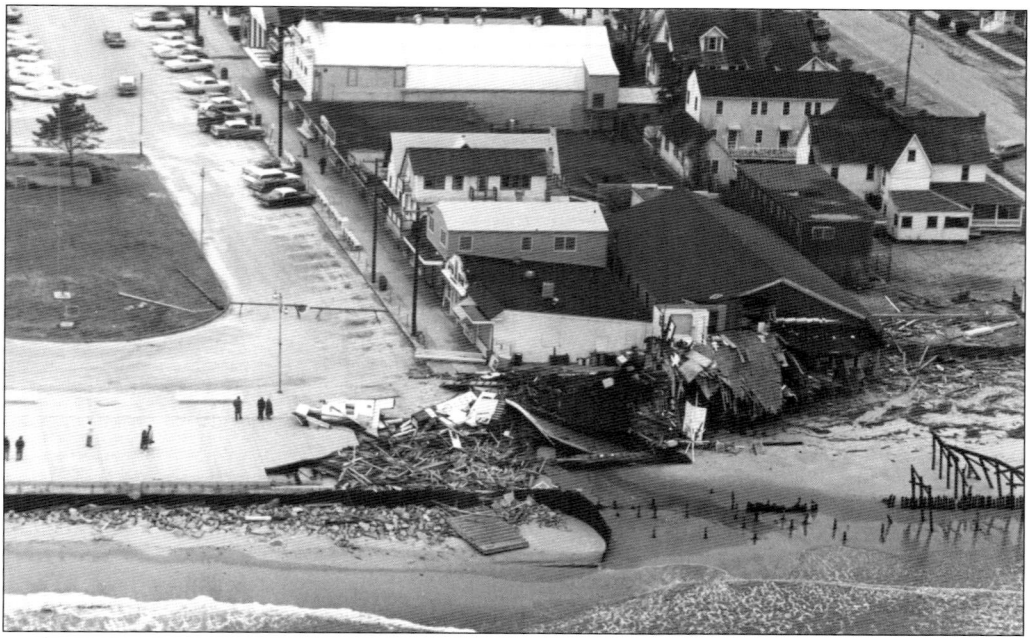

With nearly every oceanfront business battered to pieces, much of the state's largest resort community was in shambles. This aerial view (above) of Rehoboth Avenue shows what little remained of Dolle's and the boardwalk. On the opposite corner of Rehoboth Avenue, the Belhaven Hotel (below) also suffered extensive damage. As Jack Beach reported in the *Delaware State News*, "Its old front porch was always a haven for the adventurous who came to watch storms slam breakers against the boardwalk. You could stand there and feel her tremble, tasting the salt spray, but feeling secure in the knowledge that it had withstood the worst the sea had to offer over the years. Today there is no front porch on the Belhaven. In fact, the entire front half of the old hotel broke away." (Both, courtesy Delaware Public Archives.)

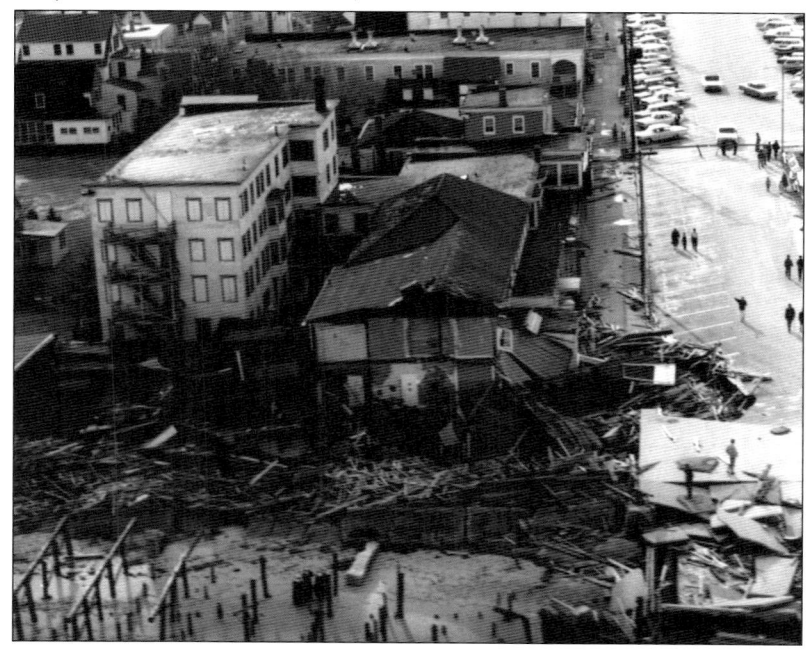

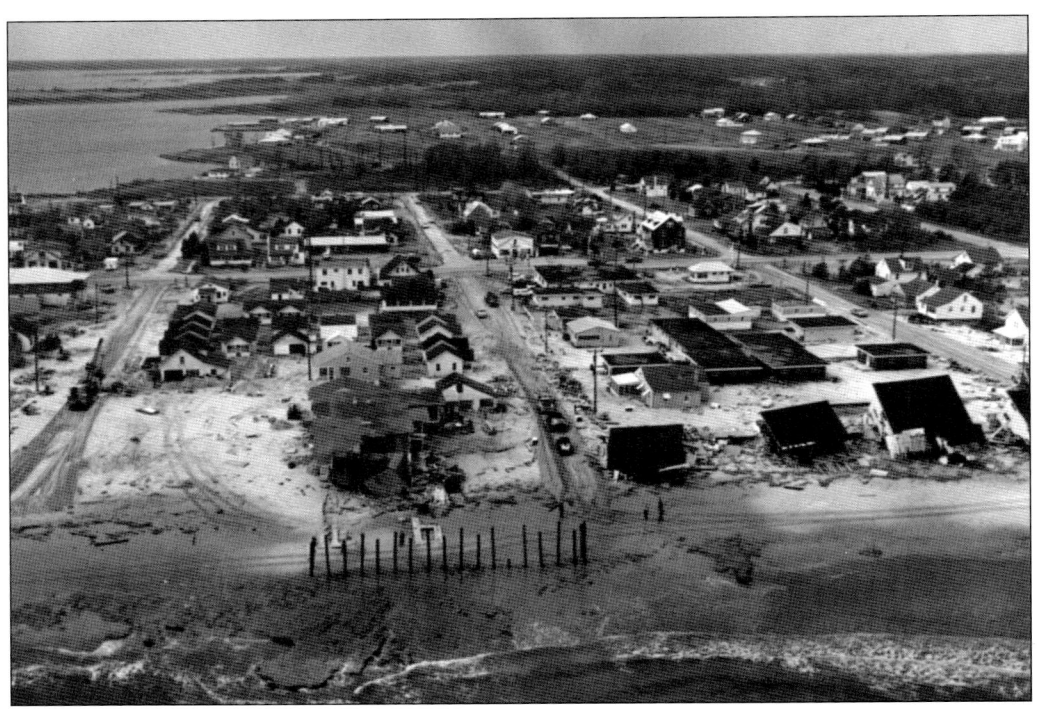

The entirety of Dewey Beach was submerged, and water flowed through the streets as the ocean met the bay across the whole community. Oceanfront homes were toppled and ruined as they were battered by 20-foot waves riding storm surges and high tides to water levels that had never been seen before. Beach sand, pieces of splintered homes, furniture, and other household belongings were either carried out to sea or across town towards Rehoboth Bay. (Both, courtesy Delaware Public Archives.)

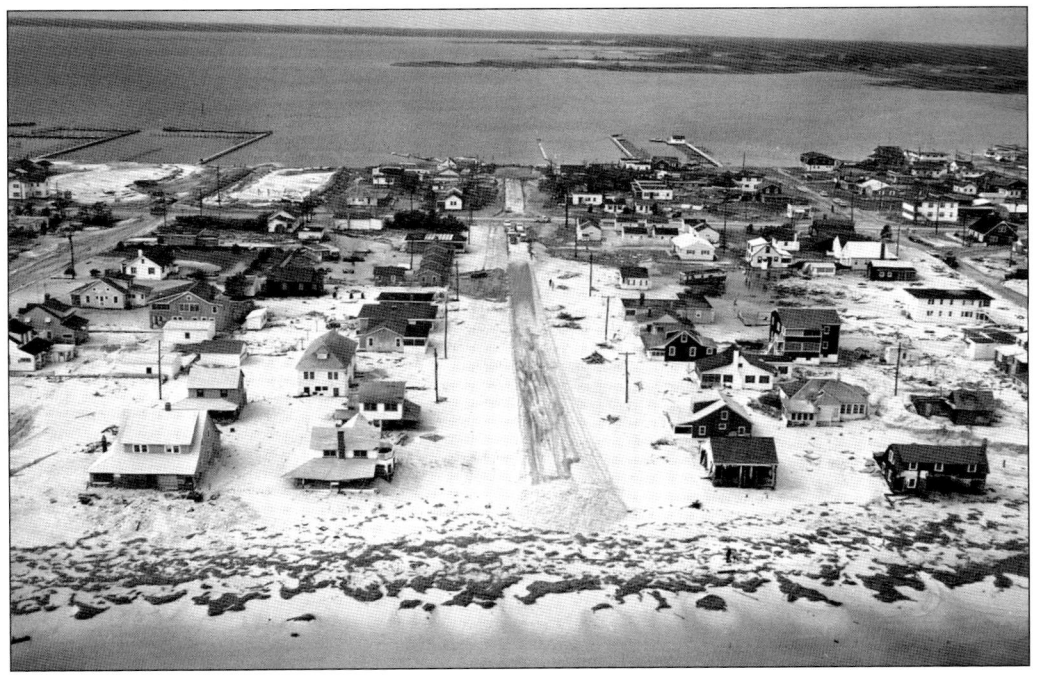

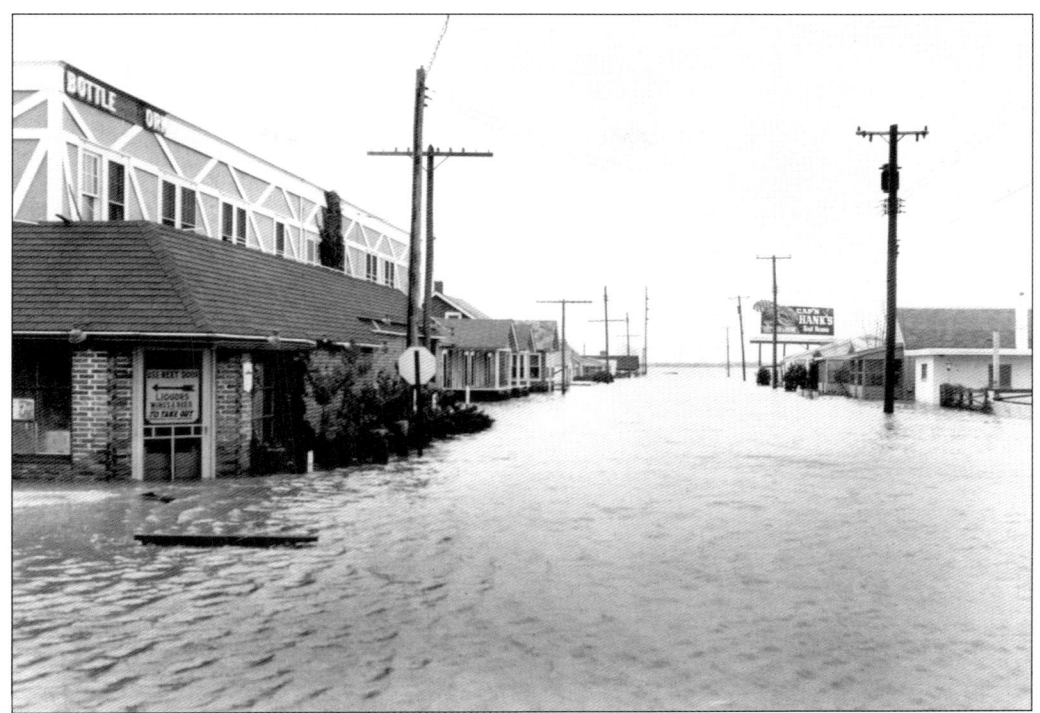

Floodwaters surged across streets of Dewey Beach, leaving thick deposits of sand in their wake. The photograph above shows the Bottle and Cork and a view down Bellevue Street towards Rehoboth Bay. The extensive flooding was a scene repeated throughout the entire town of Dewey. Up to five feet of sand accumulated in and around homes, as seen below. Although most of the bayside properties in Dewey were not left in total shambles, they suffered extensive water damage. (Both, courtesy Delaware DNREC.)

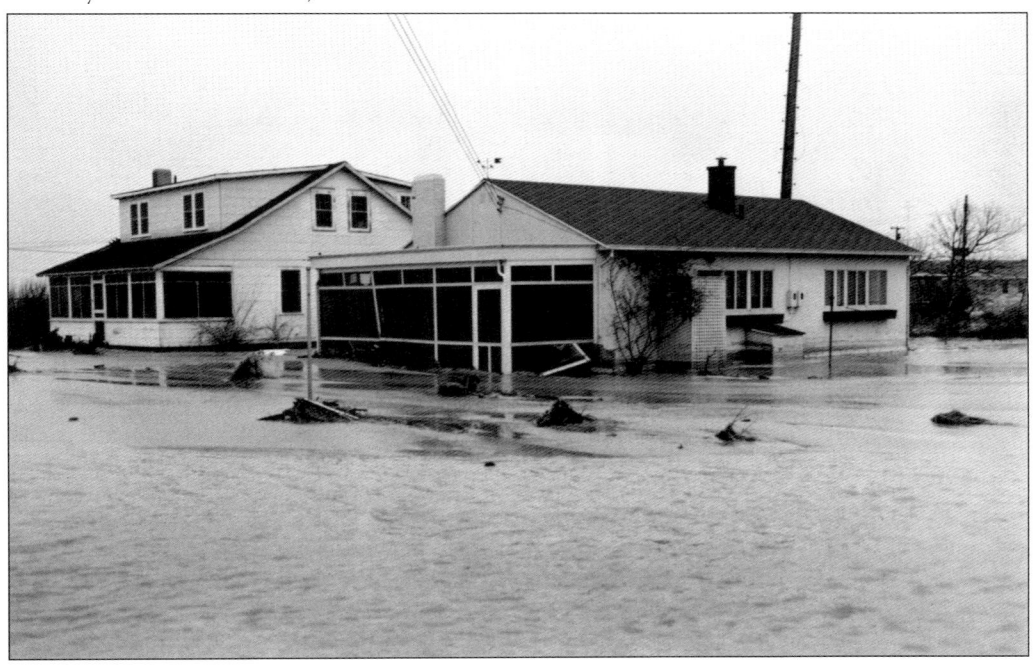

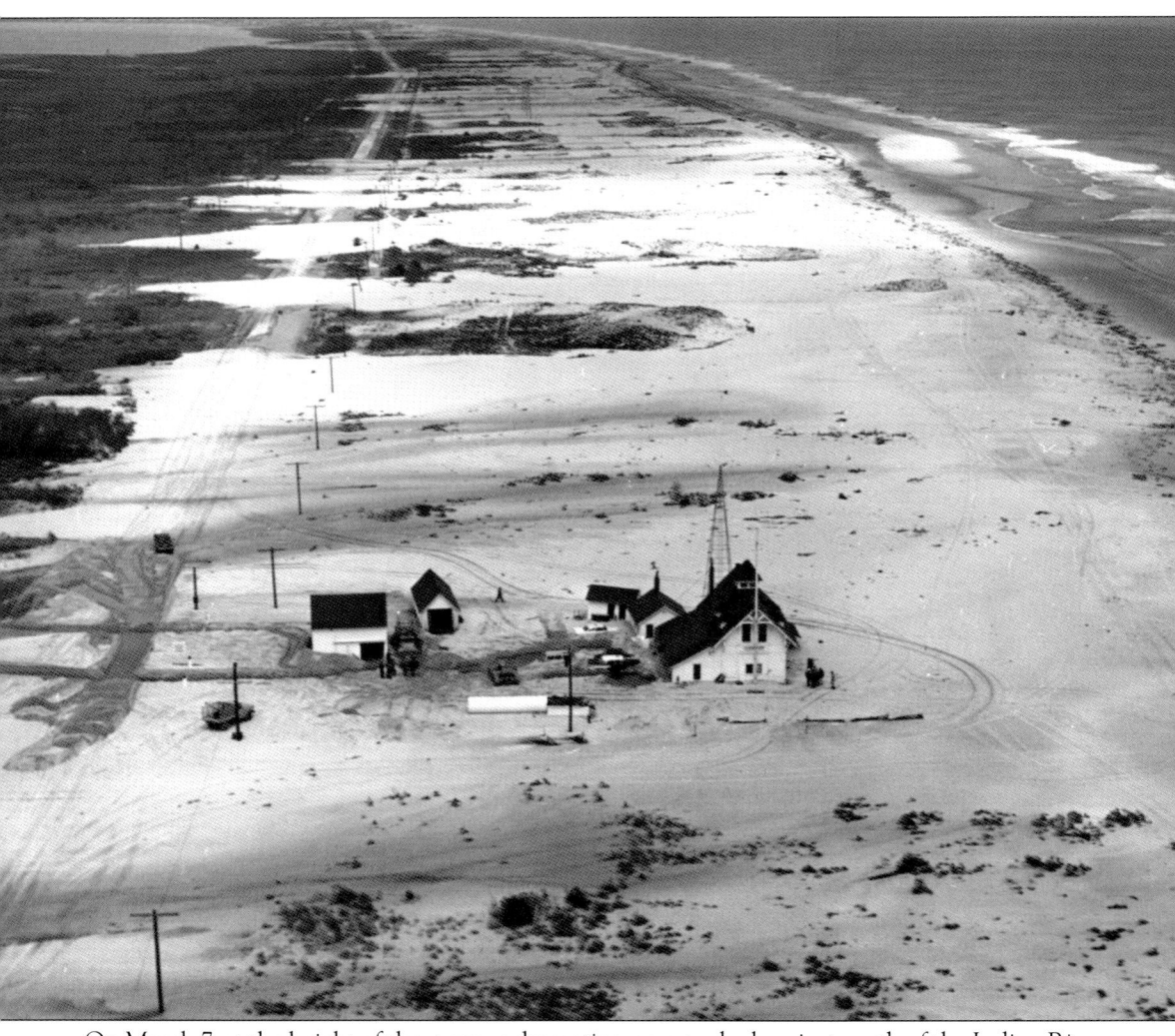

On March 7, at the height of the storm, a dramatic rescue took place just north of the Indian River Inlet. In the face of 50 mile-per-hour winds, helicopter pilot Capt. James R. Sulpizi (Delaware National Guard) rescued 10 Coast Guardsmen and National Guardsmen who were isolated at the Indian River Coast Guard Station. The stranded men had to wade in chest-deep water to a small dry area where they were picked up, one at a time, in the small two-seater helicopter and piloted to the Rehoboth Beach airport. After the storm, the US Coast Guard decided to abandon the Indian River Inlet station and build a new facility in another location. (Courtesy Delaware Public Archives.)

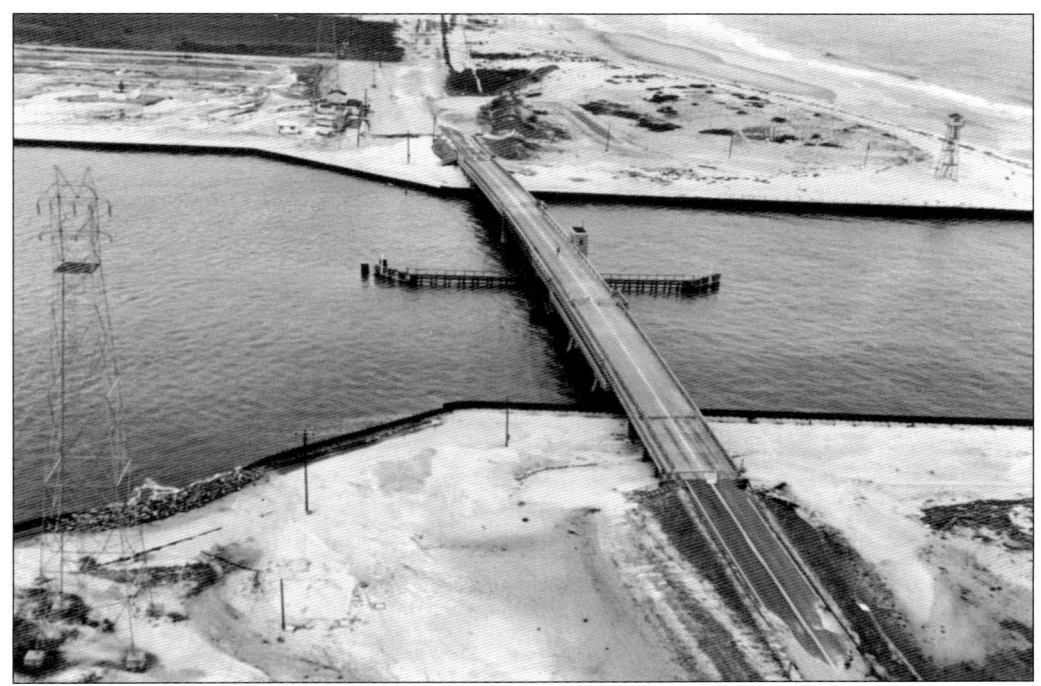

Especially vulnerable was the vicinity of Indian River Inlet where the bridge was damaged and considered unsafe (above). The highway department was faced with the task of evaluating the old road and deciding whether to keep it open in the same location. A dramatic tale of survival unfolded overnight at the Indian River Inlet trailer park (below). A US Coast Guardsman and a trailer park resident barely survived the storm. Stranded on-site by rapidly rising water levels, they took refuge in the largest trailer they could find. The trailer was battered by light poles and debris through the night and became flooded with water so high they had to sit on a stepladder and a tall table. After spending 19 hours in bitterly cold water, they were finally rescued and taken by helicopter to Beebe Hospital for treatment. (Both, courtesy Delaware Public Archives.)

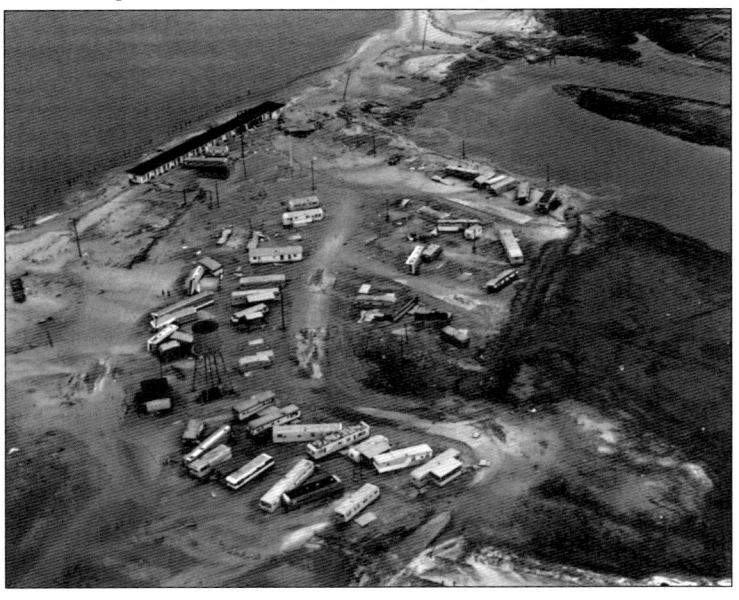

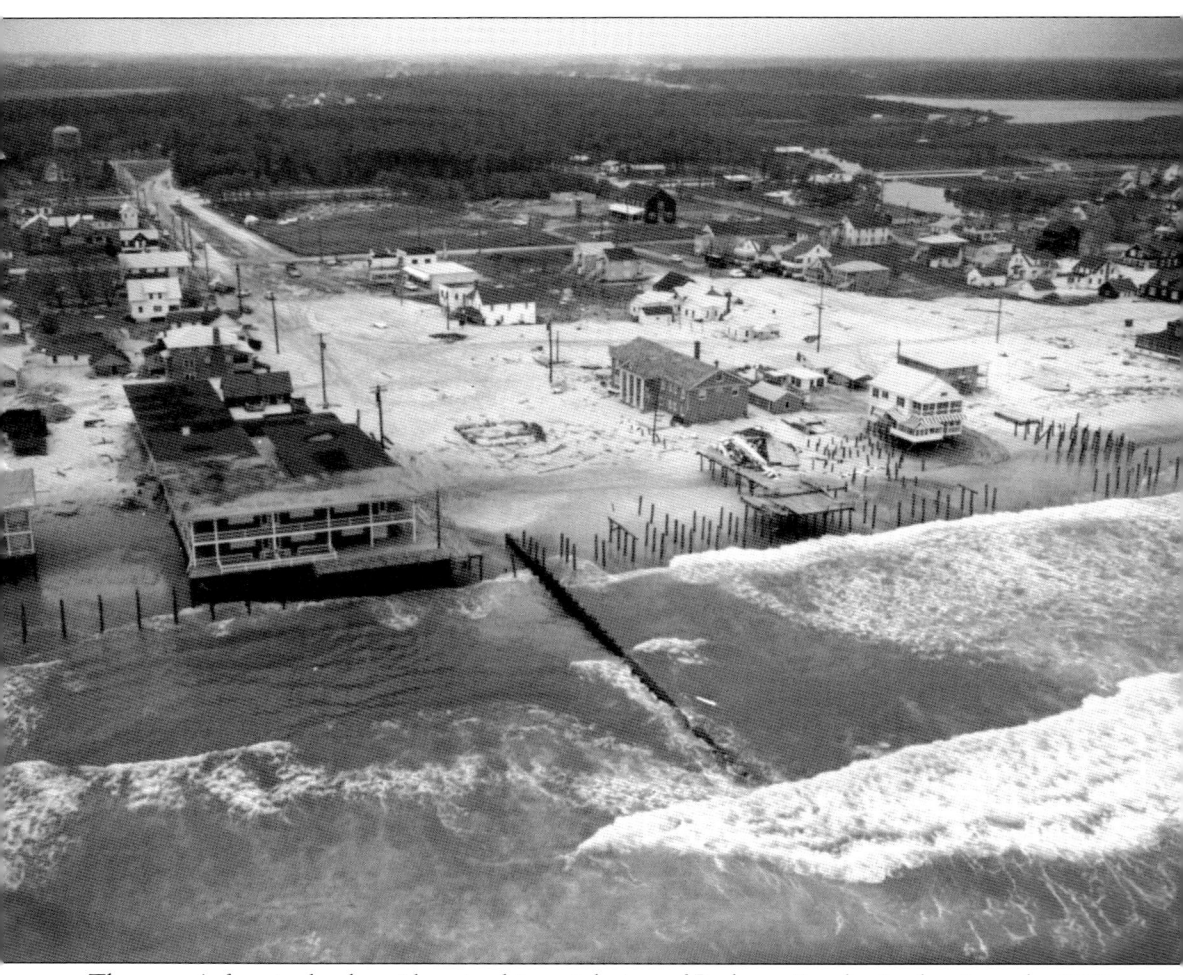

The storm's fury is clearly evident in this aerial view of Bethany Beach. At the time, the 1962 Storm was the most destructive storm in the town's 60-year history, and no coastal storm since 1962 has wreaked such devastation on the community. Landmark hotels, inns, and businesses were destroyed, including the Seaside Inn and Holiday House, as well as the town pavilion and bowling alley. The one-mile boardwalk was torn from its pilings, buildings were demolished, and sand covered the first two blocks of Garfield Parkway. The town was without power, heat, or water, and much of the town was flooded. In fact, Route 14 was under water, as was Route 26 to Ocean View and beyond. (Courtesy Delaware DNREC.)

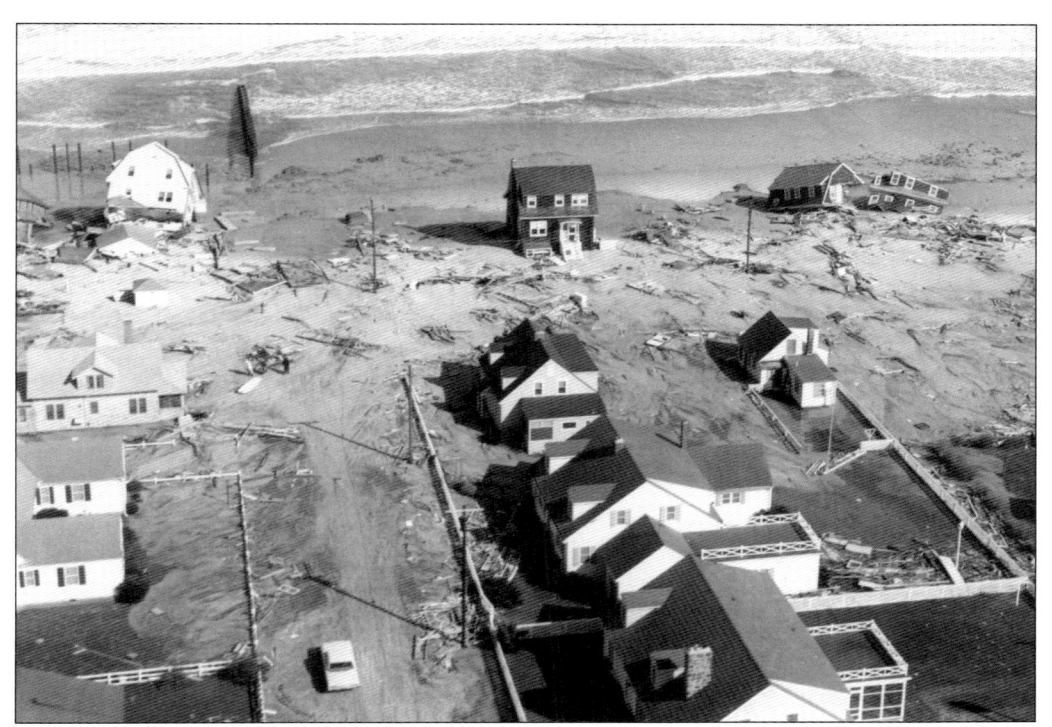

Pounding seas washed over dunes and flooded the streets in Bethany Beach. Dunes were demolished and beachfront homes were totally wrecked, tilted on foundations, or washed away. Debris and sand accumulated on all streets leading to the beach. (Courtesy Delaware Public Archives.)

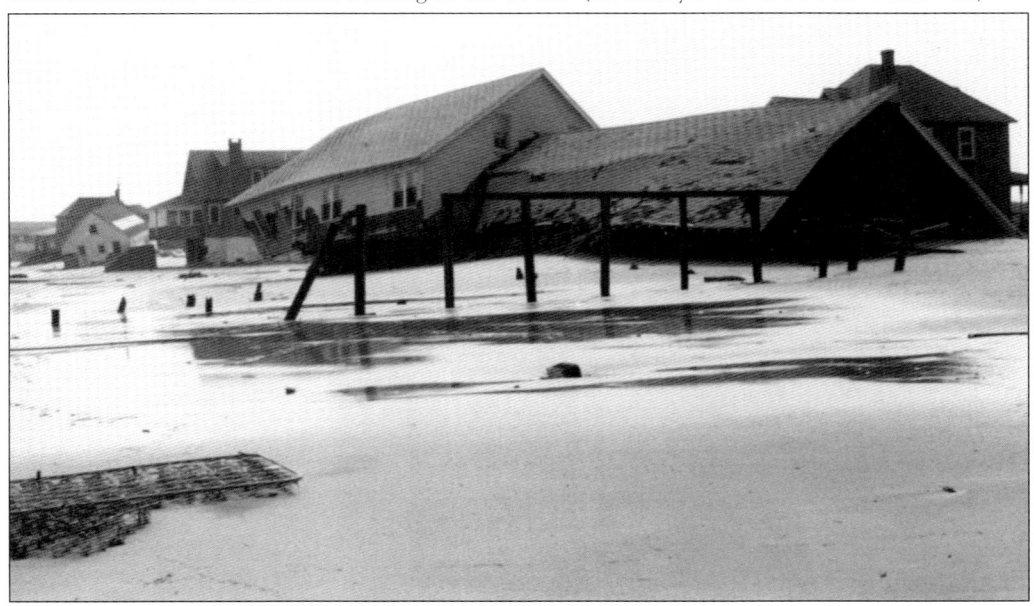

After storm tides receded, widespread wreckage was all that remained along the beach in Bethany. Of the 29 oceanfront houses in the town, 28 were destroyed. Portions of homes rested on sand, and some houses were missing entire sections of living areas. The only thing remaining of the bowling alley (shown above) was the roof. Note the remnant mattress springs in the foreground. (Courtesy Town of Bethany Beach.)

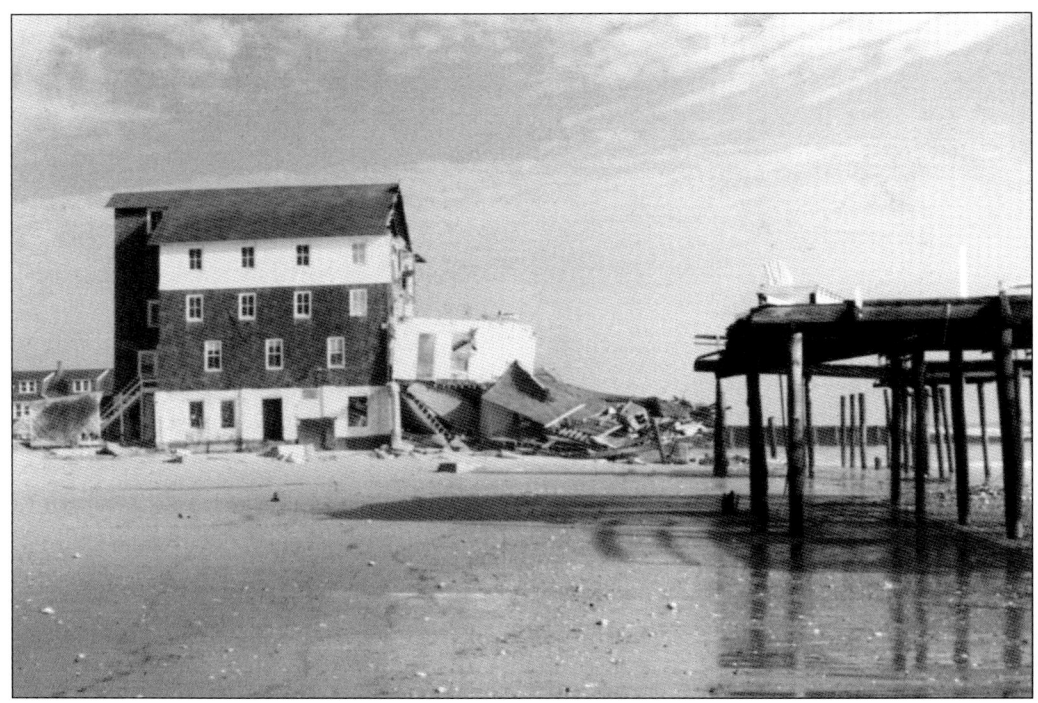

The scale of the disaster is evident in these photographs. Scenes of total destruction were everywhere as savage seas surged across the entire community; homes were ripped apart, sections of houses were piled against one another, and homes were upended and tossed by waves. The photograph above shows what remains of the Seaside Hotel and the boardwalk in Bethany Beach. Below is a view of oceanfront cottages at the southern end of town. (Both, courtesy Town of Bethany Beach.)

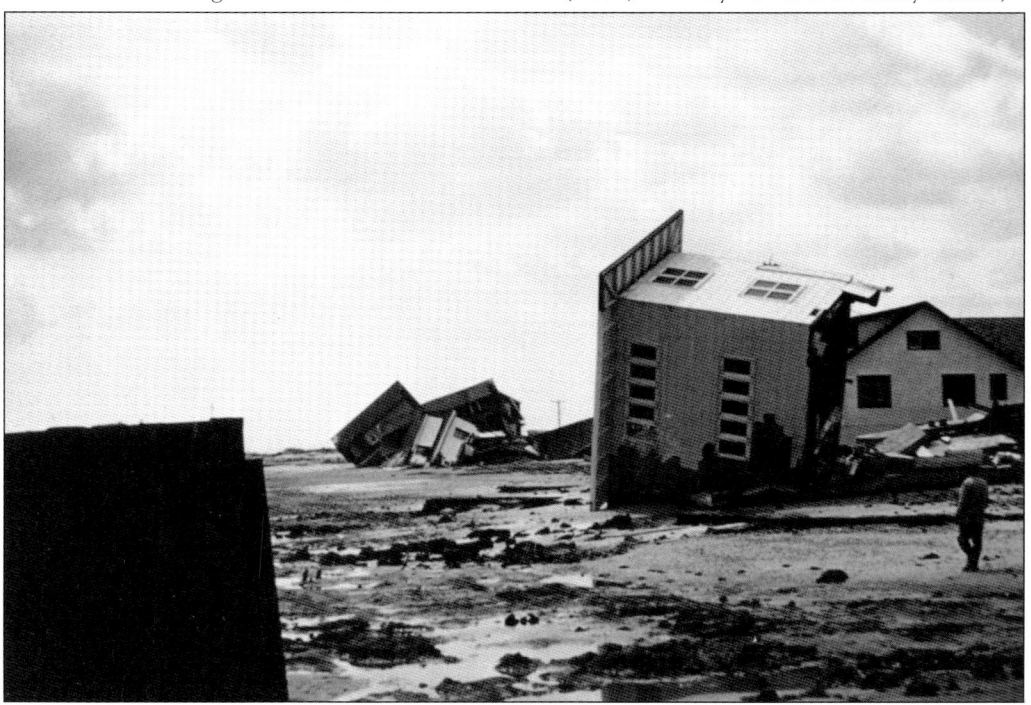

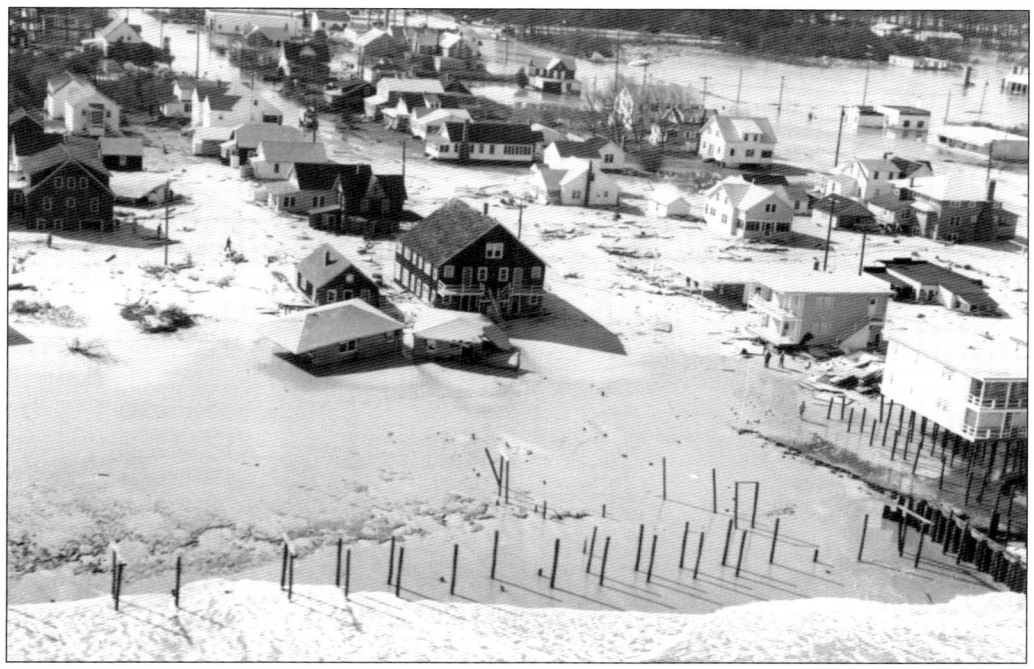

Homes collapsed as they were undermined and removed from original foundations. Pilings in the foreground are all that remain of the Bethany Beach boardwalk. Parts of town that were not covered with sand and debris were covered with water (note flooding in upper right of photograph). As seen below in a view of Atlantic Avenue, many side streets were under three to four feet of water for days after the storm. (Above, courtesy Delaware Public Archives; below, courtesy Town of Bethany Beach.)

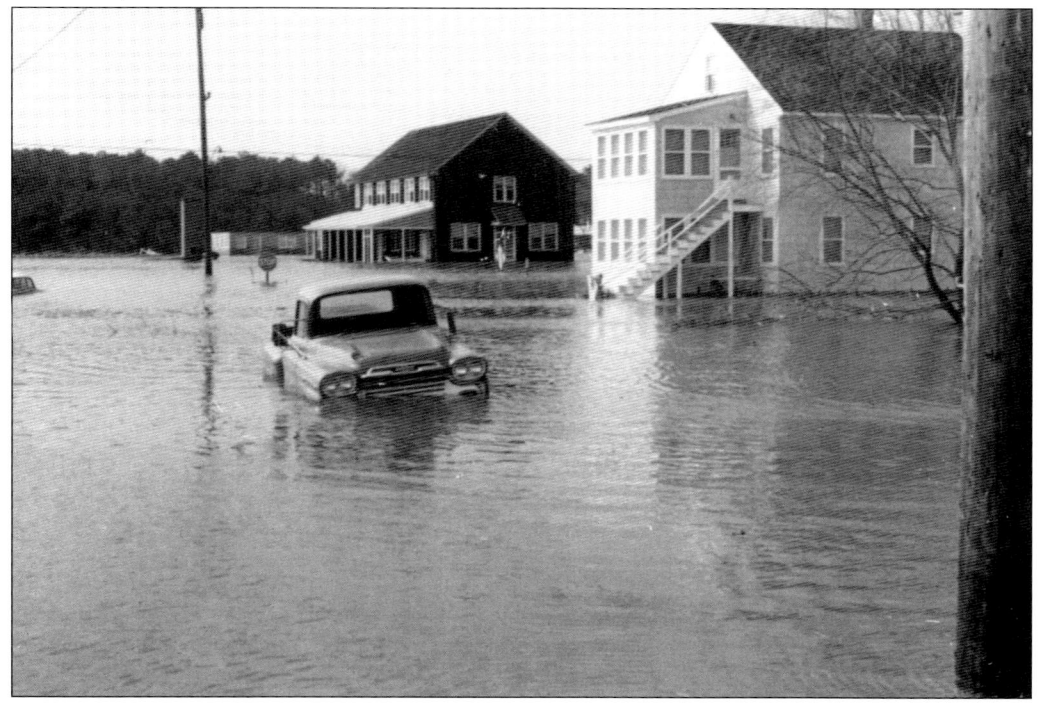

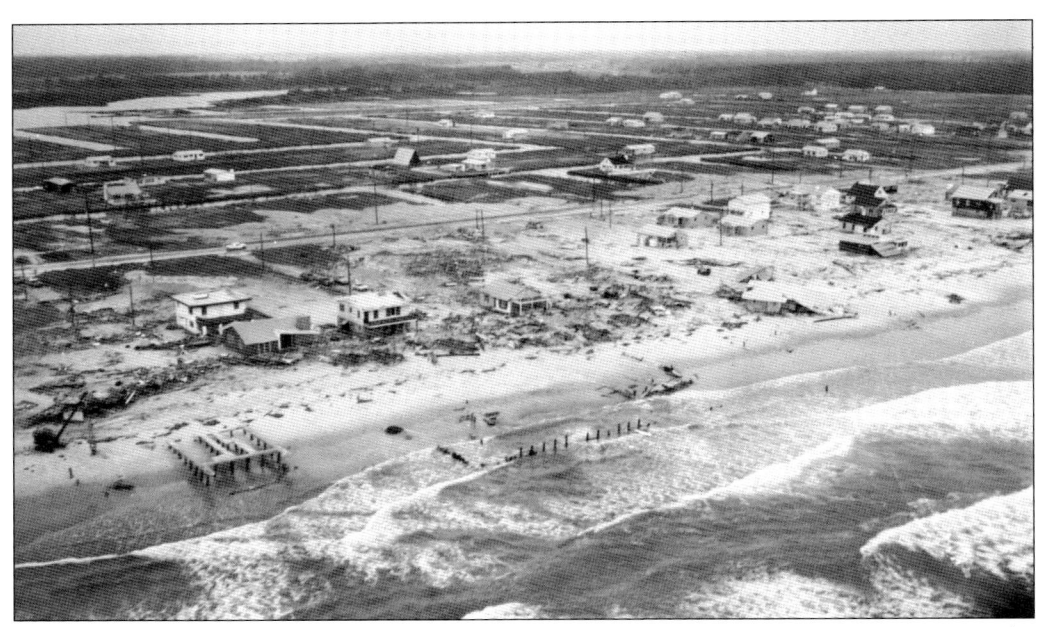

In South Bethany, ravaging floodwaters and pounding waves left a trail of destruction across the entire stretch of coast, from the ocean to the bay. The entire front row of oceanfront houses was swept away by the sea. Shattered dreams in the form of splintered lumber and broken concrete were strewn across the beachfront. Some property owners returned to find their homes or parts of homes moved by the tides to a different location—either down the block or across the highway. In the photograph below, it is hard to imagine the size and power of the waves that turned this cottage on end and battered it to pieces. Remnants of the slab foundation can be seen in bottom right corner, along with a bathtub and chair. (Above, courtesy Delaware DNREC; below, courtesy South Bethany Historical Society.)

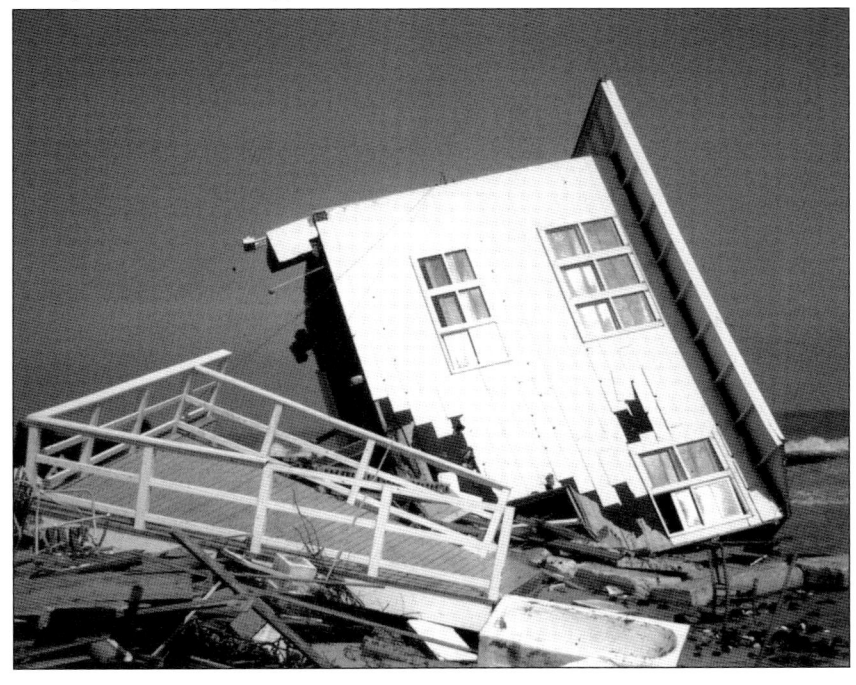

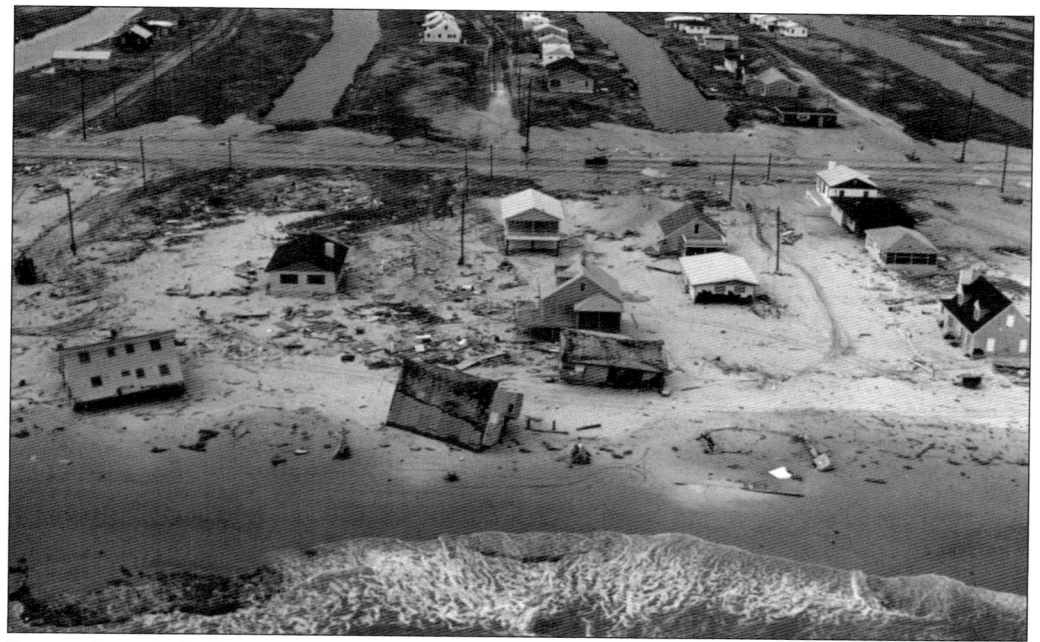

Extraordinarily high tides carried South Bethany's oceanfront homes off foundations as 20- to 30-foot waves turned them over and broke them apart. Not only were 23 homes totally destroyed, but the beach itself was totally changed; sand was carried hundreds of feet inland across Route 14 and into canals and marshland. Before the storm, the beach was relatively wide, and intermittent sand dunes offered a measure of protection from average coastal storms. (Both, courtesy Delaware Public Archives.)

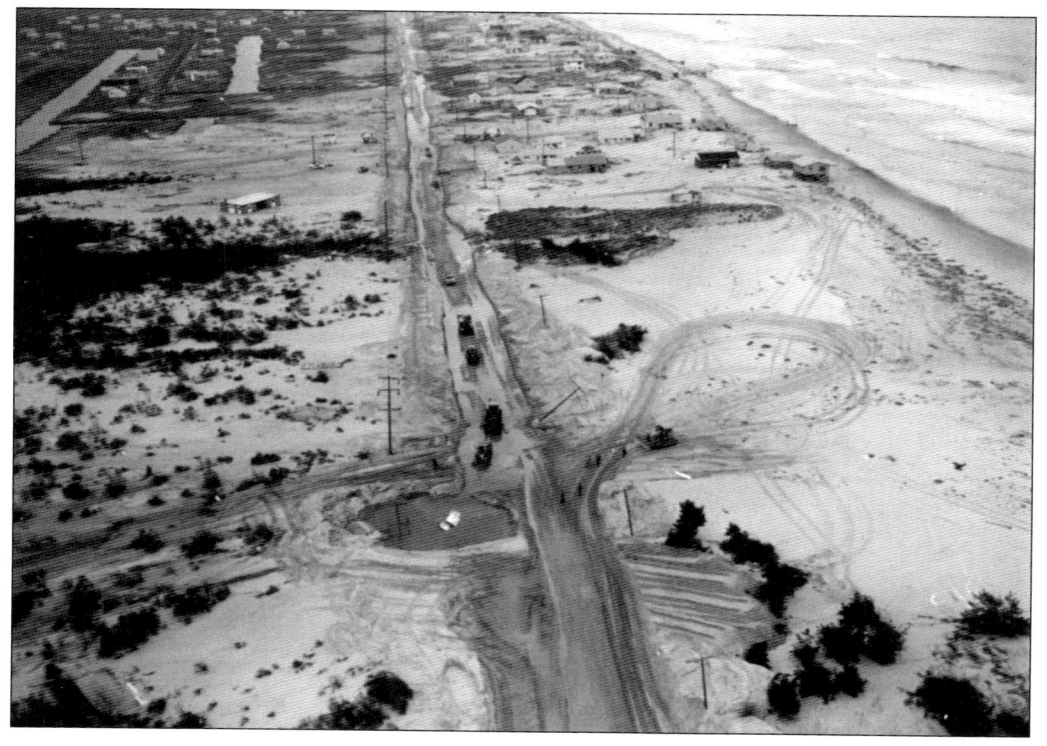

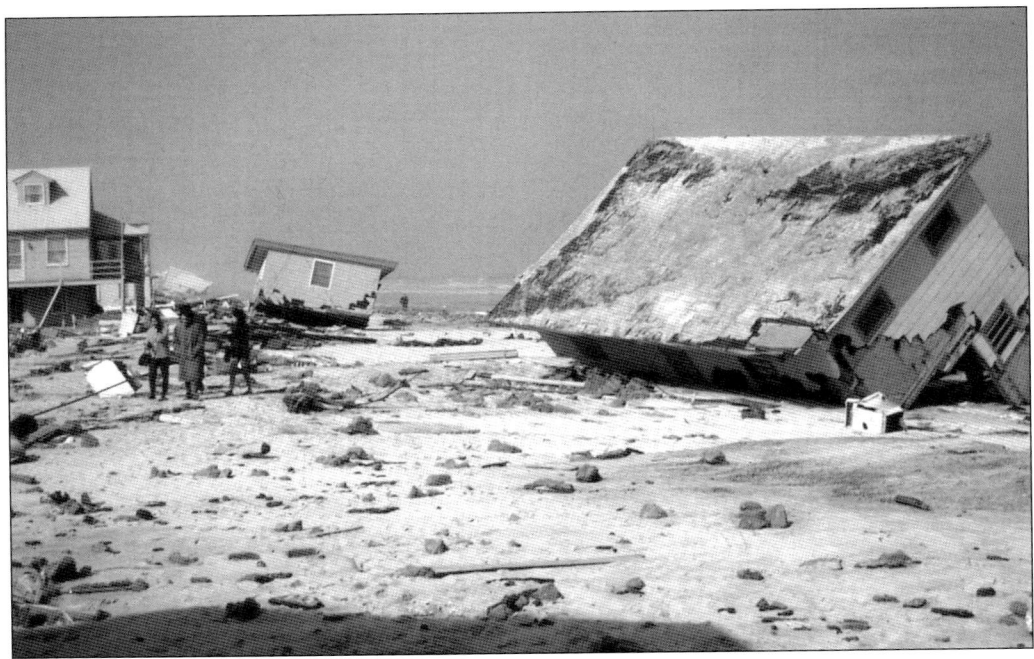

Nothing remained of the sand dunes and front line of houses in South Bethany. The entire ocean block was covered with debris: concrete blocks, roofs, walls, and windows. The beach was covered not only with broken homes, but also with pieces of broken lives: refrigerators, sinks, furniture, clothes, beds, photo albums, and memories. (Both, courtesy South Bethany Historical Society.)

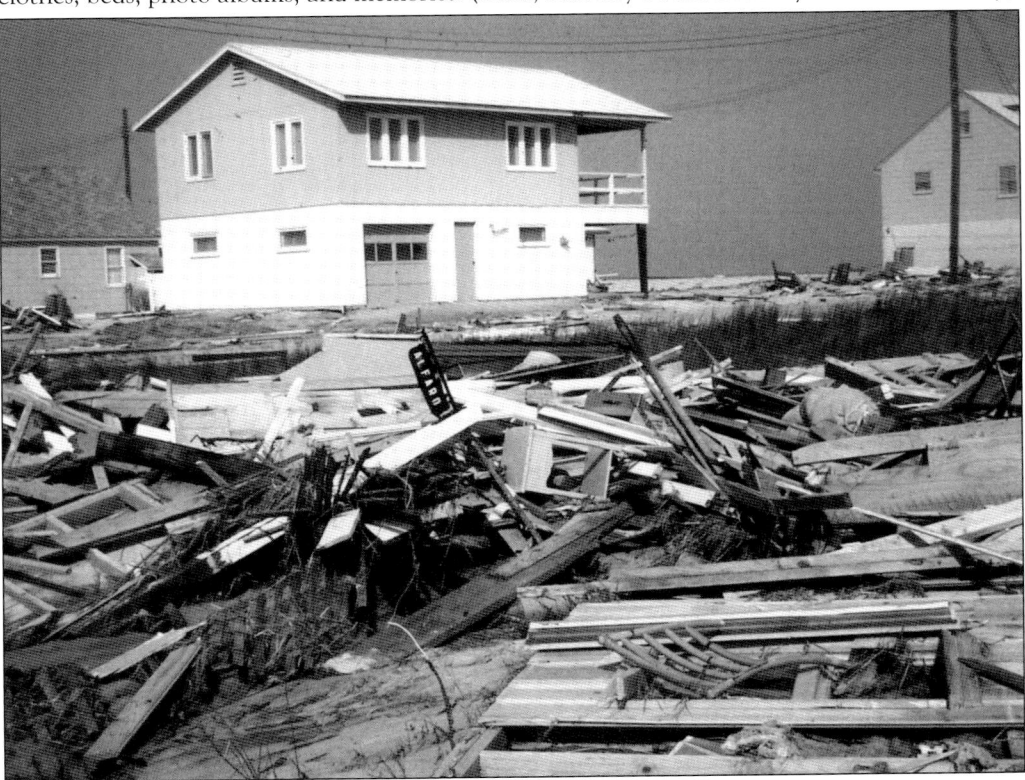

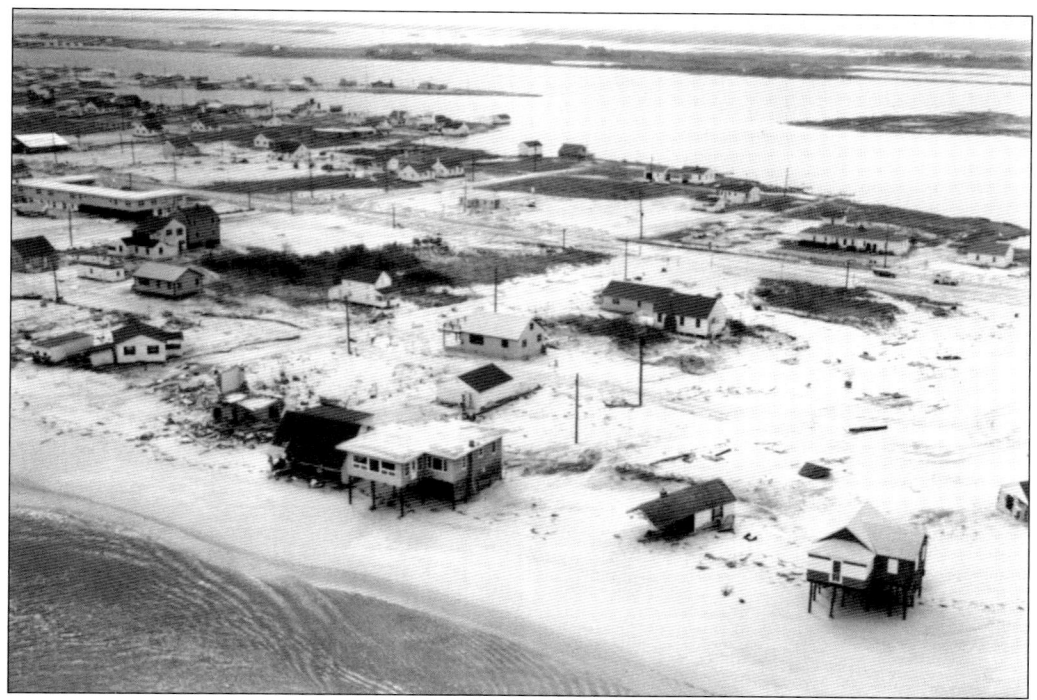

Initial accounts of damage in Fenwick Island revealed that dunes were flattened, more than half of the oceanfront cottages were totally destroyed, and many others were badly damaged. Ocean waves and tides poured across the beach and dunes, moving homes from foundations and toppling even newly constructed houses end over end. (Above, courtesy Delaware Public Archives; below, courtesy Colonel McGarraugh via Marna Cupp.)

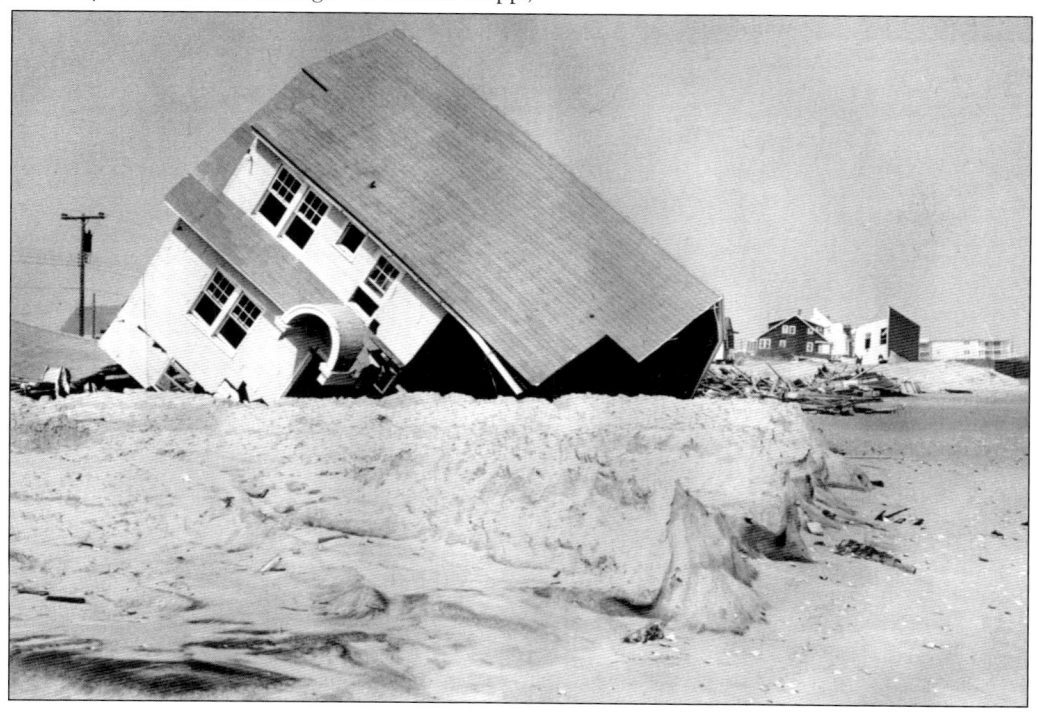

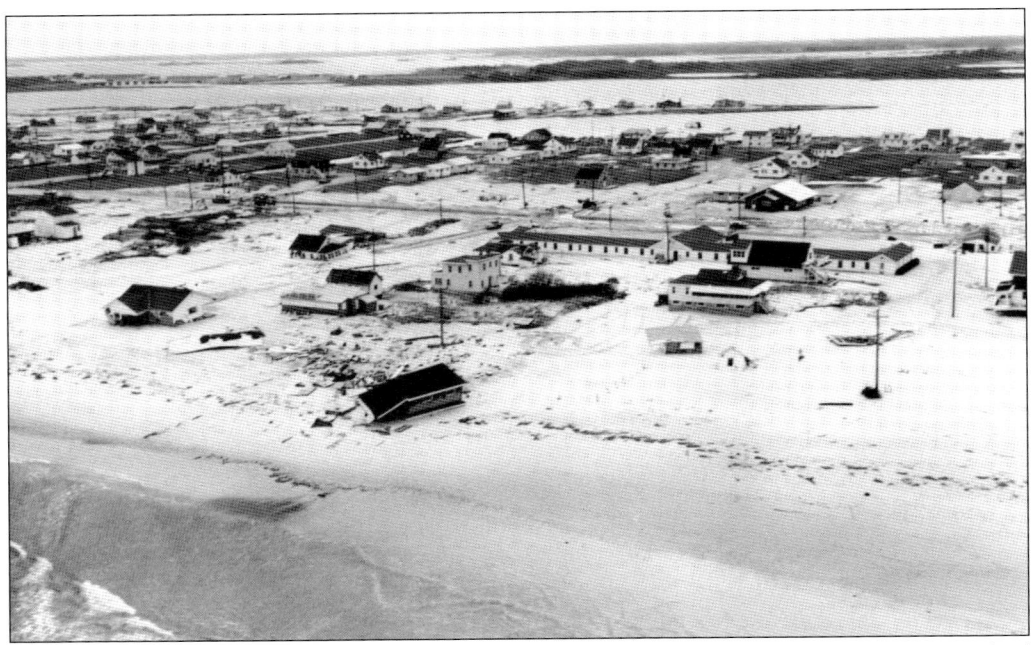

Throughout the town of Fenwick Island, continuous pounding of waves and tides wreaked havoc on oceanfront homes—most were broken apart, totally undermined, or transported off foundations. The late Mary Pat Kyle, an eyewitness to the devastating destruction, described the scene as viewed from a high vantage point on Route 54 saying, "And what a sight it was. Although we were approximately three miles inland, we could see huge breakers coming in to the shore and completely washing over the beach into the bay near the area of Fenwick Towers [built since the storm]. The huge breaking waves are a sight I will never forget." (Both, courtesy Delaware DNREC.)

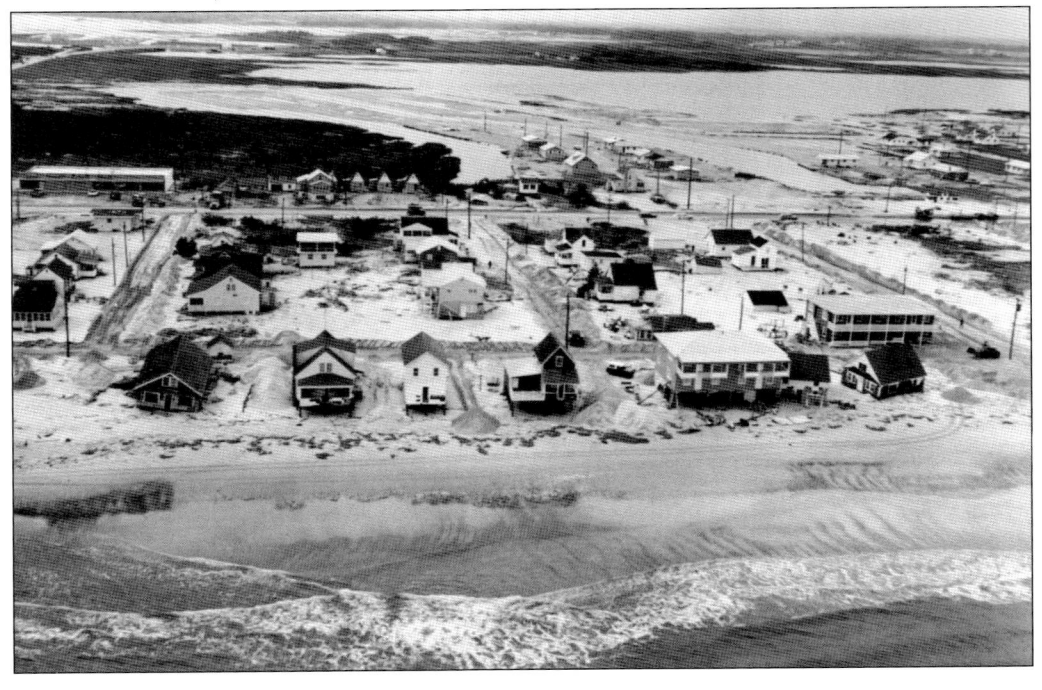

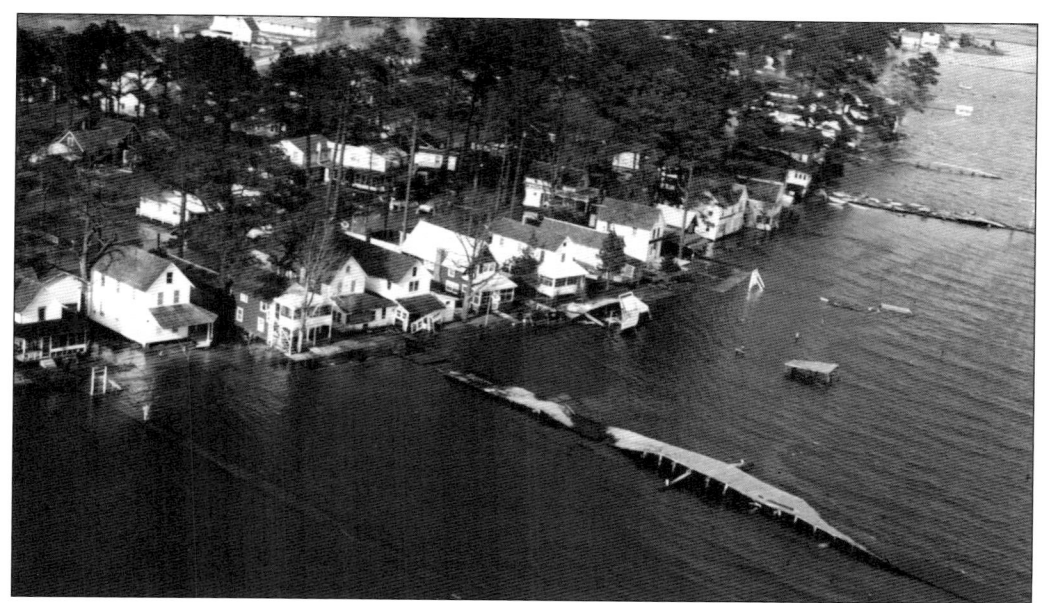

Roadways and properties surrounding the Inland Bays were flooded by three-foot wind-driven waves and tides that were four feet above normal. Members of the Indian River Fire Company worked day and night to provide assistance to local residents. Preliminary property damage estimates in the Indian River area alone were projected to be $400,000. Along the north side of Indian River Bay, residents of Oak Orchard reported that homes were ruined and flooding was so extensive that the only access to properties on the bay front was by boat. Much of the shoreline along the Indian River had been washed away and several boathouses were smashed to pieces. The *Evening Journal* cited an eyewitness account, "There are gas tanks and boats all over the place and six inches of water in the Indian River Fire House." (Both, courtesy Delaware Public Archives.)

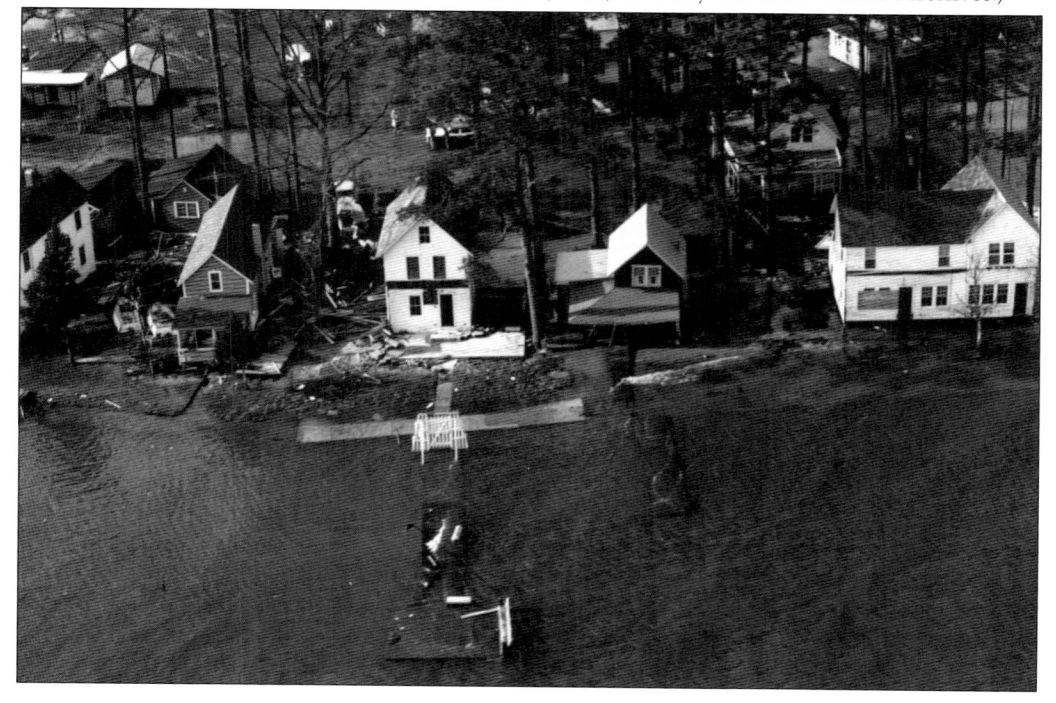

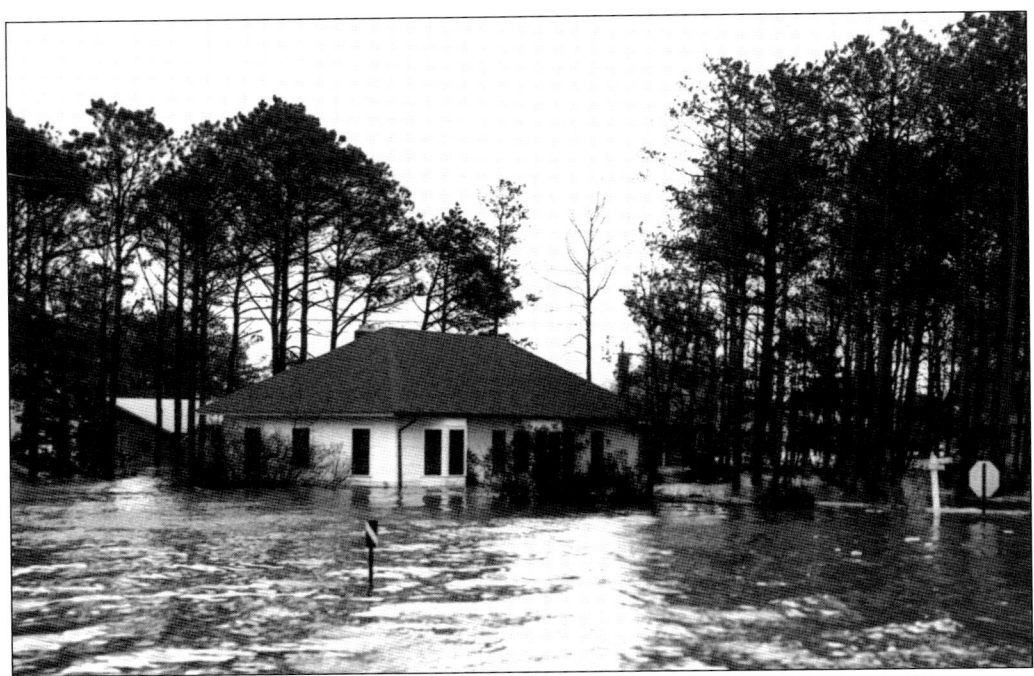

Road damage was significant on major highways and local streets alike, from one end of the state to the other. As of March 8, William J. Miller, director of operations for the Delaware State Highway Department, reported that road damage was severe, but that it was too early to assign dollar estimates for repairs. Miller also emphasized that it was impossible to make even rough estimates because most of the roads were still covered with water. Additionally, most highway department personnel were still involved in rescue operations. (Both, courtesy Delaware Public Archives.)

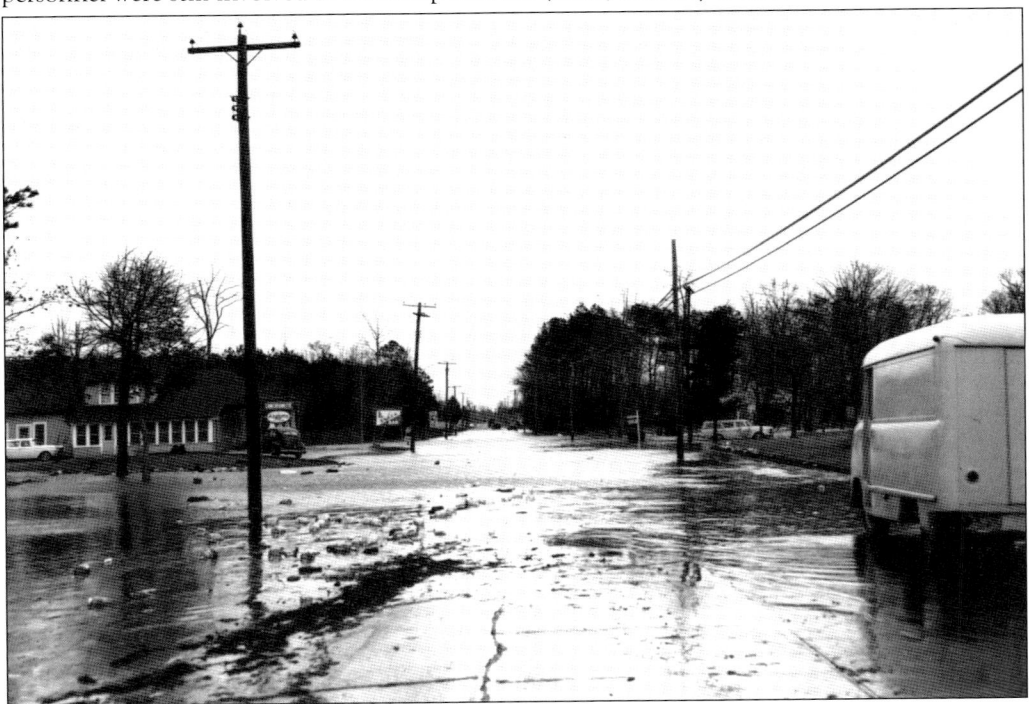

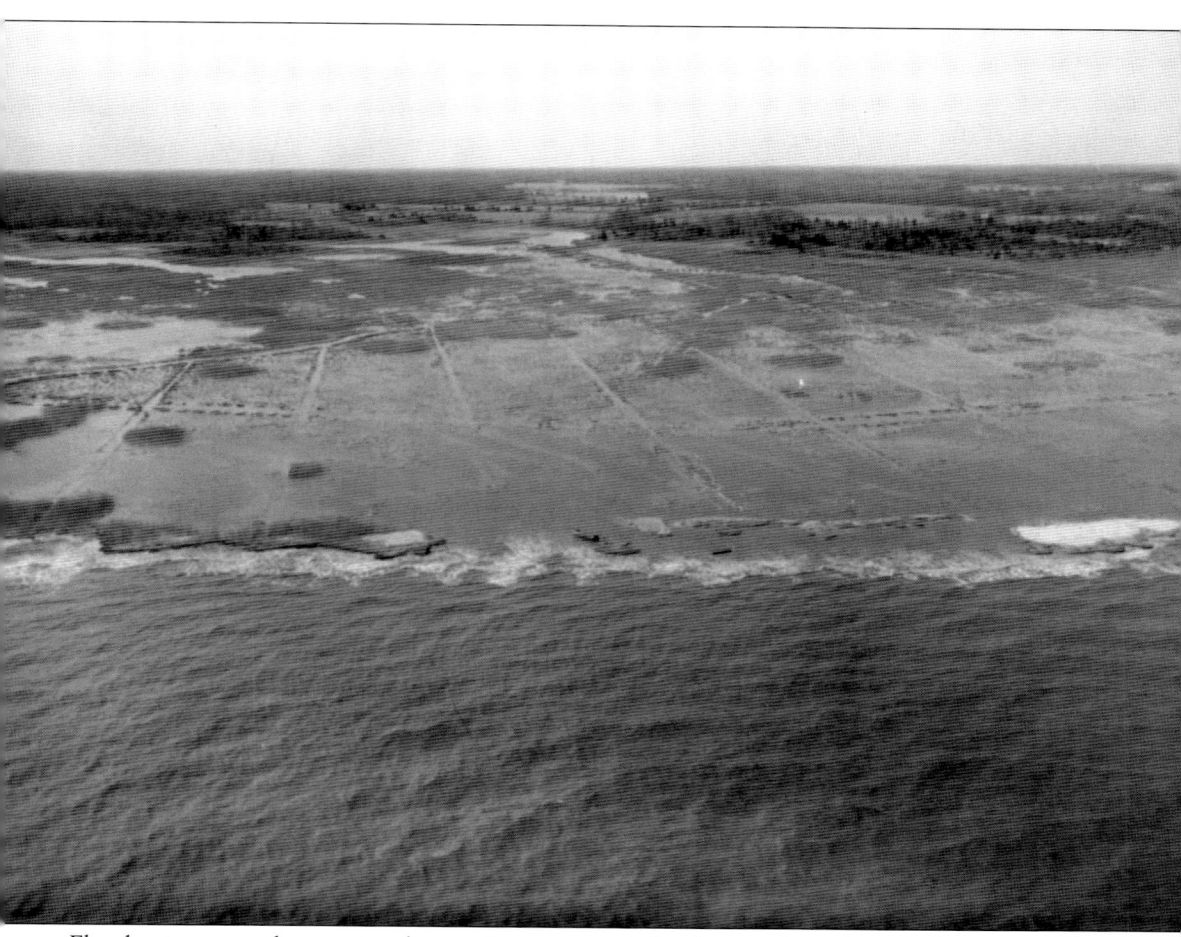

Floodwaters caused extensive devastation in many inland areas throughout Delmarva. It was reported that as many as half a million broiler chickens were lost in Sussex County as streams swollen from storm surge and rain flooded brooder houses. Much of this type of damage occurred between Route 113 and the coast, concentrated in the low-lying areas around the Inland Bays. Farmland throughout the state was flooded with seawater. This photograph shows that even as late as March 22, Delaware Bay floodwaters still encroached over the beach-marsh system, flooding adjacent low-lying land. In Kent County alone, approximately 20,000 acres of cropland were under water at one time. Research teams from the University of Delaware's School of Agriculture initiated work to test salt concentration in fields from Smyrna to Oak Orchard and advised farmers on planting conditions. The highest soil salinity concentrations were found in the area south of Lewes, and the lowest were found in Kent County. Salt was expected to leach out of the soils before the late-April and early-May planting seasons. (Courtesy Delaware DNREC.)

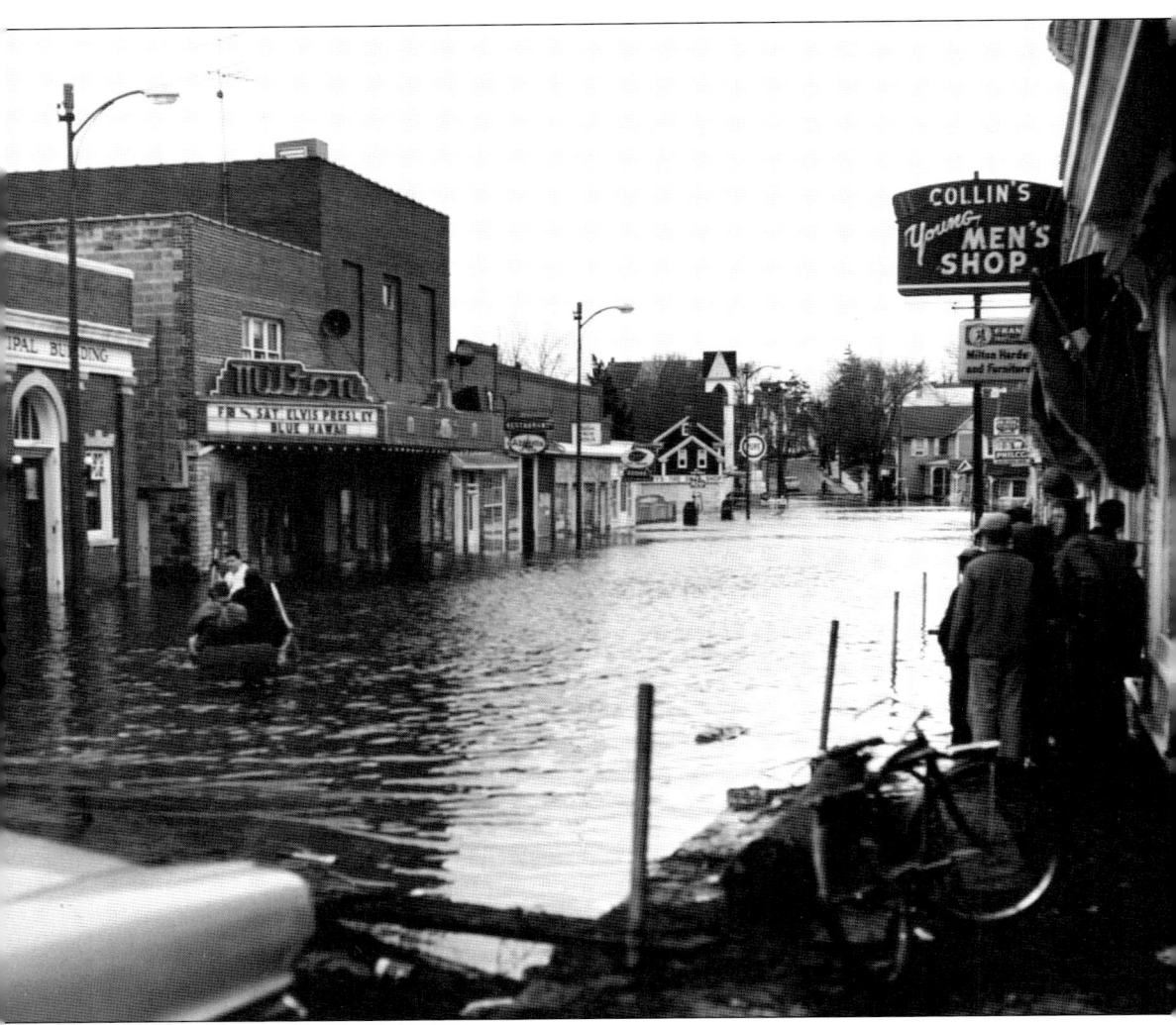

Widespread flooding occurred throughout Delaware's inland communities as tidal tributaries spilled over their banks. In Milton, police reported that it was impossible to travel through town because water from the Broadkill River had surged across main streets as shown in the photograph above. Union Street was closed to traffic for two days, and the first five rows of seats in the Milton Theatre were completely under water. Similarly, overflow from Mispillion River poured through the center of Milford, flooding much of the business section. Walnut Street was impassable, and shopkeepers throughout downtown Milford had to move their stock off the floors as water surged through the shops. (Courtesy Delaware Public Archives.)

Four

WIDESPREAD WRECKAGE

As the storm subsided, the wind dropped out, waves and tides flattened, and the sun returned to the sky, the devastating aftermath was visible in full dimension for the first time. For those who have not walked outside of homes or shelters or driven back into a disaster area following a major weather event, it is difficult to imagine what it feels like to people who have seen their vibrant, happy, productive neighborhoods laid flat, devastated by a short three days of high winds, waves, and tides. "I just enjoyed dinner with good friends in that house last weekend, and it and everything around it is gone" must be the kind of thought that goes through people's minds in a variety of scenarios when they see the loss for the first time.

The photographs in this chapter bring people who have not lived through it as close as one can get to the feeling of the loss. These are grim reminders of the power of the sea, just as Hurricanes Sandy, Katrina, and Ike have been recently in different parts of the country. Damages to buildings and infrastructure in coastal storms are due to three primary forces: high wind, flooding, and direct wave strikes. Waves and high tides also bring about land erosion, most notably at beaches and dunes, where the sand is swept away and the land surface is significantly lowered. Building foundations and infrastructure (roads, pipelines, utility poles, etc.) that rely on the land surface to support them are very often lost in the storm. The photographs in this chapter show many striking examples of the devastating wreckage wrought by the Ash Wednesday Storm.

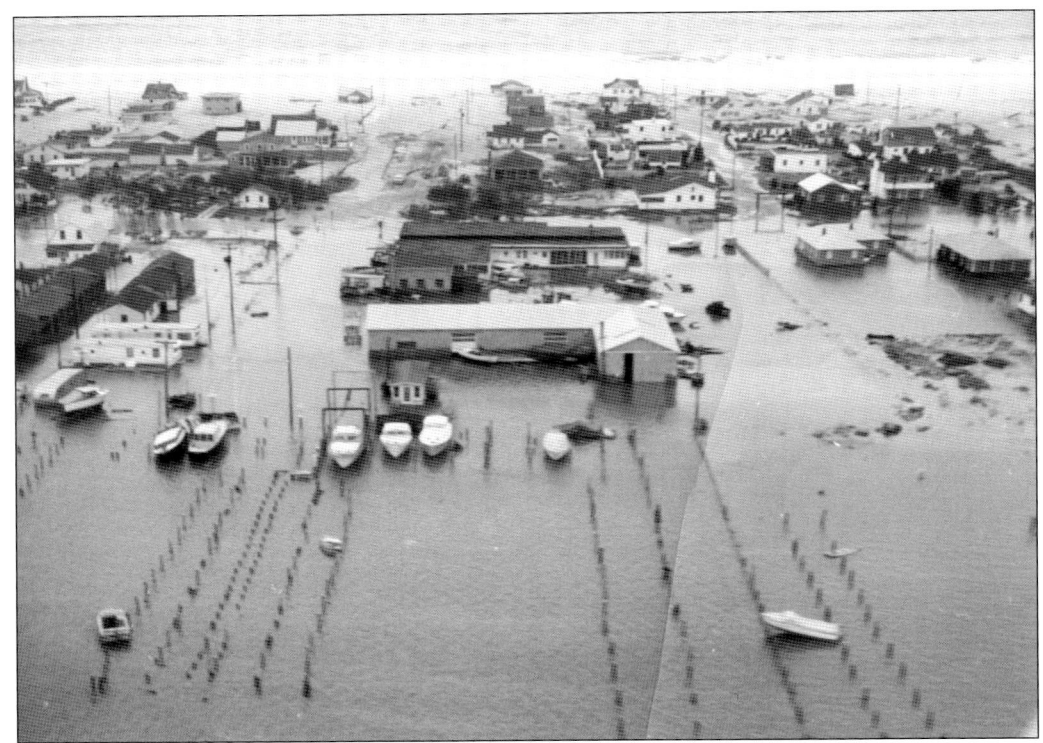

Flooding was by far the storm's most widespread impact. The above view, looking east from Rehoboth Bay, shows ocean and bay waters connecting across the entirety of Dewey Beach. This storm's surge still holds the record for the highest tide ever recorded in Delaware as of 2014. Low-lying areas were completely inundated, and as the sea flooded over the coast, ocean and bays were united as one. (Courtesy Norman Rossiter.)

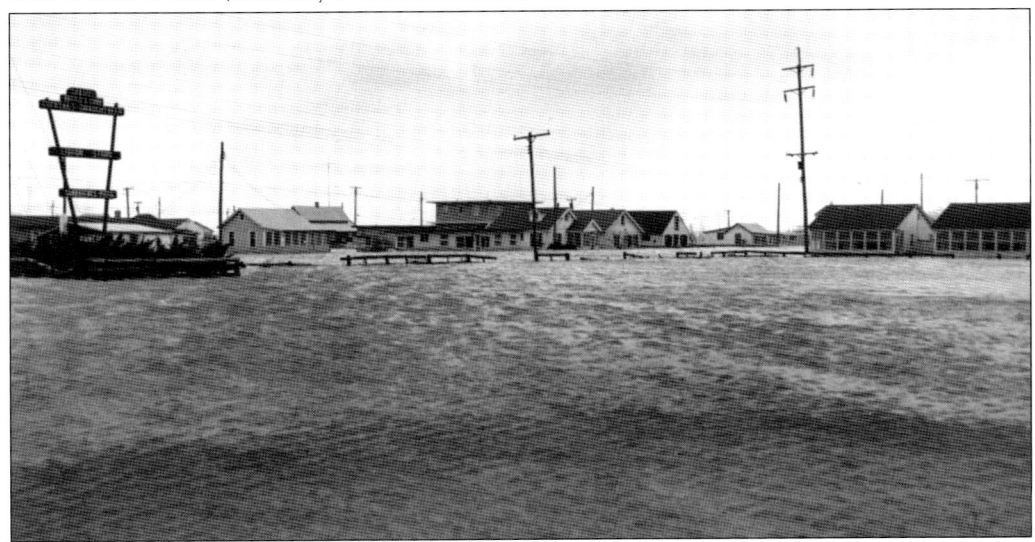

Bayside cottages in the 1950s and earlier were typically built with the first floor right at ground level, with little or no knowledge or concern about how high floodwaters may rise. This view of the Rehoboth Bay shore of Dewey shows cottages flooded out, with everything inside of them soaked with saltwater. (Courtesy Delaware Public Archives.)

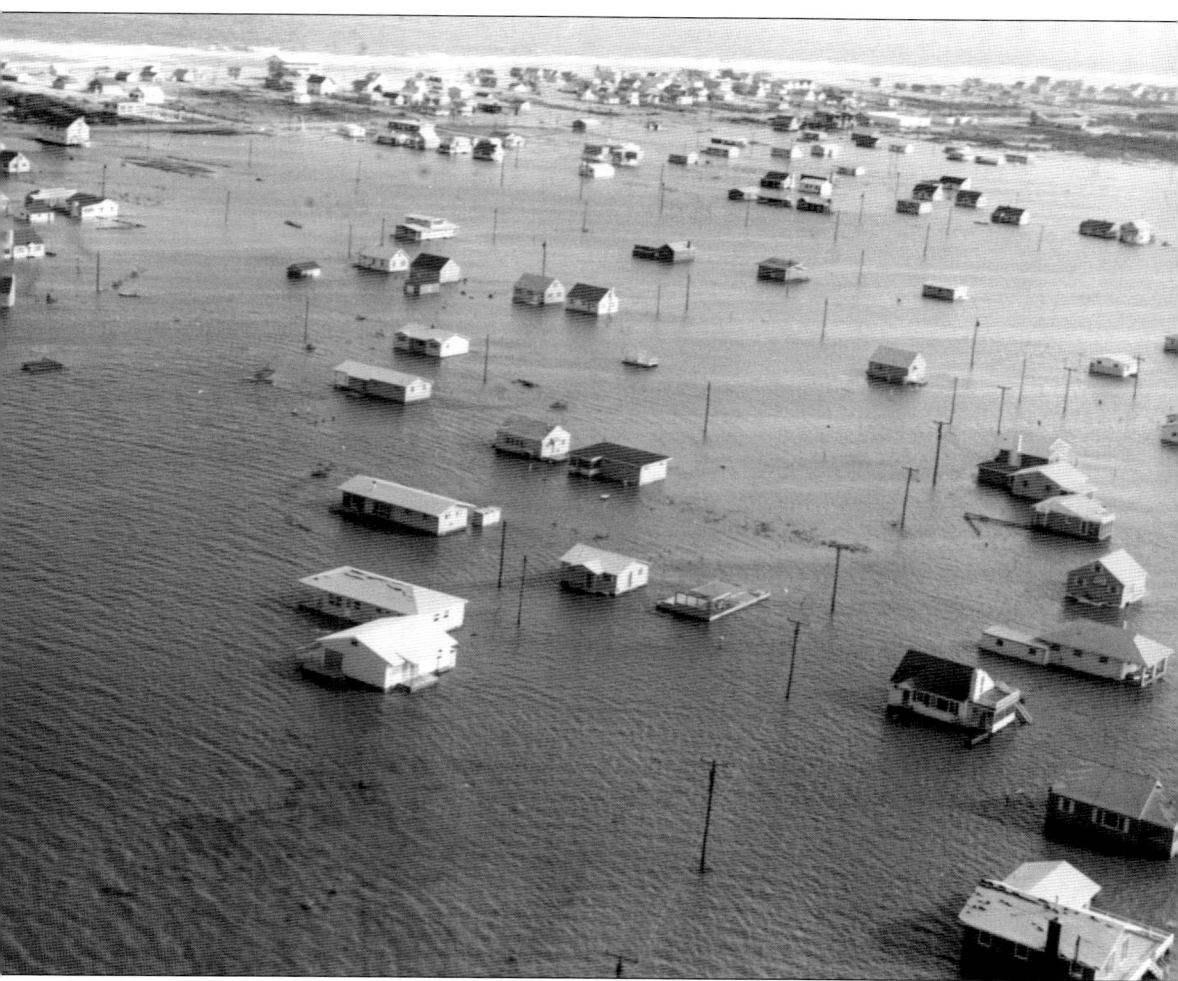

Coastal communities developed on narrow barrier beaches are especially vulnerable to flooding. Fenwick Island, built between the Atlantic Ocean and Little Assawoman Bay, was completely submerged during the 1962 Storm. Unlike many northeast storms, which typically subside after one or two tidal cycles, this storm persisted through five high tides. Mary Pat Kyle reported that all of Fenwick was flooded except for an area near the lighthouse. Not only did ocean water flow into the bay, but the bayside was also inundated with water washing back in from the west. This photograph shows bayside flooding that covered Route 14 and even appeared to connect to the ocean in the top center of the image. Nearly all homes on the west side of Route 14 in Fenwick suffered flood damage. (Courtesy Delaware Public Archives.)

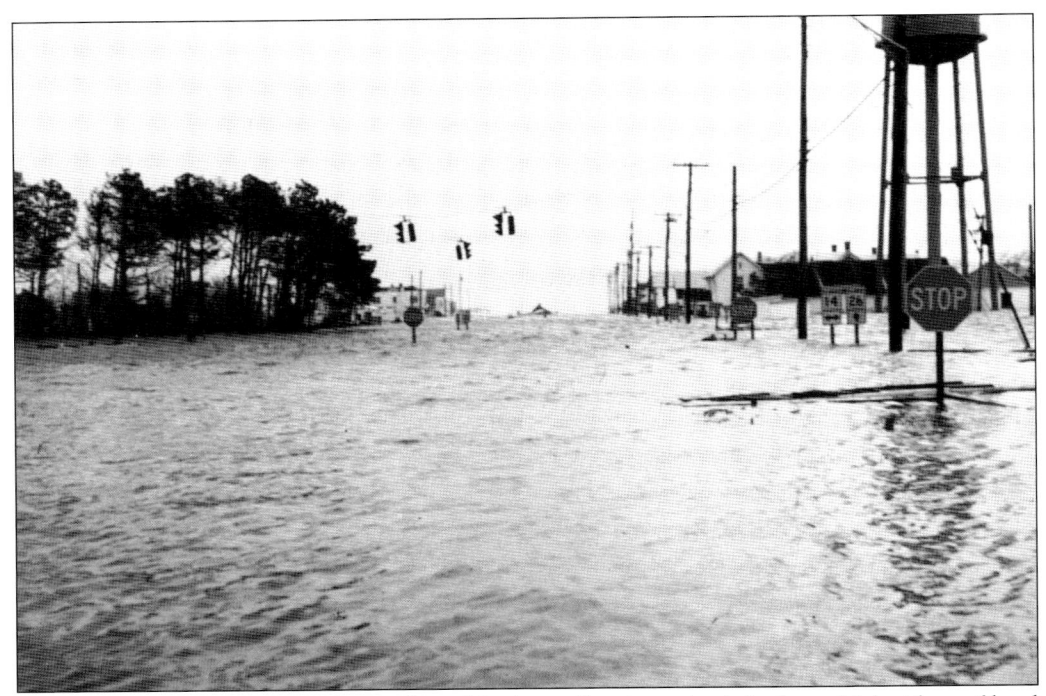

The communities of Rehoboth Beach and Bethany Beach are both built on high ridges of land that extend out to the sea with no back bay west of them. Bayside flooding was not an issue in Rehoboth; rather, all damages were right along the oceanfront. Bethany, however, is linked to the inland bays through a canal that had been created to bring boats into town. This canal allowed access for tidal water flow, and as water also came over or through the dune, the result was substantial flooding of downtown Bethany (shown in photographs above and below), a problem that occurs even today during severe coastal storms. (Both, courtesy Town of Bethany Beach.)

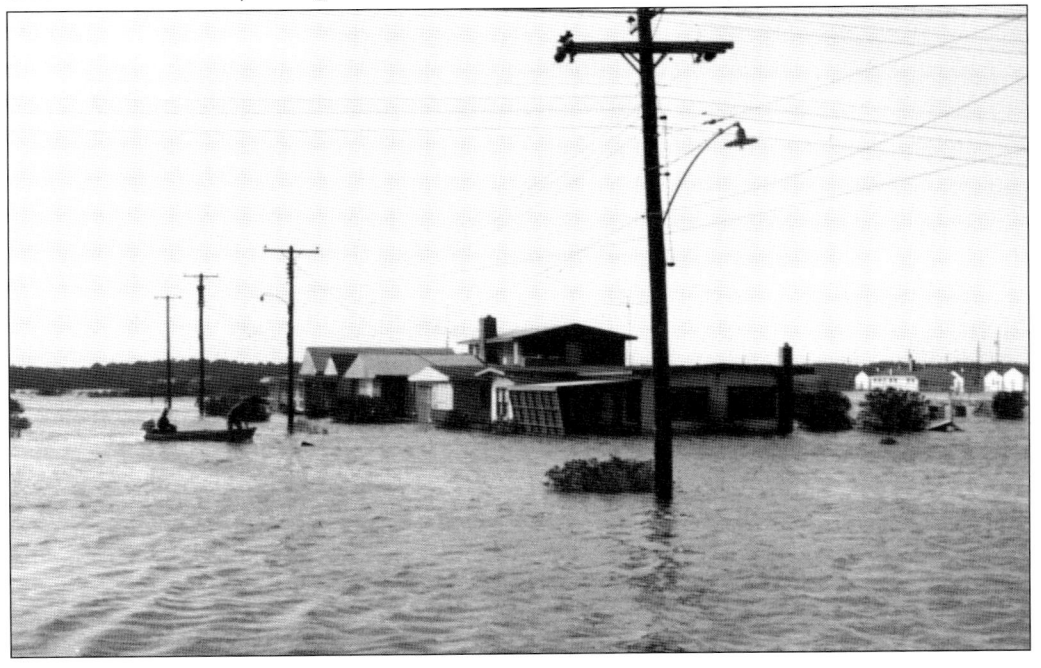

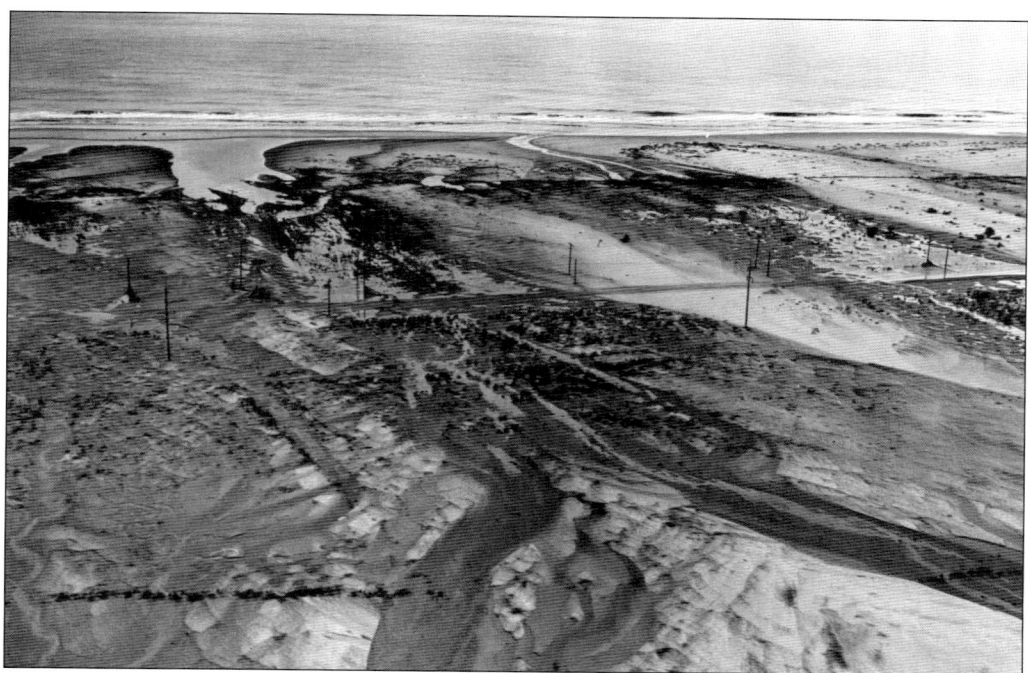

The photograph above is a post-storm view of the stretch of highway between Dewey Beach and Indian River Inlet. Telephone poles mark the location of Route 14 (now Route 1). Water flooding over the dunes and washing back into roads behind them carried huge amounts of sand as it flowed. Once the water level went down, the results of the flooding were revealed. The photograph below shows deep deposits of sand left on the roads, in some ways similar to snow covering roads after a winter storm but far heavier and more difficult to get rid of. (Above, courtesy Delaware DNREC; below, courtesy South Bethany Historical Society.)

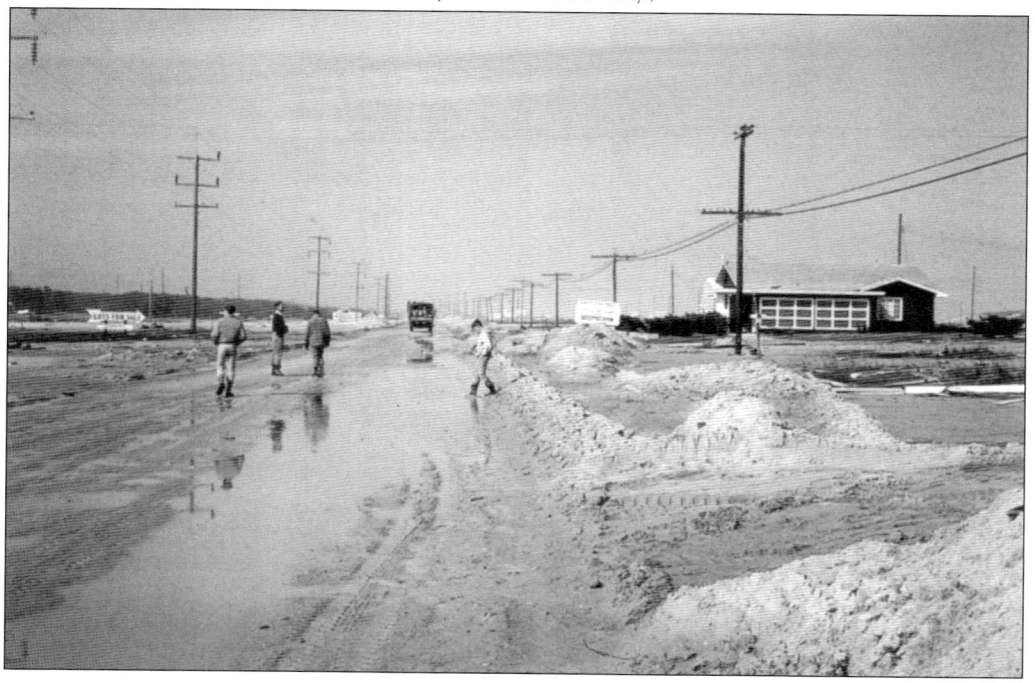

61

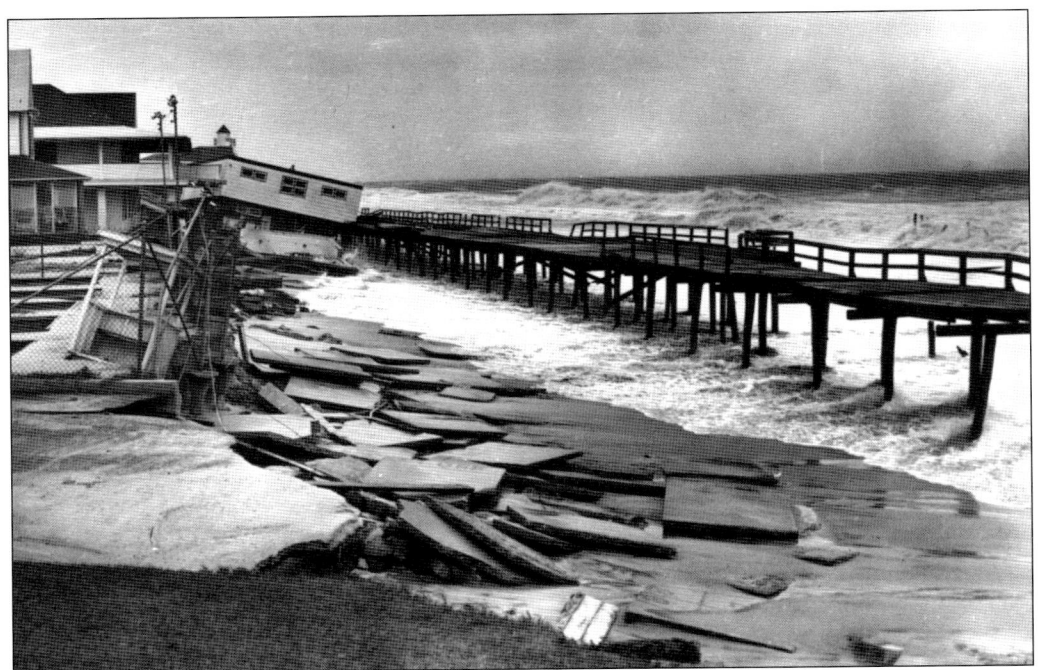

Regular beach visitors may have noticed a small vertical cliff form in the beach at the top reach of high tide. Kids love to slide down these small bluffs when they form. This feature is called a scarp and is the result of waves eroding, or lowering, the outer edge of the beach. The higher mid-portion of the beach breaks off and the cliff develops as a drop-down to the lower beach area in front of it. The larger the erosion event, the higher and farther back the scarp will form on the beach. In the 1962 Storm, the scarp was several feet high and it moved—or was excavated—landward into roads and lots in many locations, such as Rehoboth, shown here. (Above, courtesy Delaware Public Archives; below, courtesy Colonel McGarraugh via Marna Cupp.)

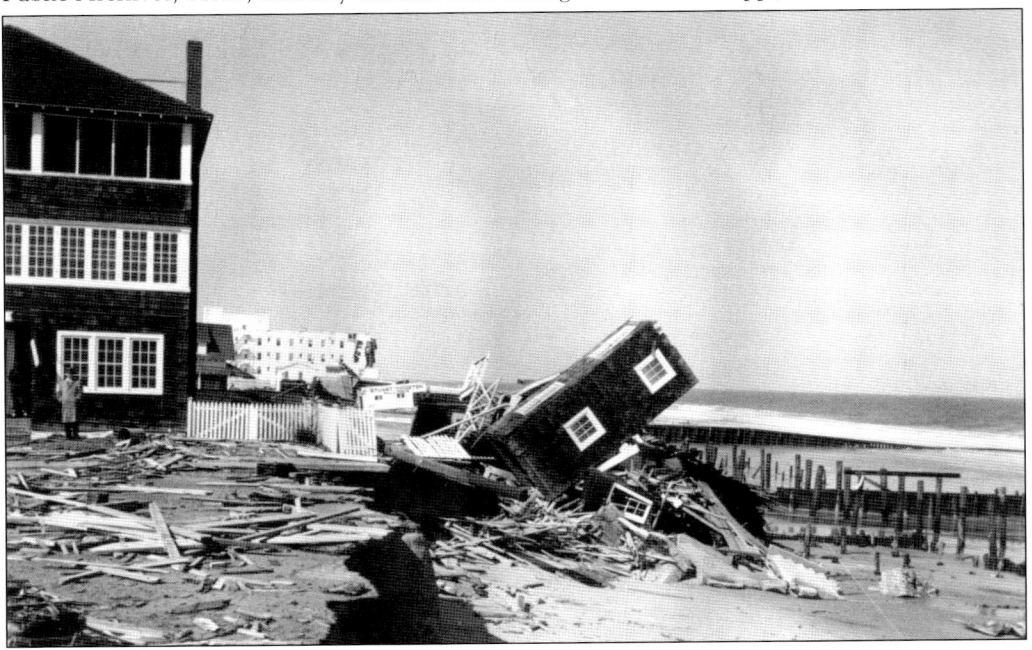

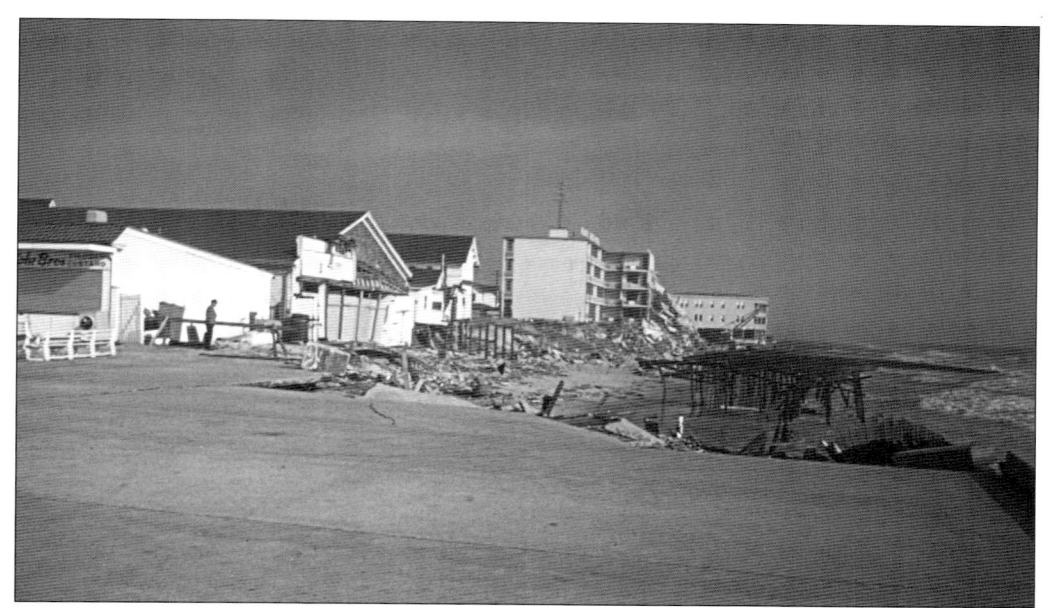

At the east end of Rehoboth Avenue in Rehoboth Beach, there was a concrete section of the boardwalk that was not supported by timbers or pilings; it lay directly on the earth below it. This concrete slab was unsupported as waves and tides excavated the sandy soils, and eventually the erosional scarp moved beneath it. Large portions of this concrete section of the boardwalk dropped down to the eroded beach below. (Above, courtesy Lewes Historical Society; below, Delaware Public Archives.)

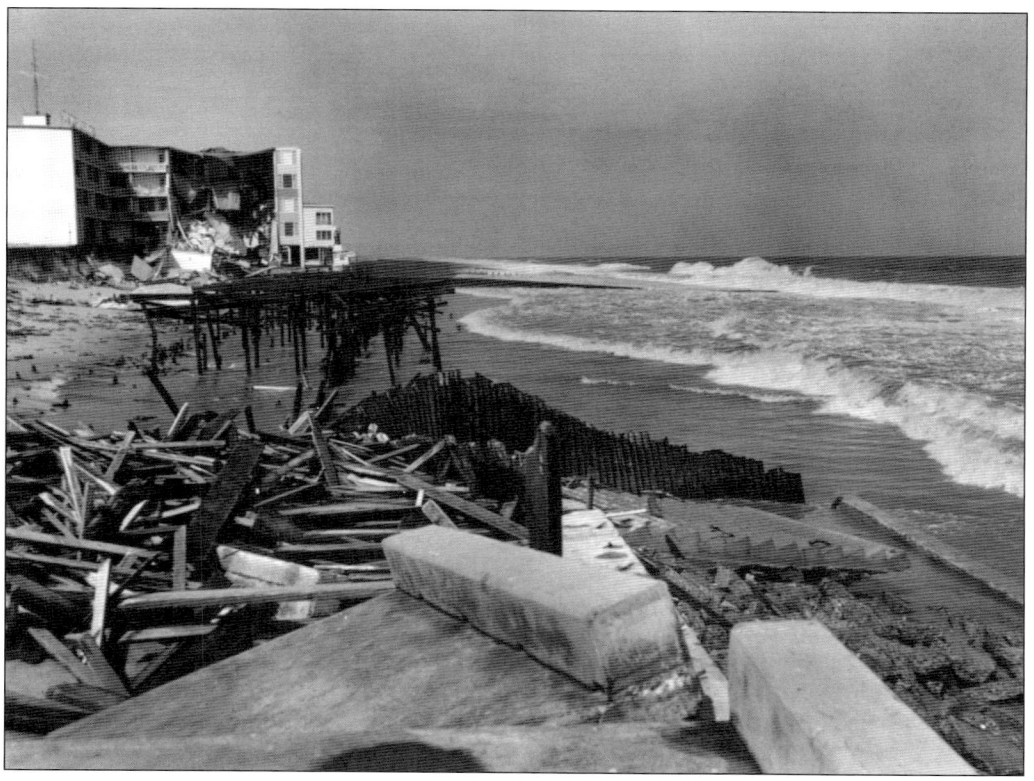

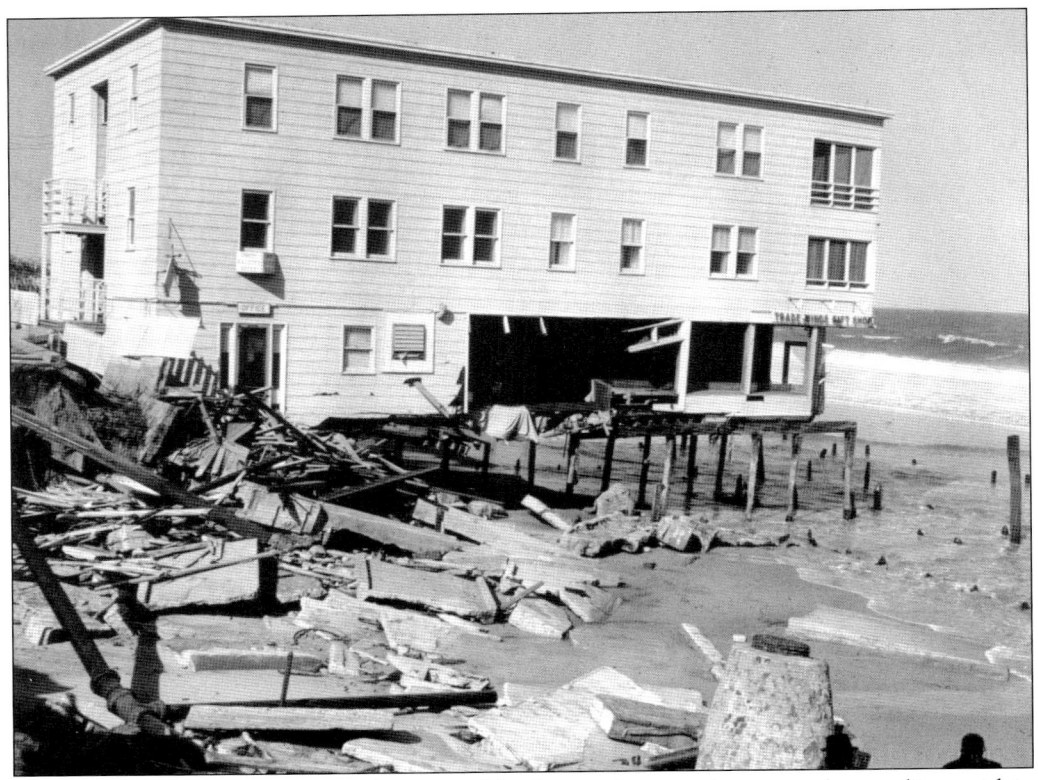

Roads collapsed where the scarp line moved back into them, and sewer and water lines within the eroded area were severed. These two photographs were taken in Rehoboth Beach. The above image shows an exposed concrete manhole (in the foreground) that was under the road. The round steel cover at the top of the concrete manhole was at street level, a good indicator of the extent of vertical erosion. The photograph below illustrates how cottages also toppled into the sea as the ocean removed the sediments that had previously supported foundations. (Above, courtesy Colonel McGarraugh via Marna Cupp; below, courtesy Delaware Public Archives.)

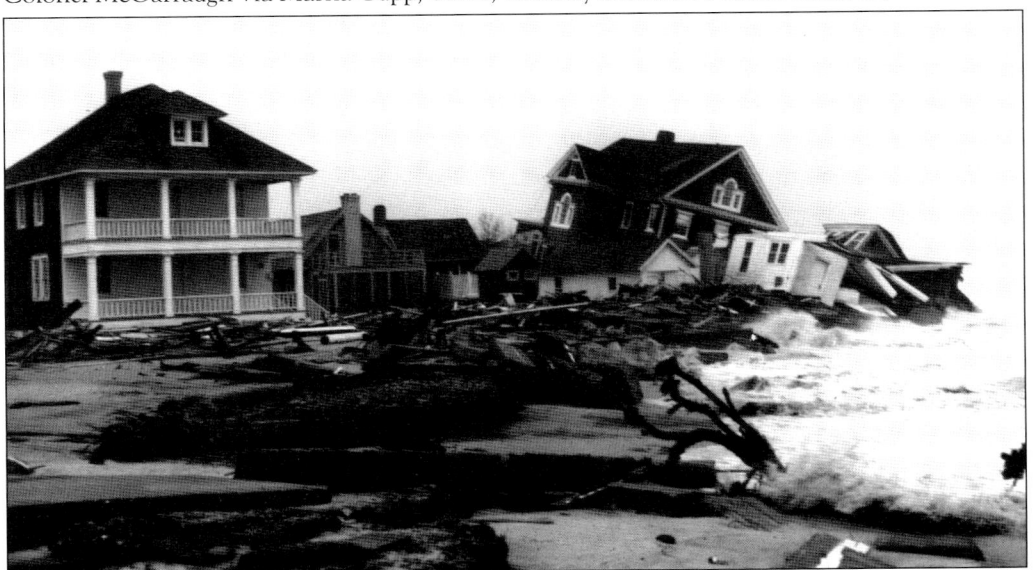

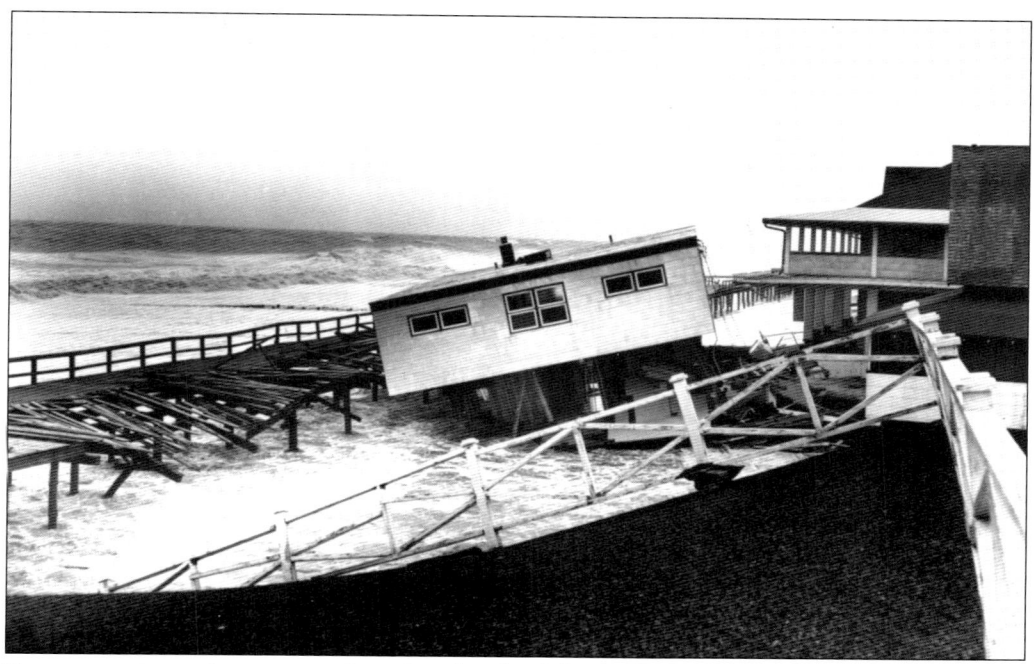

Extreme erosion and consequent loss of sand and soil that had provided foundation support resulted in catastrophic collapse. The above photograph shows an oceanfront house tilting into the sea as its foundation has been undermined—there was simply nothing left to keep it upright. The image below shows a collapsed road, probably Surf Avenue at the north end of Rehoboth. Note the remnants of boardwalk pilings in front of what remains of the Henlopen Hotel. At left center of the photograph is the still-standing groin—a coastal structure that was normally covered by beach sand. (Above, courtesy Delaware Public Archives; below, courtesy Delaware DNREC.)

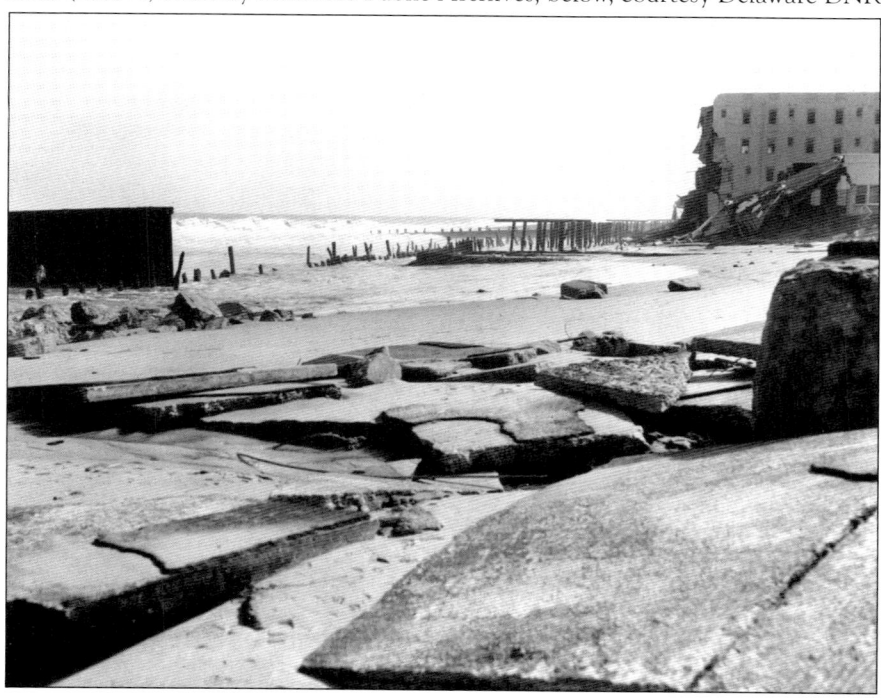

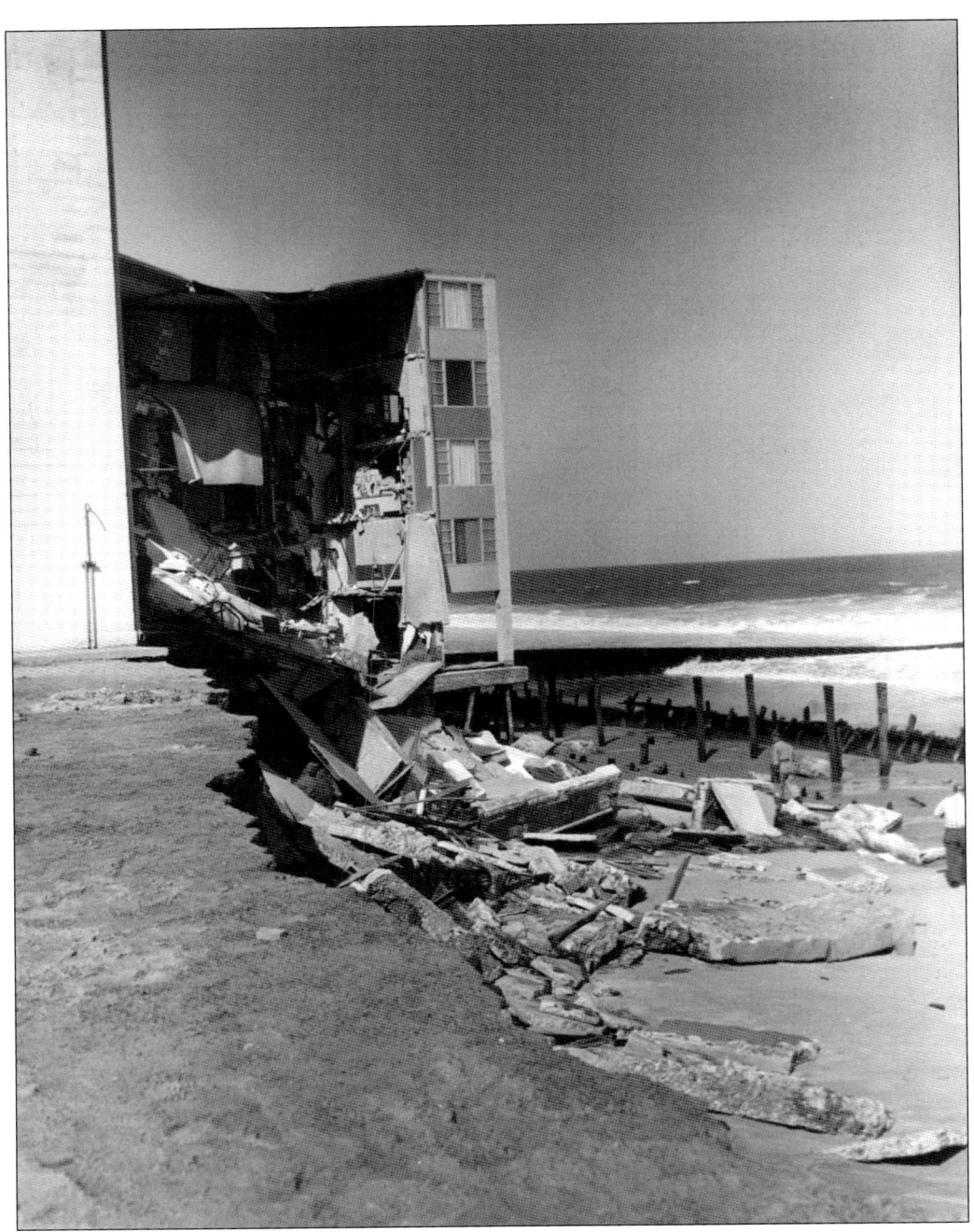

An iconic image of the Ash Wednesday Storm, and arguably one the most catastrophic single building losses, the Atlantic Sands Hotel in Rehoboth is shown here as the erosional scarp line has moved about midway through the building. The hotel's front section was undermined, the foundation was lost, and eventually all floors collapsed—from ground level to the roof. The building buckled in a domino-like falling sequence. Foundation failure led to the collapse of the first floor, which had supported the second level, followed by the collapse of the second and uppermost floors. (Courtesy Delaware Public Archives.)

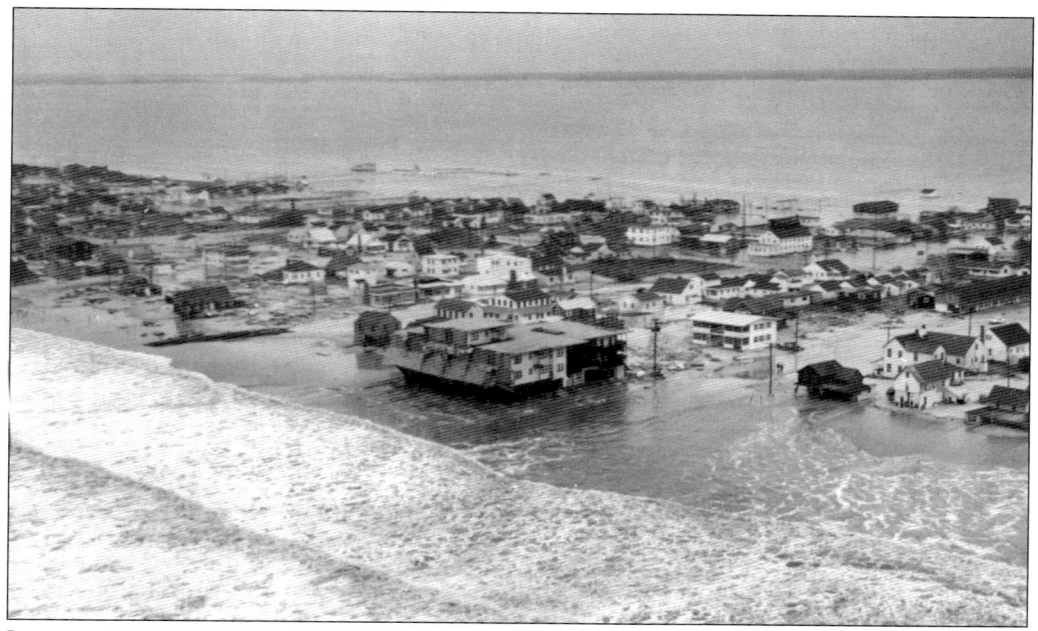

In many areas, no erosional scarp developed; rather, waves raced across the beach horizontally with great speed. Storm-driven waves rushed up and over the beaches and dunes and into the landward towns, roads, and buildings. This was by far the more common form of destruction in the 1962 Storm. Ocean waves riding high on the storm surge tides traveled well into communities and completely across barrier beaches where inland bays backed shoreline areas. The photograph above shows how the ocean connected to Rehoboth Bay in Dewey Beach. The photograph below illustrates how far waves penetrated into Bethany, depositing sand and debris two to three blocks into town. (Above, courtesy Norman Rossiter; below, courtesy Delaware DNREC.)

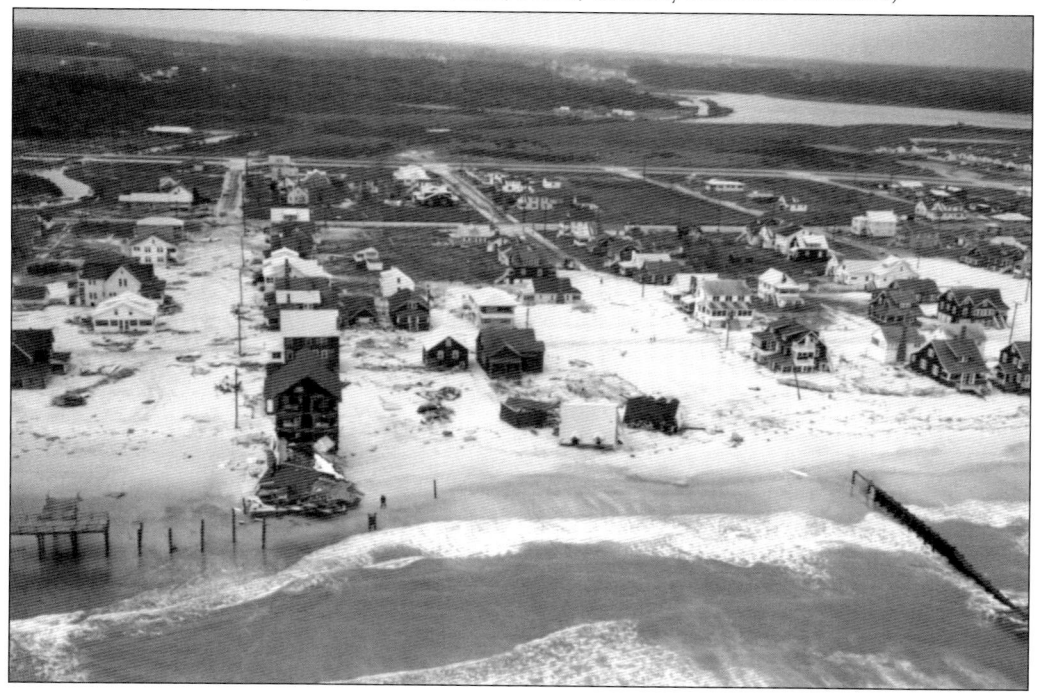

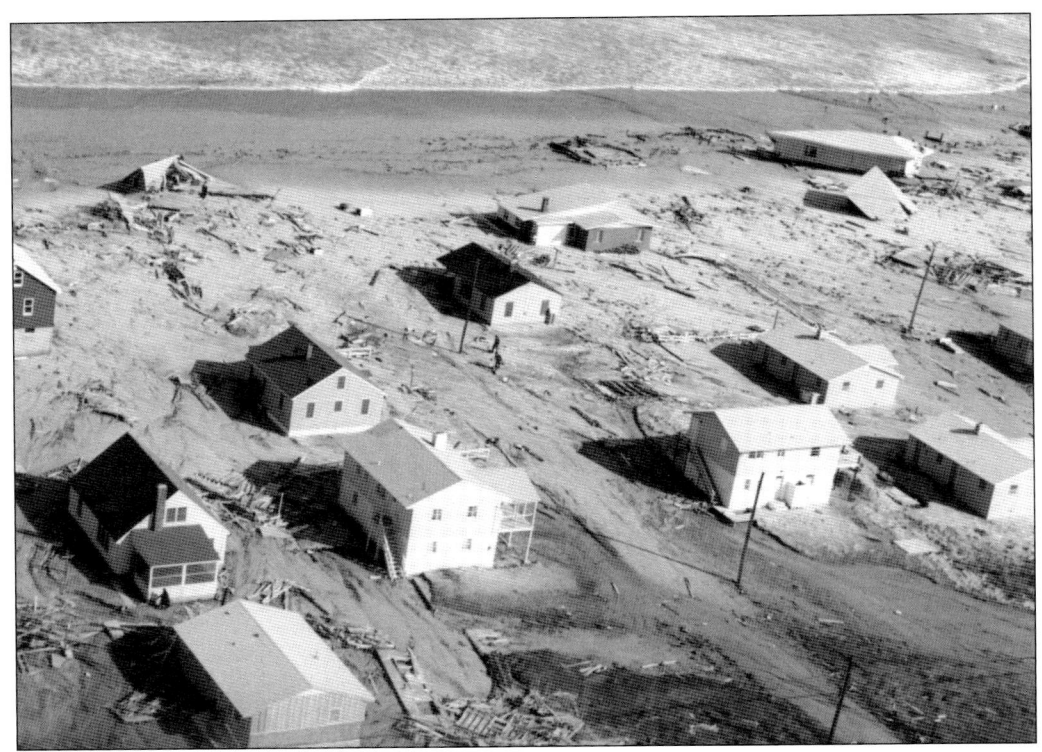

These two photographs of the Bethany area clearly show evidence that water raced over and beyond the beach and overwhelmed neighborhoods. Everything in the path of the powerful surf fell victim to its destructive force. As waves picked up and transported debris, pieces of timber and other building materials became water-borne battering rams, causing added damage to surrounding structures. (Both, courtesy Delaware Public Archives.)

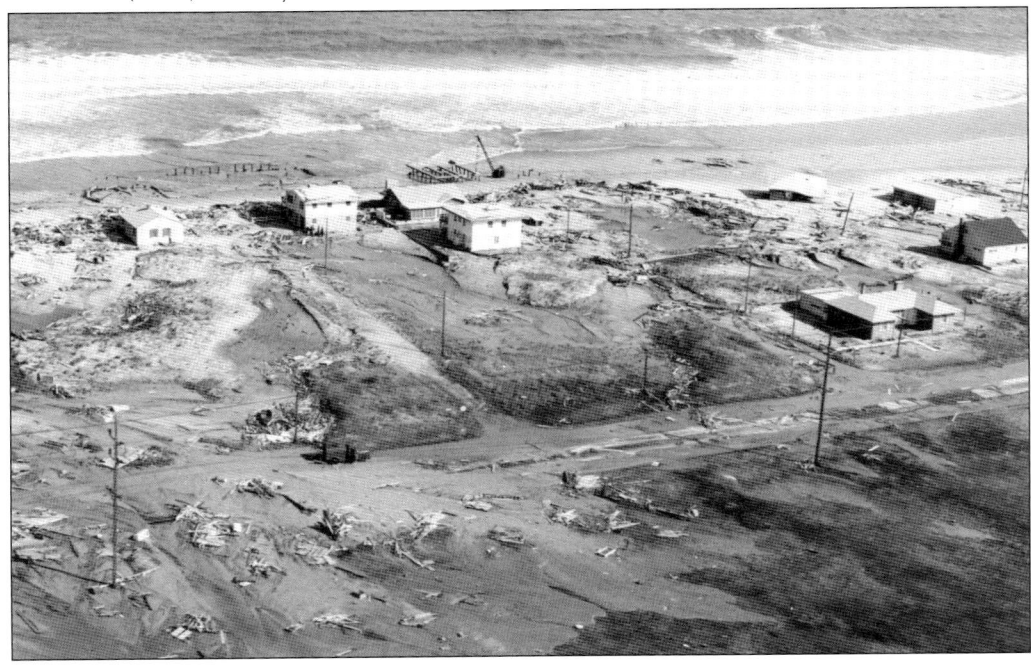

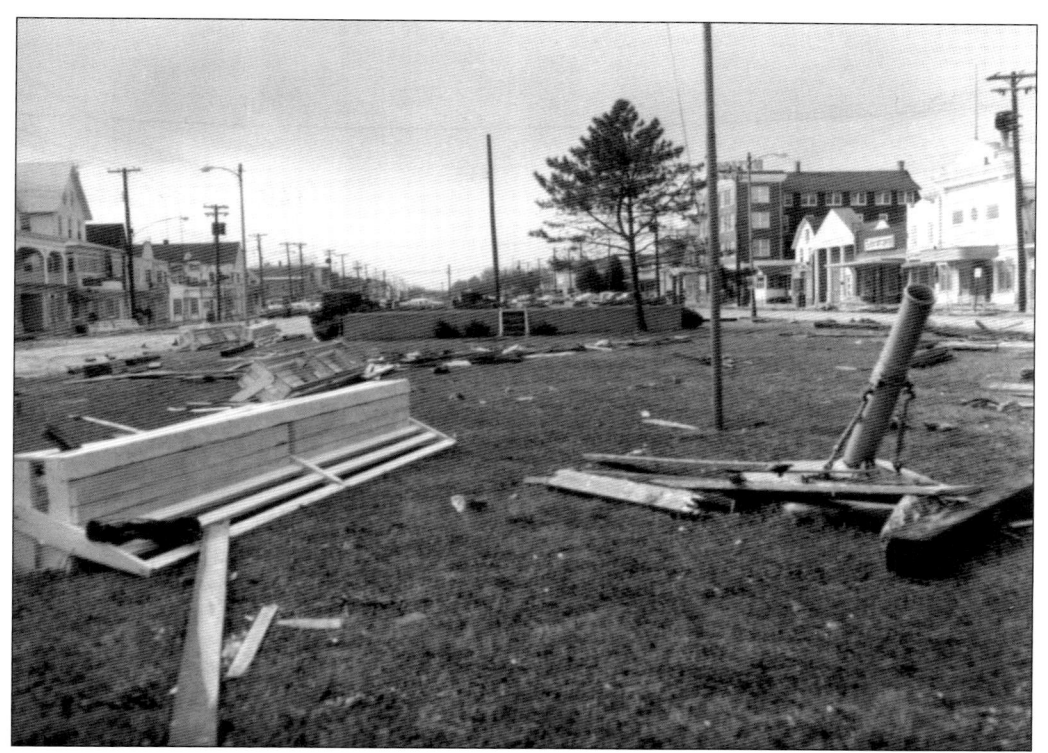

Even in Rehoboth Beach, where there was a very pronounced erosional scarp or cliff, water washed over the upland, scattering debris as it flowed. On Rehoboth Avenue, shown here, seawater, rubble, timber, and remains of battered structures were strewn throughout a large area of the first block back from the ocean. (Both, courtesy Delaware DNREC.)

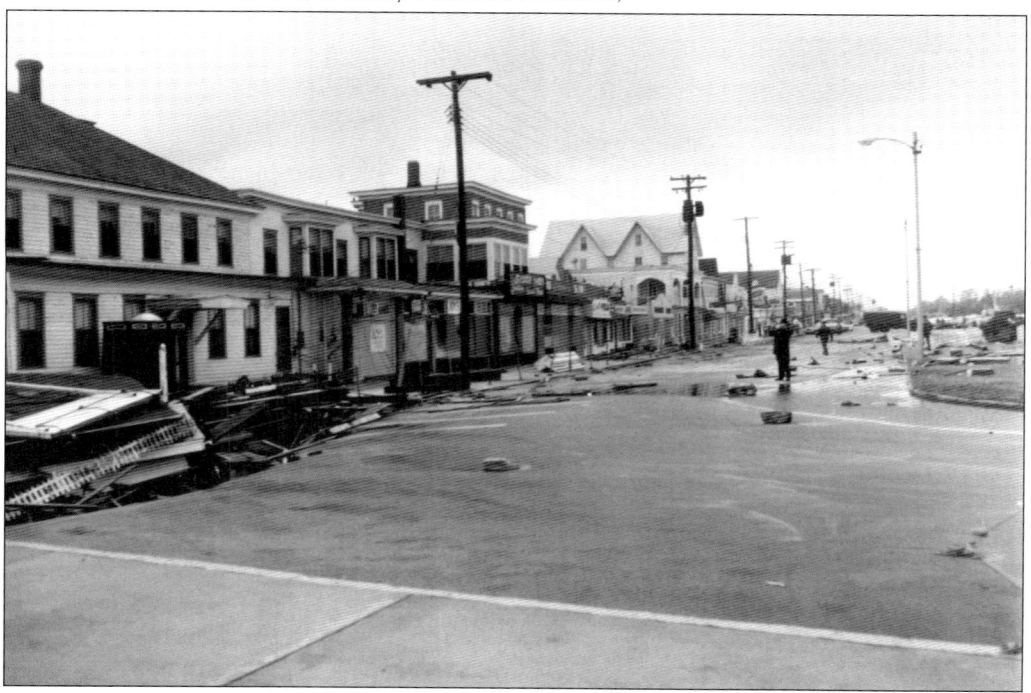

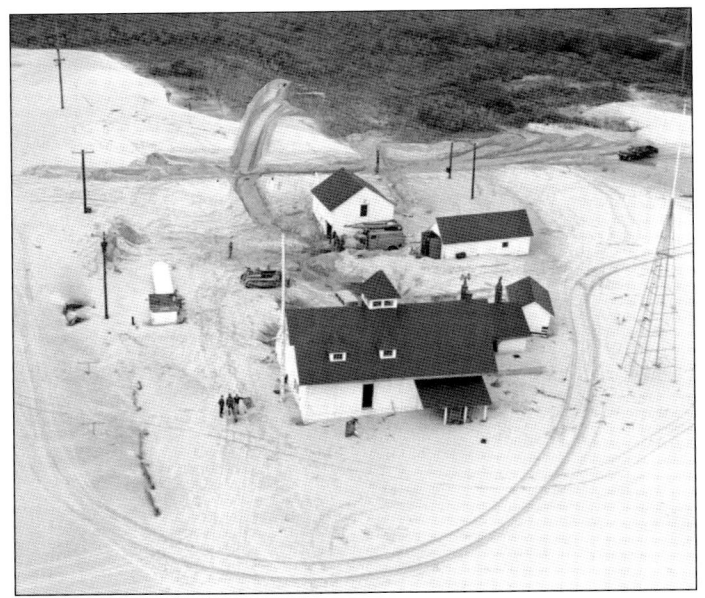

Waves carried large volumes of beach and dune sand into building lots and roads. Barrier beaches naturally evolve as sea levels increase and storms increase land elevations via overwash events. However, when sand is transported into yards and neighborhoods, it is removed almost immediately. This photograph shows extensive sand deposits, up to the first-floor windows at the life saving station north of Indian River Inlet. (Courtesy Delaware DNREC.)

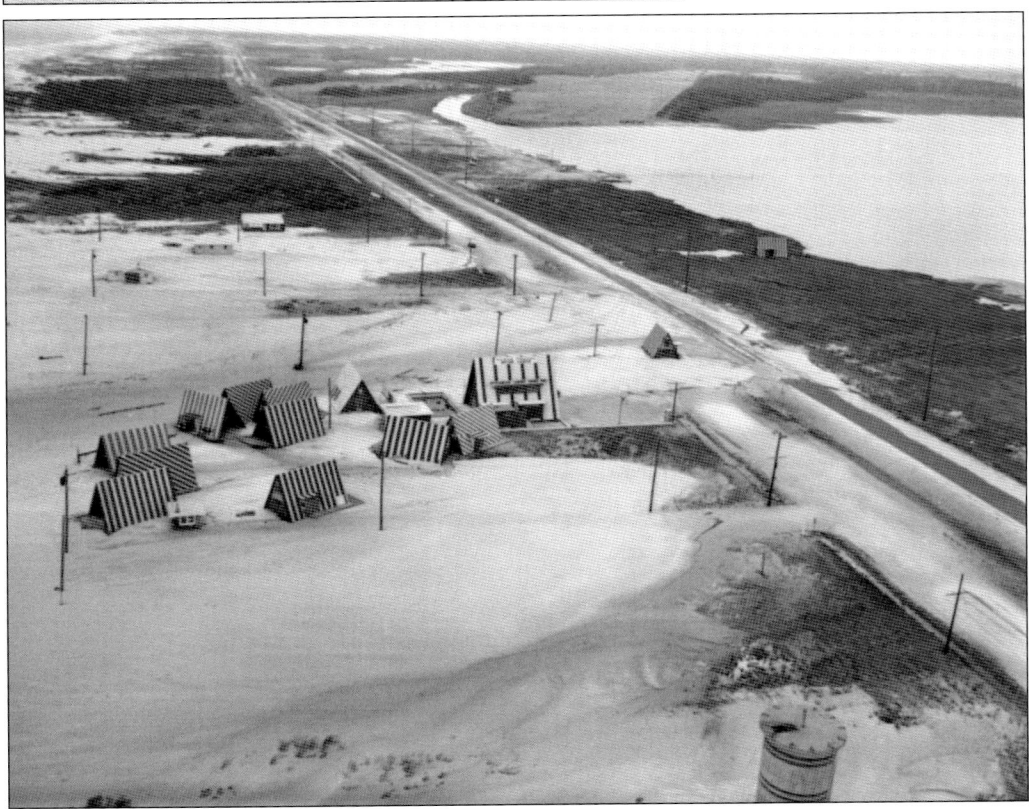

Nomad Village, located just south of Indian River Inlet, consisted of several striped-roof A-frames, many of which were relocated during the storm. The buildings were strewn about like children's toys, with one building ending up in the marsh on the west side of the highway. The photograph above shows the A-frame in the marsh and the extensive overwash area that went right through Nomad Village. (Courtesy Delaware DNREC.)

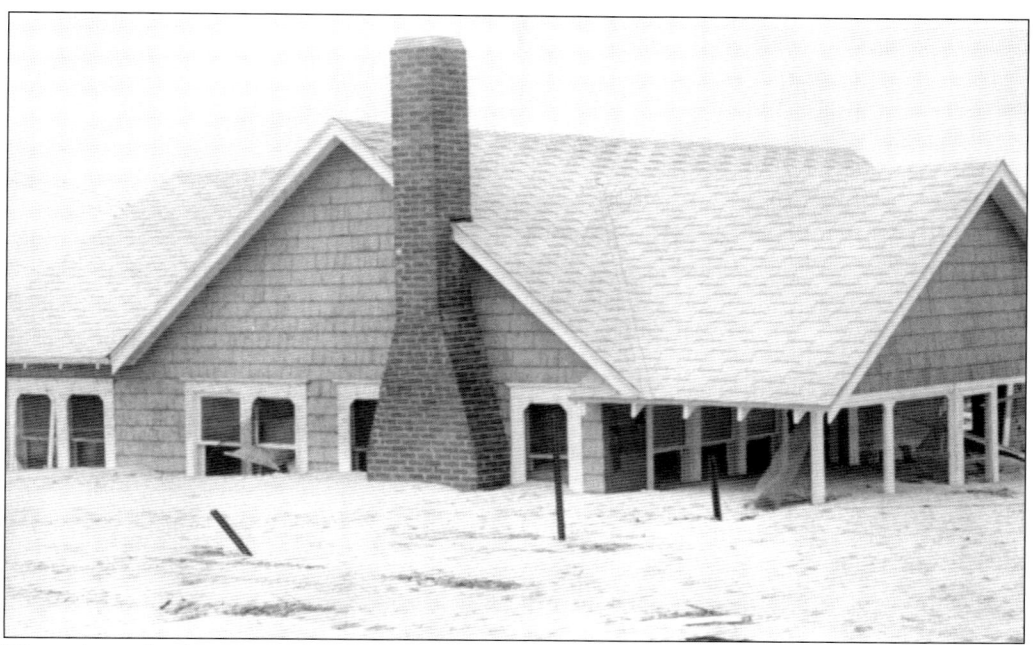

Throughout the duration of the storm's high tides, water-borne sand was pushed across the coast the way snow is driven by wind in a blizzard. Similar to blowing snow that seemingly infiltrates every available space, sand flowed into every open nook and crevice, creating nightmarish conditions to clean up. The photograph above shows a house in Dewey with sand deposited above the bottom of the first-floor windows. The photograph below illustrates sand removal efforts along the coast. (Above, courtesy *Delaware State News*; below, courtesy Delaware DNREC.)

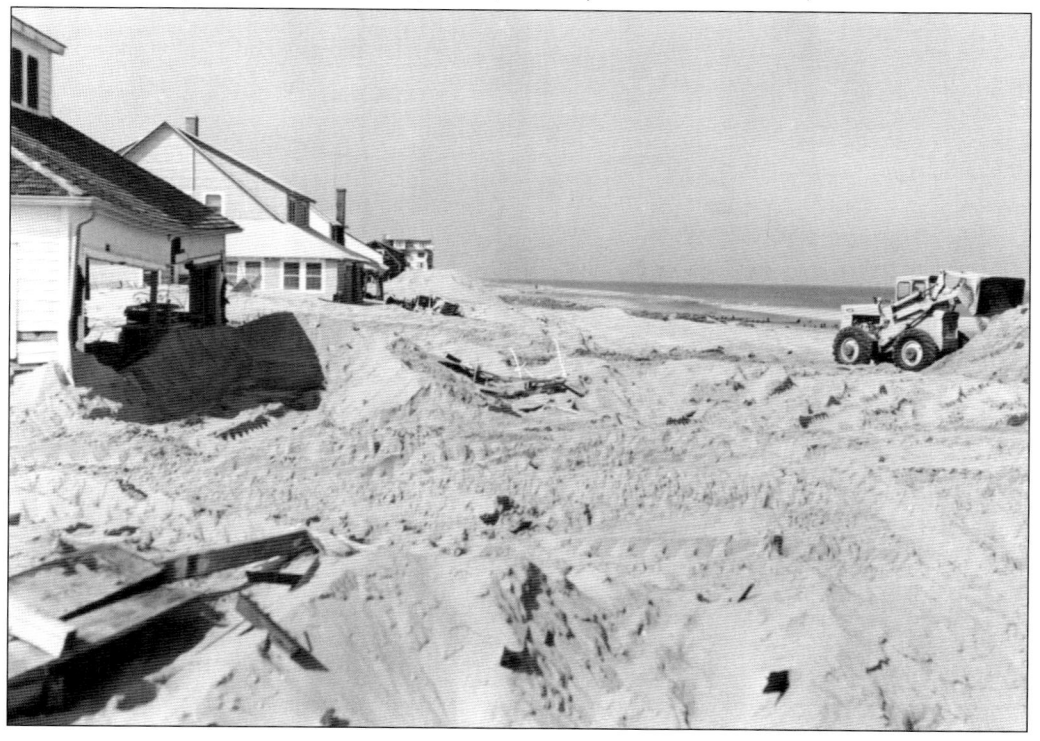

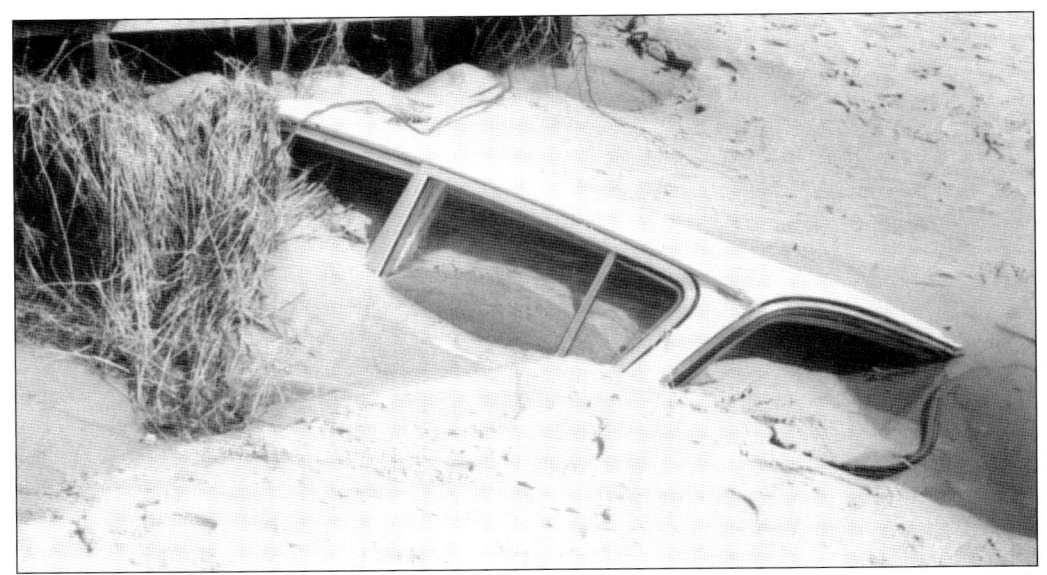

A Delaware State Police car that ventured onto Route 14 for a rescue mission went into a ditch that the driver had not noticed because sheets of floodwater were pouring over the road. In fact, the roadway collapsed, and the vehicle plunged into five feet of water. The troopers and the rescued highway employees decided to abandon the vehicle and walk to higher ground, where they were eventually rescued by the National Guard. The photograph above illustrates how little of the car remained in almost six feet of storm-deposited sand. The photograph below shows the flattened and overwashed dune at what is now Cape Henlopen State Park. (Above, courtesy *Delaware State News*; below, courtesy Colonel McGarraugh via Marna Cupp.)

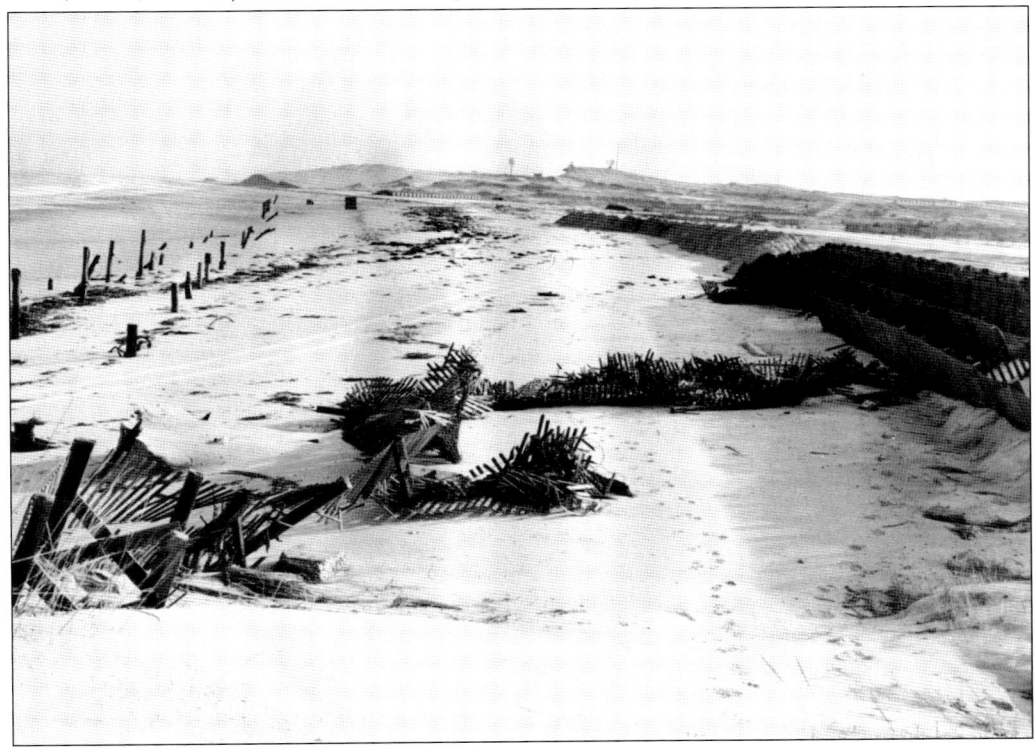

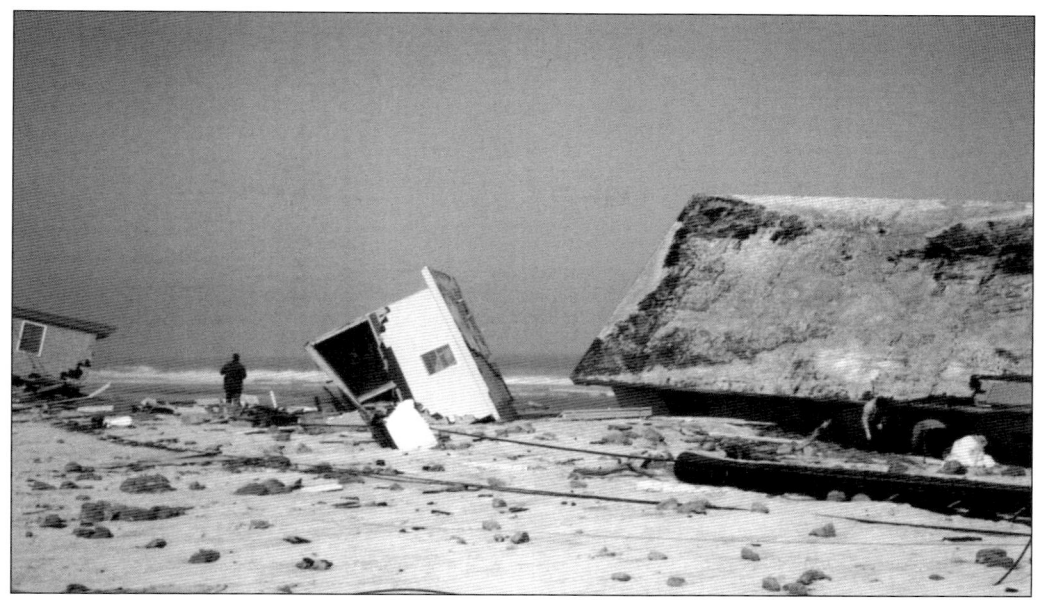

This storm caused unprecedented building damage in Delaware. The consequential widespread wreckage was by far the most devastating aspect of the storm. Reports indicated that every oceanfront home in South Bethany was destroyed in the storm. The Bethany and Rehoboth boardwalks were obliterated. Houses, cottages, hotels, motels, restaurants, and stores were turned into splinters and then washed throughout communities. The photograph above depicts the oceanfront area of South Bethany, showing the kind of devastation wreaked there. The image below shows Bethany with a pile of debris that was once a beach cottage. (Above, courtesy South Bethany Historical Society; below, courtesy Town of Bethany Beach.)

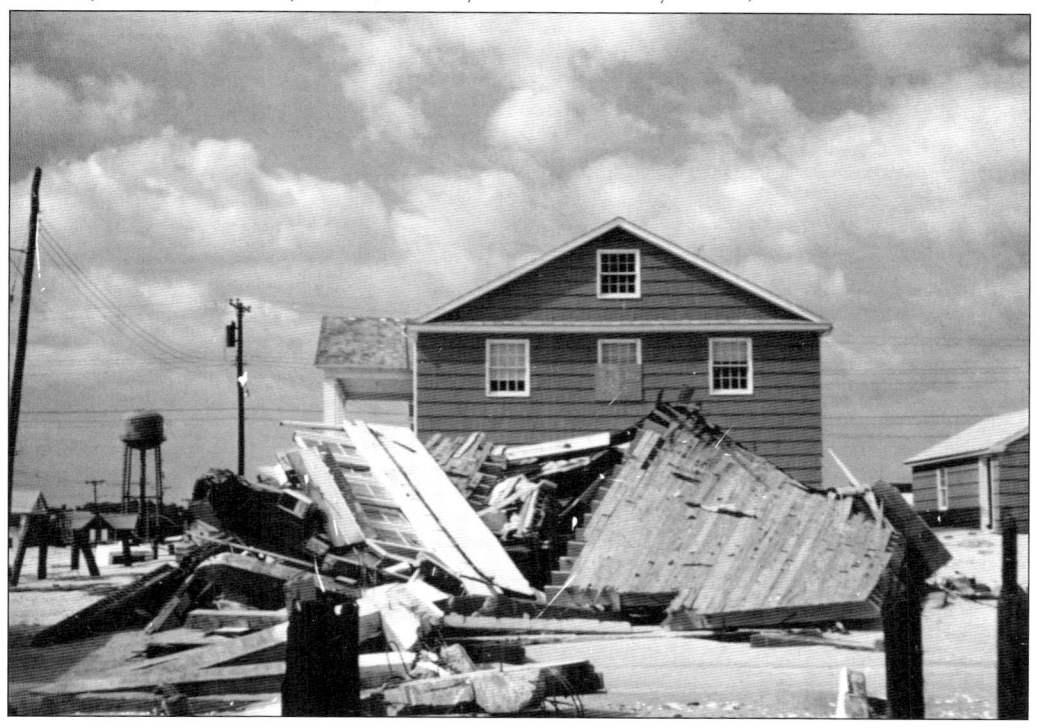

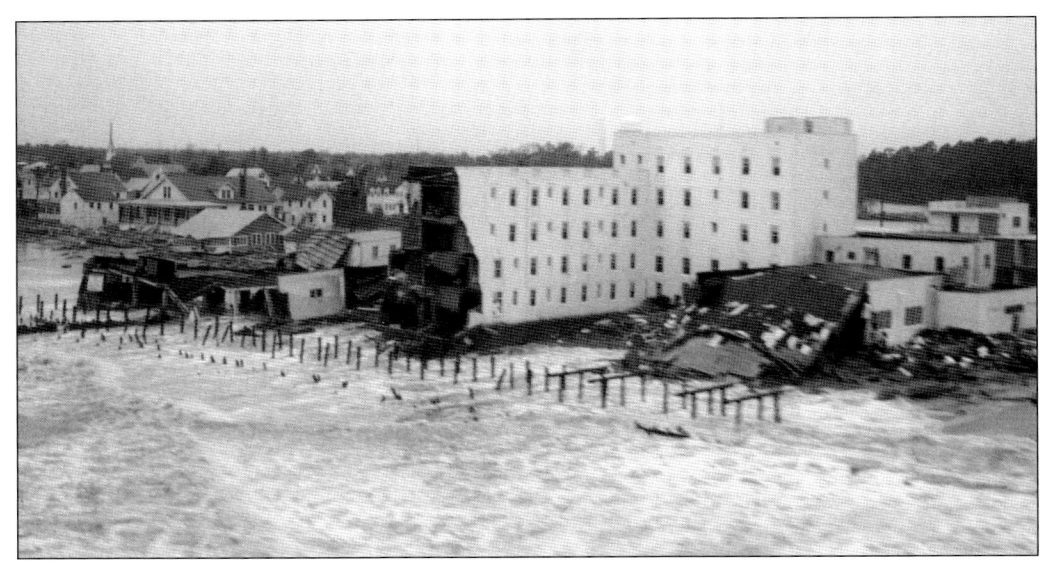

A critical factor leading to such widespread loss of buildings was the mistake of building foundations being supported entirely by the earth directly under the structure. Block foundations are perfectly fine when the ground supporting them is stable. But in a location where the ground washes out in a storm, the building collapses. The two most compelling images of this category of storm loss include the Henlopen Hotel (above) and the Atlantic Sands Hotel (below). An entire front section of the Atlantic Sands collapsed when foundation supporting the whole building was lost to the erosive effects of the waves. (Above, courtesy Norman Rossiter; below, courtesy Colonel McGarraugh via Marna Cupp.)

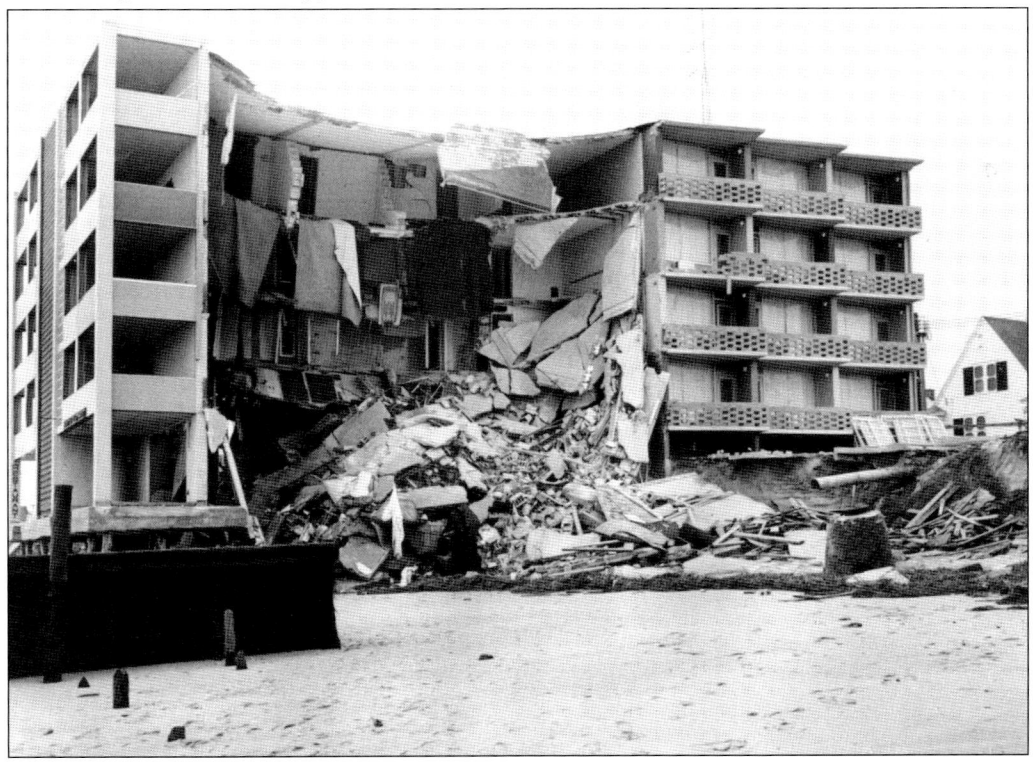

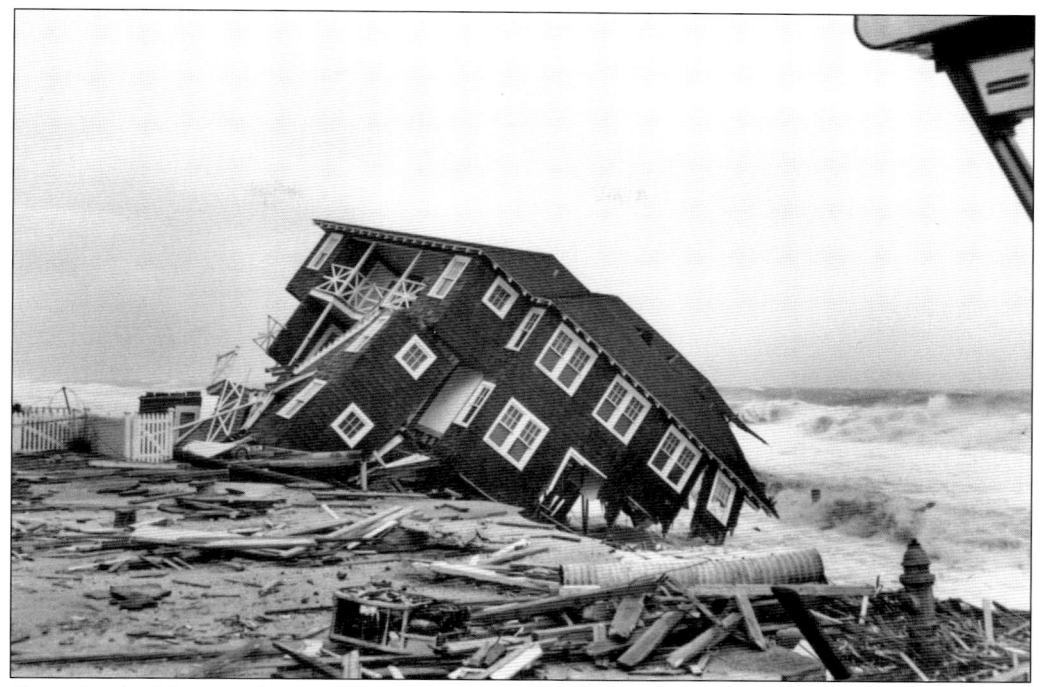

Countless buildings and homes were lost in the same manner as that which caused the Henlopen Hotel and Atlantic Sands to collapse. Some structures completely collapsed into the violent surf and became timber flotsam, and others experienced undermining of a portion of the foundation resulting in the building tipping toward the sea. The photograph above shows such a collapse at Maryland Avenue in Rehoboth, and the photograph below is of two unidentified buildings that experienced the same demise. (Above, courtesy Delaware Public Archives; below, courtesy Colonel McGarraugh via Marna Cupp.)

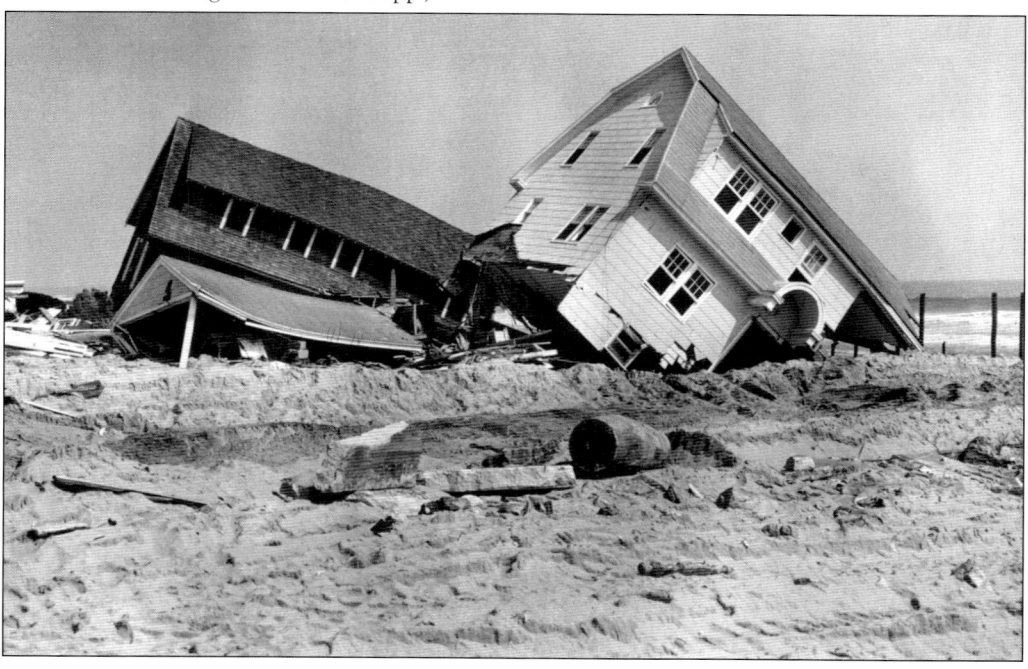

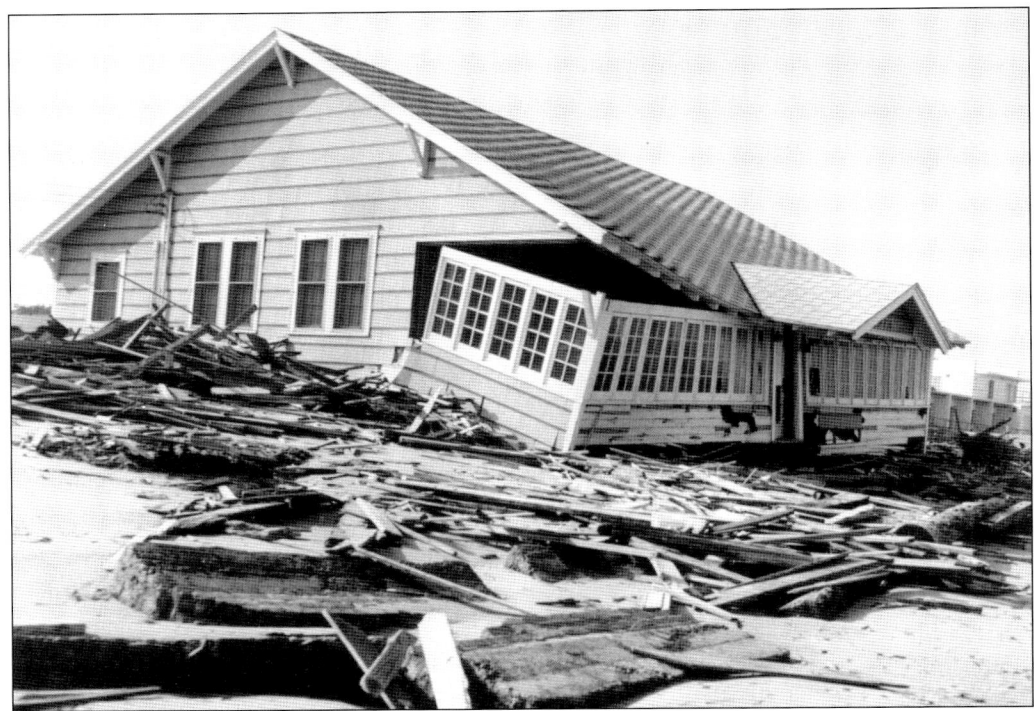

Some homes experienced partial collapse, as shown in the photograph above, where the building's front section is slightly undermined—it pulled away from the rest of the structure and settled a couple of feet. Behind the vast field of debris in the foreground of the photograph below, a post has been used to hold up the front part of a building that might otherwise lean forward into the sea. (Above, courtesy Colonel McGarraugh via Marna Cupp; below, courtesy Delaware Public Archives.)

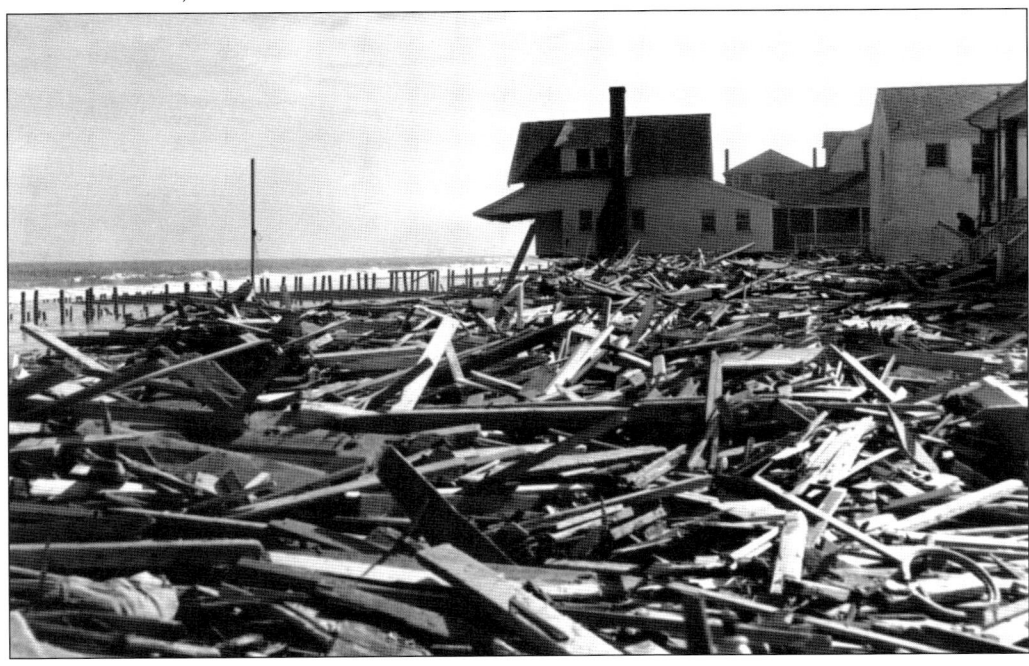

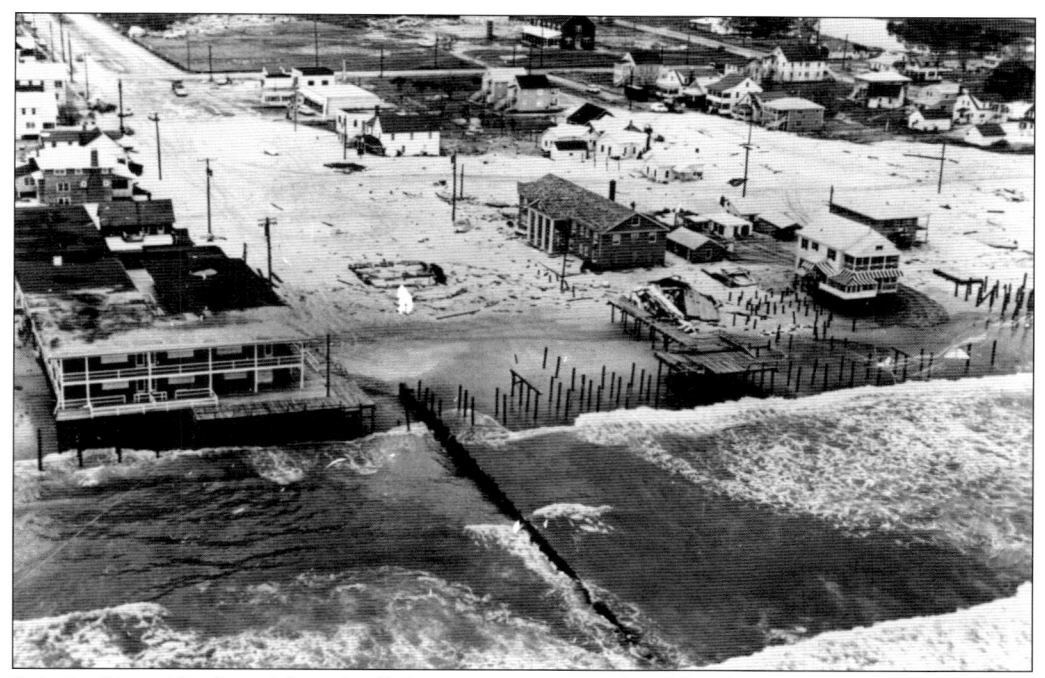

Rehoboth's and Bethany's boardwalk frontages were considered familiar landmarks and prime real estate, thus many of post-storm damage photographs were taken of these areas. Both boardwalks were stripped of their decking, as seen in the aerial shot of the Bethany boardwalk (above), and the buildings along the boardwalks in both towns were very badly damaged. The shot from ground level behind the Rehoboth boardwalk shows the eroded level of the beach and associated breakdown of buildings. (Above, courtesy Town of Bethany Beach; below, courtesy Delaware Public Archives.)

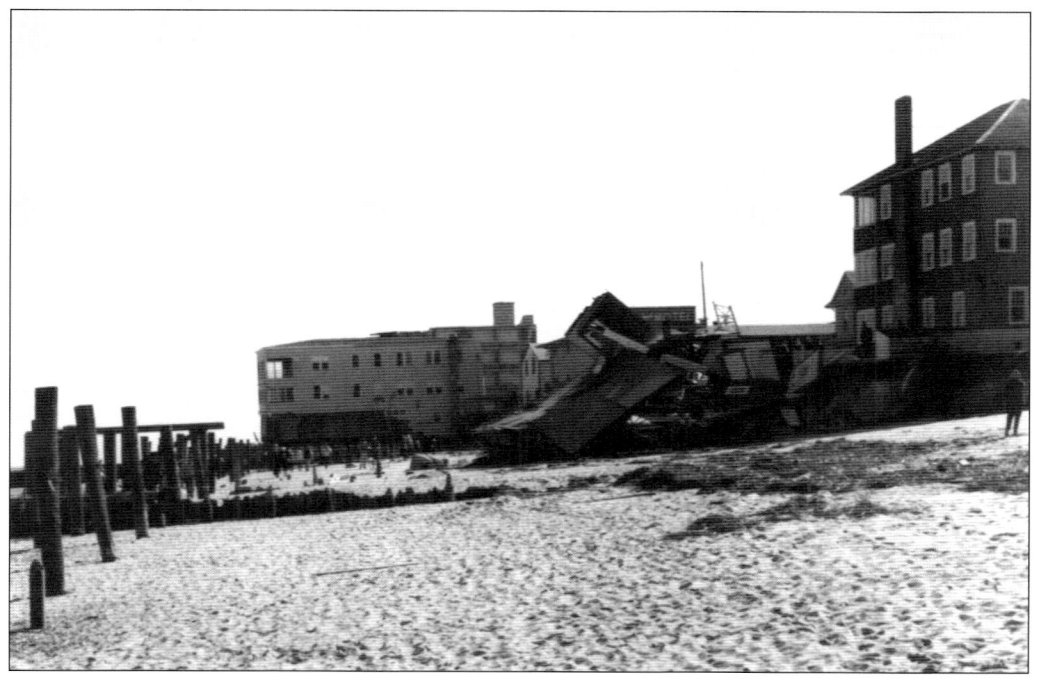

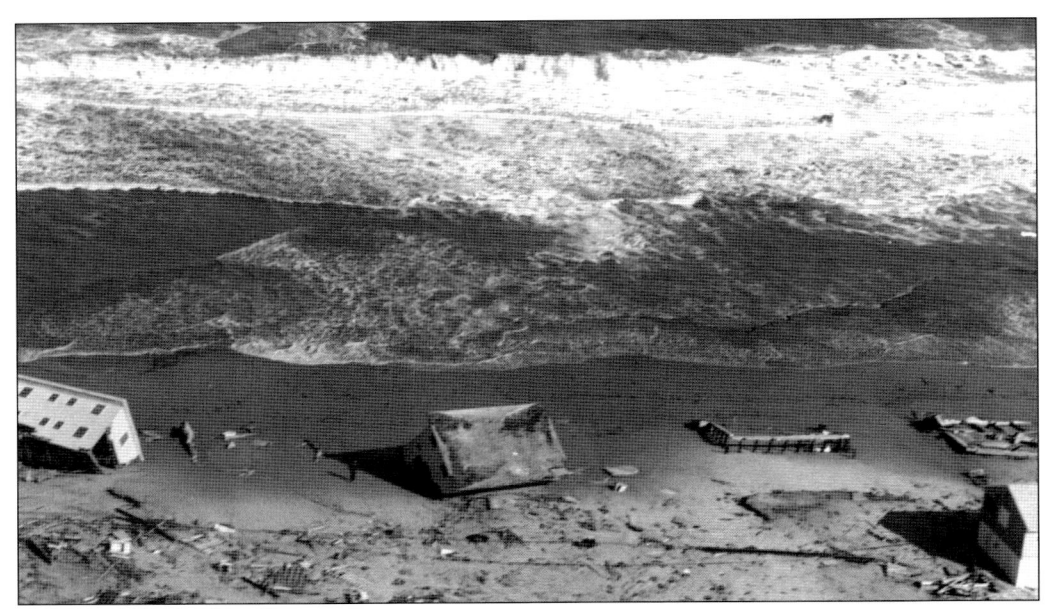

It is difficult to visualize the force of the waves that swept through the oceanfront structures in the coastal towns. The aerial photograph above is of Bethany Beach and typifies the result of the huge mass of water that flowed through the dunes, taking everything in its path with it and leaving vast debris in its wake. A ground view of the Atlantic Sands is shown in the photograph below. (Above, courtesy Delaware Public Archives; below, courtesy Colonel McGarraugh via Marna Cupp.)

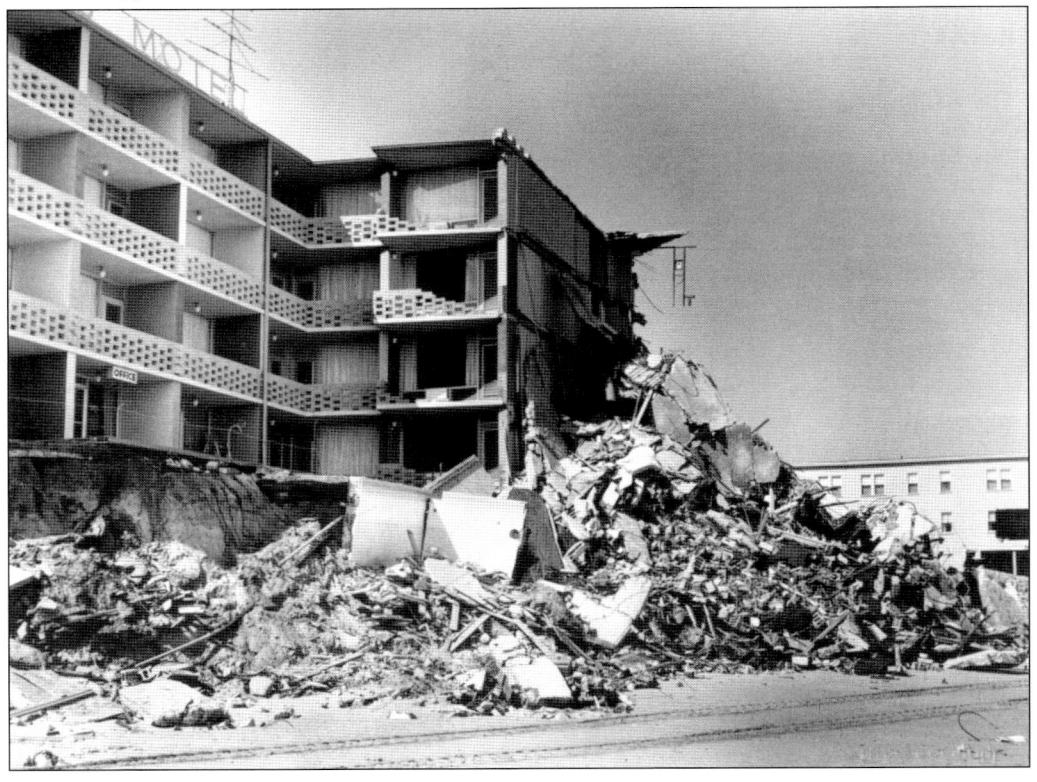

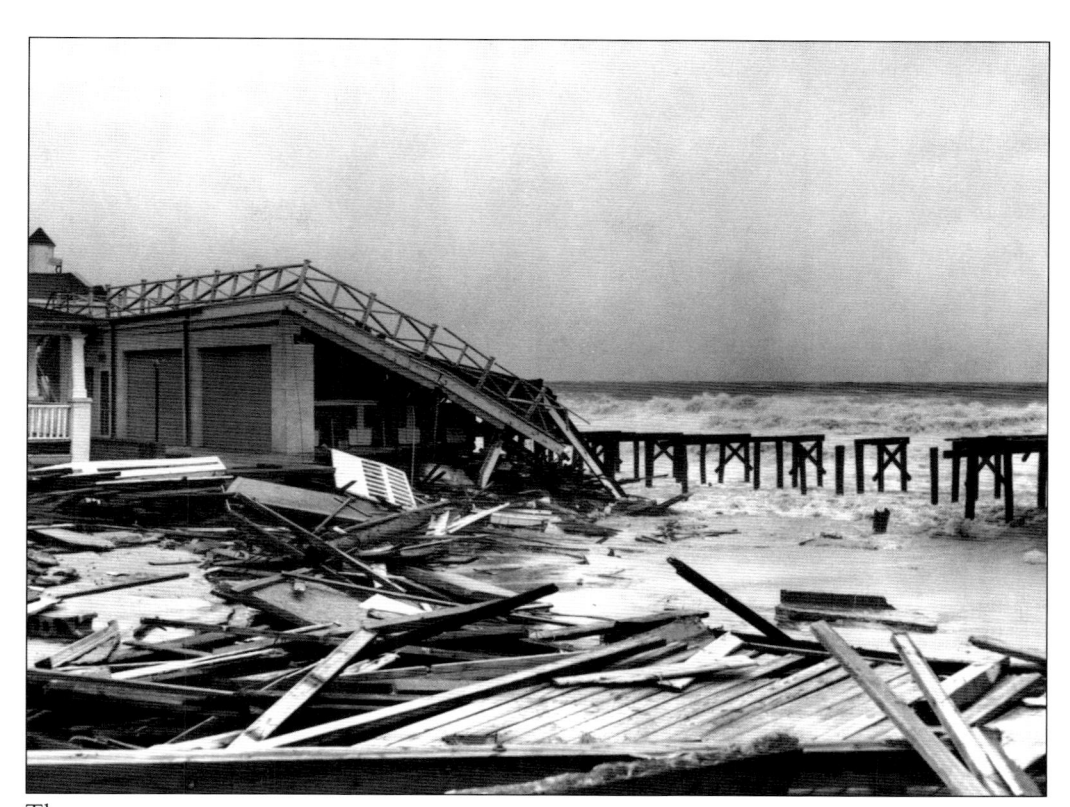

These two photographs, both taken in Rehoboth, illustrate the wreckage resulting from the high tides and waves. Note the scarp in the photograph on the right, which shows just how deeply the vertical erosion was. One can only wonder how much more damage would have occurred if waves or tides were just a foot or two higher, or if the storm had persisted through one additional high tide cycle. (Both, courtesy Delaware Public Archives.)

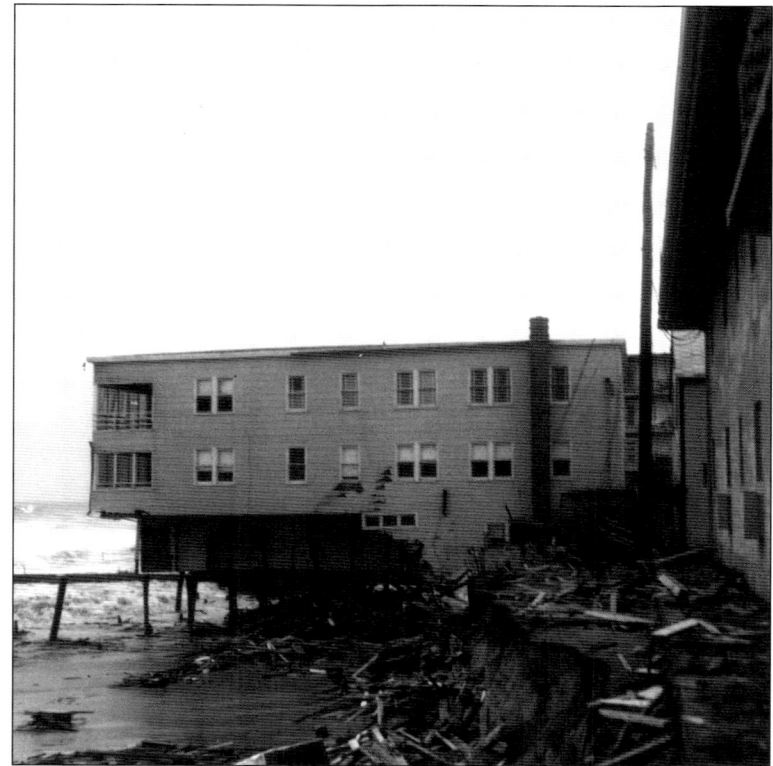

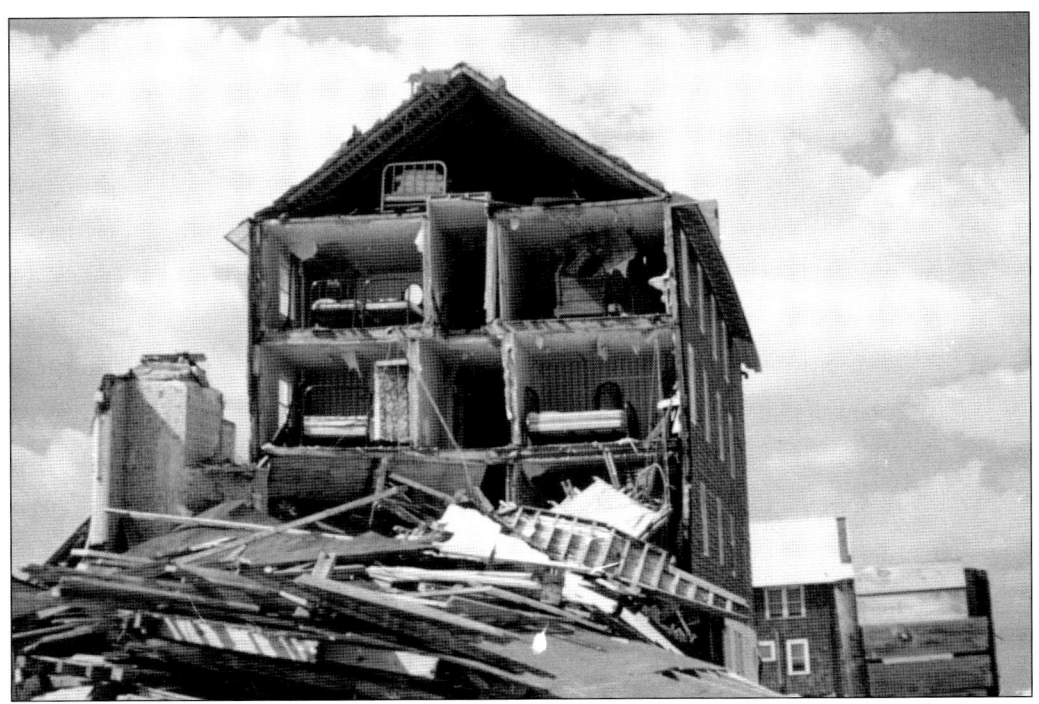

Storm forces ripped walls and roofs off homes and turned structures inside out and upside down—sometimes with results that seem to defy logic. The Bethany home in the photograph above looks as though a knife sliced it in half, exposing interior bedrooms that look like someone had just walked out of the space. The photograph below shows an upside-down bathroom. Someone left the seat up! (Above, courtesy Town of Bethany Beach; below, courtesy Lewes Historical Society.)

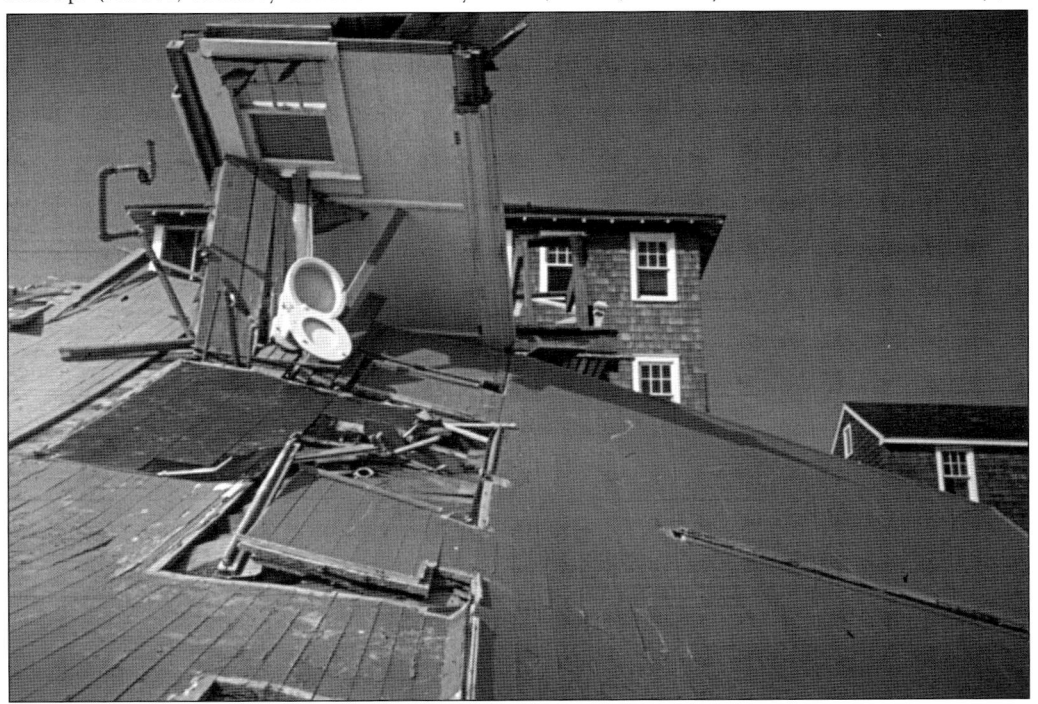

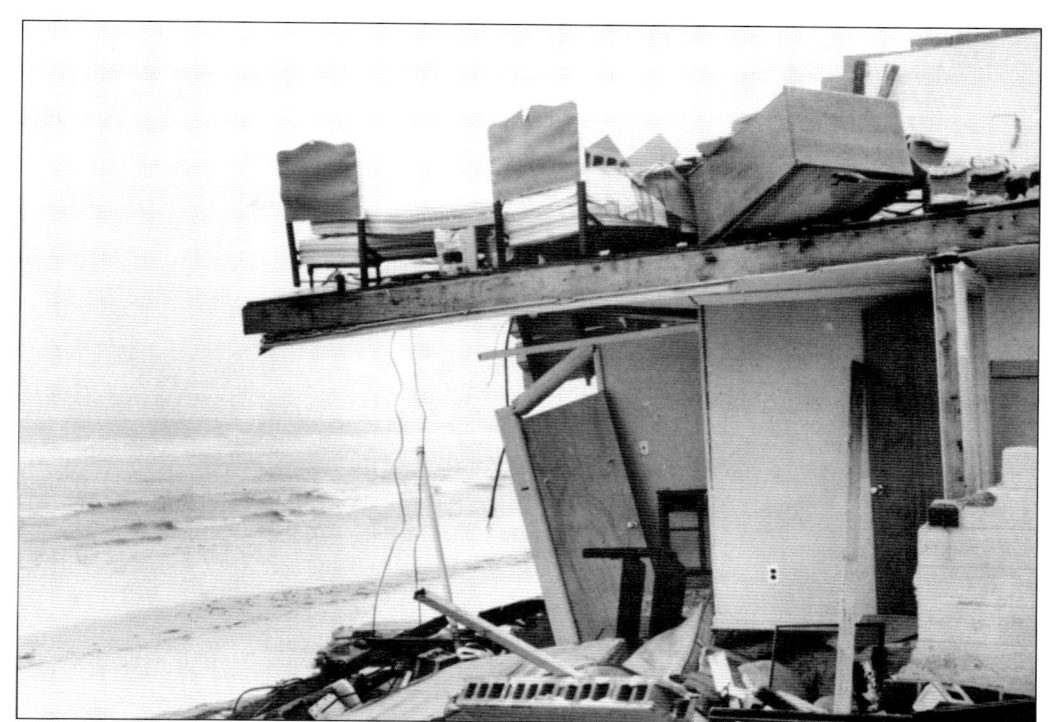

The Fenwick cottage above shows a teetering second floor with twin beds about to slide off onto the beach below. The photograph on the right is of a summer rental. This summer cottage is a little too breezy for most. While these images might hint at a bit of levity in the face of adversity, there was no cheer in this disaster area. Yet positive and determined human spirit motivated the massive cleanup effort and rebuilding work that allowed the Delaware coast to be back in business by the summer of 1962. (Above, courtesy *Delaware State News*; right, courtesy Colonel McGarraugh via Marna Cupp.)

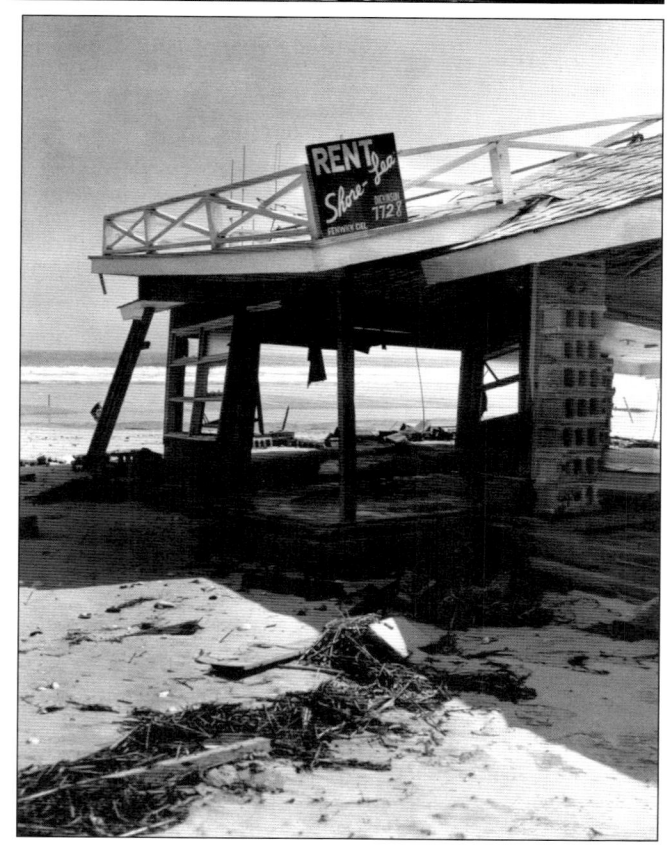

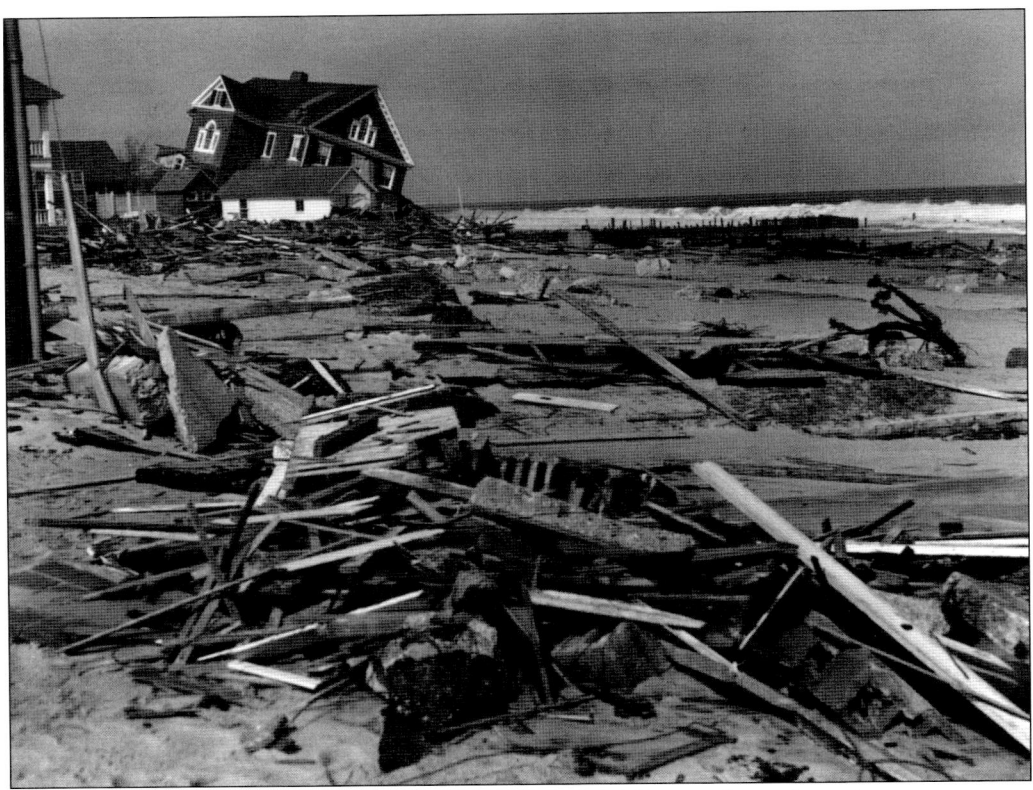

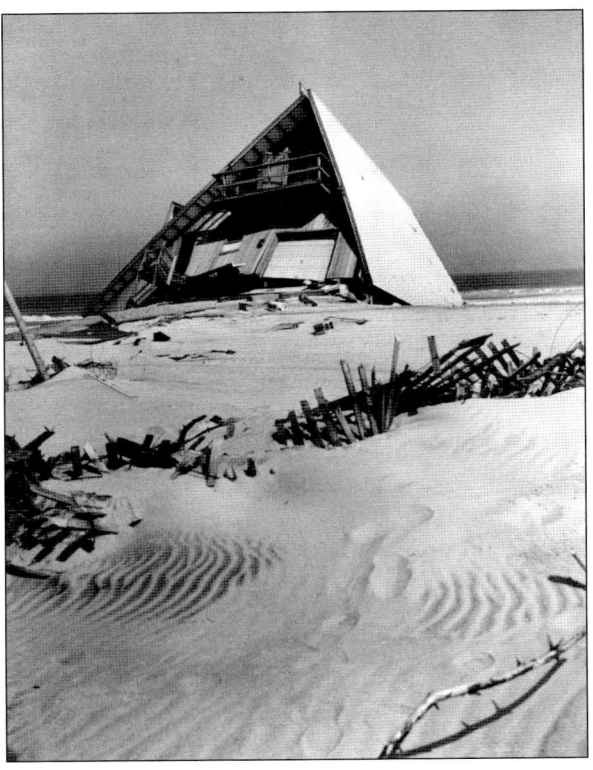

The wreckage along the eastern seaboard resulting from the Ash Wednesday Storm was widespread. Seen in these photographs are individual lots or groups of lots that are representative of the category of damage that had been generated along the coast from North Carolina to Long Island—encompassing nearly 500 miles of Atlantic coast. Ground zero for this storm was the mid-Atlantic, including Maryland, Delaware, and New Jersey. This page, and the following four, illustrates the variety and scope of damage. The photograph above is the debris field at the north end of the boardwalk in Rehoboth and on the left is a collapsed A-frame. (Above, courtesy Delaware Public Archives; left, courtesy Colonel McGarraugh via Marna Cupp.)

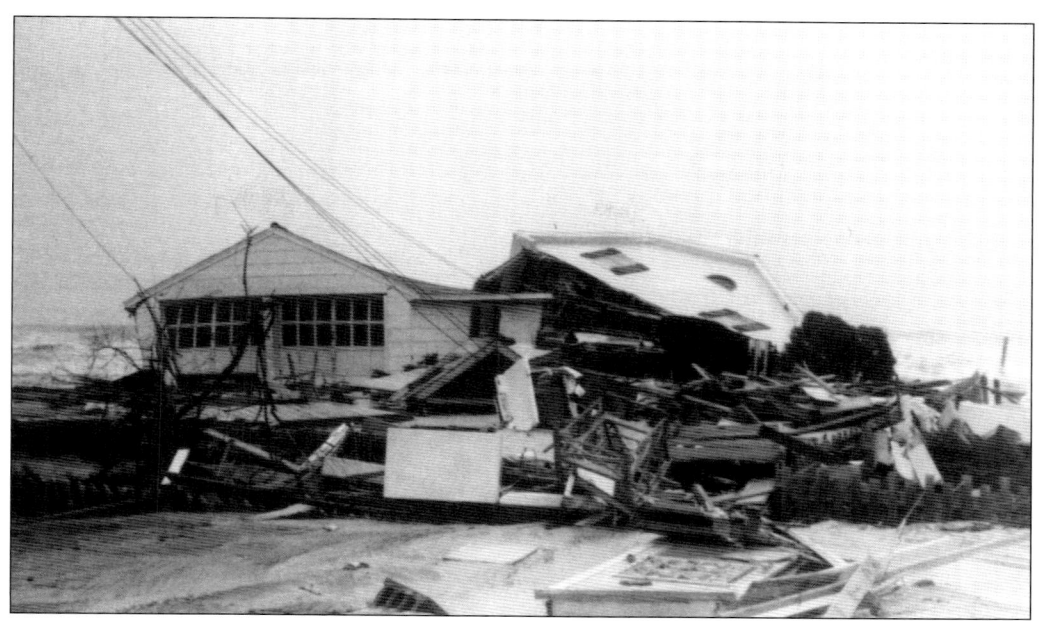

These two scenes could have been side-by-side lots but are in fact taken in Bethany (above) and Rehoboth (below). Mile after mile after mile, from North Carolina to Long Island, this was the condition of oceanfront communities. Shops, hotels, homes, and buildings of all types were reduced to massive piles of shattered boards, chunks of concrete, broken glass, tangles of wire, shingles, clothes, bedding, dishes, photographs, and artwork. Material objects of every variety became saltwater-soaked mounds of debris. (Above, courtesy Town of Bethany Beach; below, courtesy Colonel McGarraugh via Marna Cupp.)

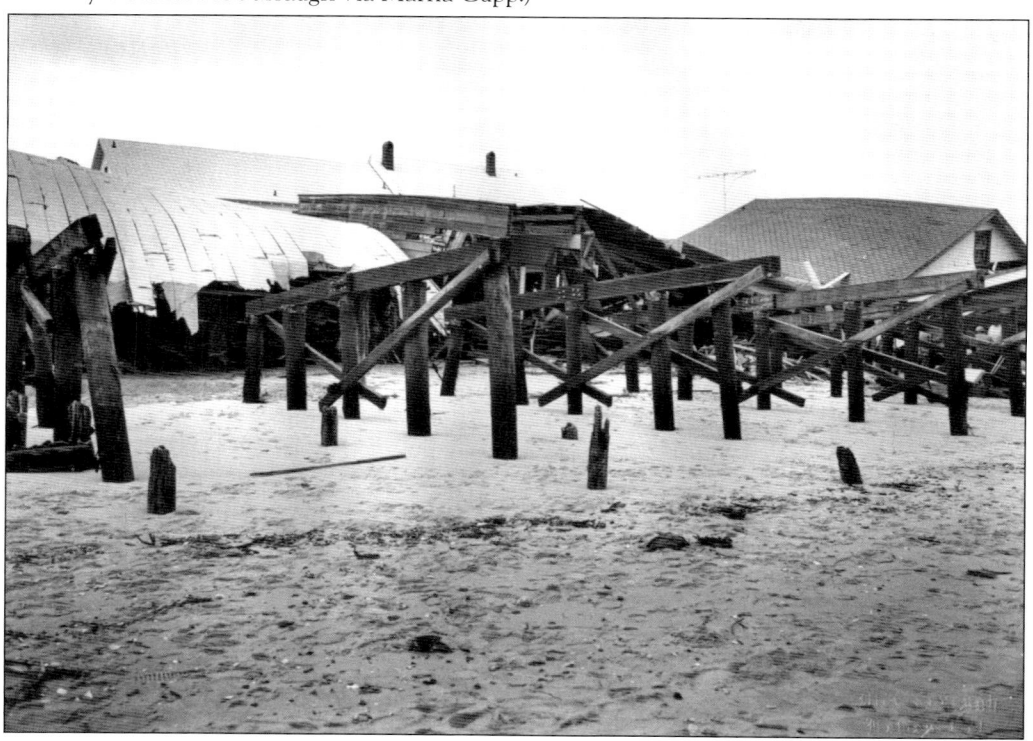

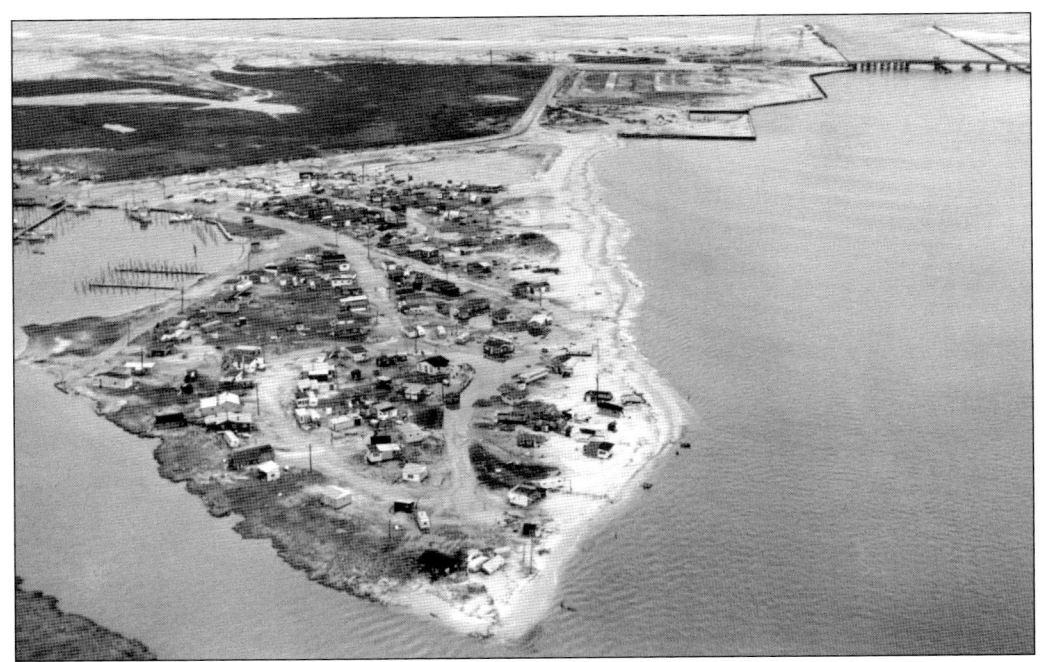

More than the physical and material losses, the storm—as do all major storms—destroyed human connection to things that had been loved through experience. Yes, people will return to the beach and smell the salt air and get the same sunburn, cool off in the same ocean, eat flounder and crabs and corn and tomatoes with family and friends after beach communities are rebuilt. But never again will they walk into the cottage they grew up in, or smell the interior of the restaurant they went to every year for 17 consecutive summers, look at pictures now gone, or visit some businesses that did not financially survive the disaster. Above is a mobile home community along Indian River Inlet shoreline. Below is South Bethany. (Above, courtesy Delaware DNREC; below, courtesy South Bethany Historical Society.)

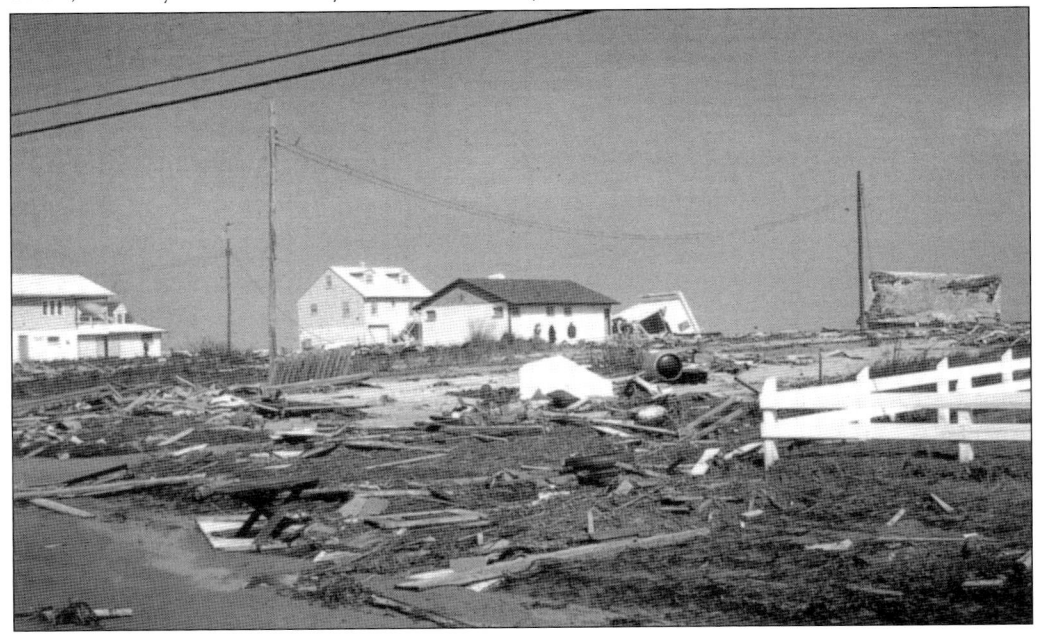

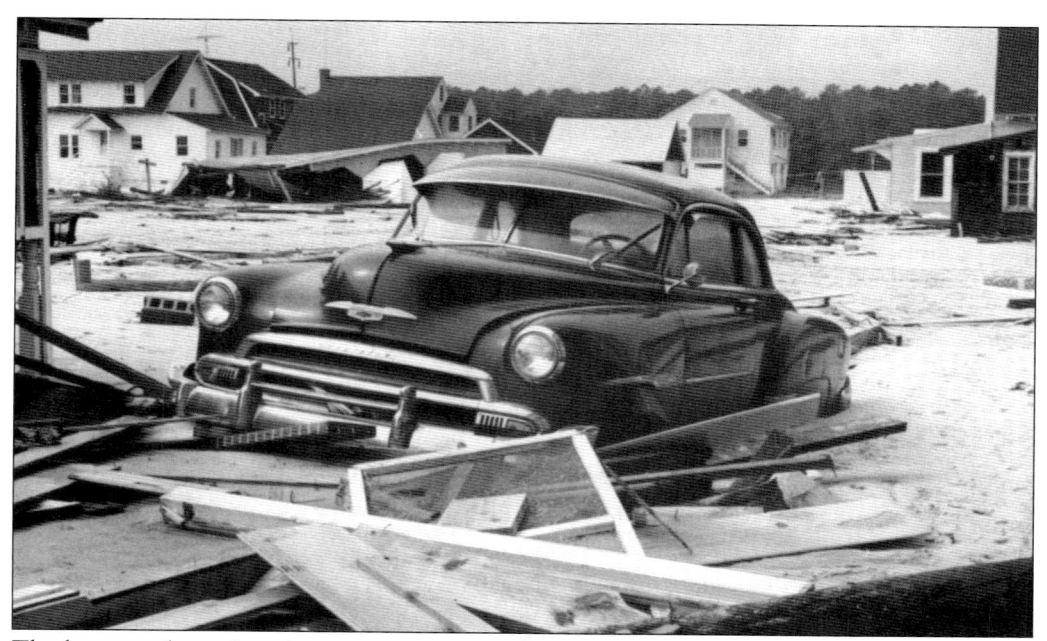

The losses spoken of on the previous page are fleeting losses: memories, sensory (smell, sound) stimulants, the comfort of revisiting physical space associated with good times of the past. Deeper losses are also suffered of course. Wreckage includes things that people cannot or choose not to photograph. Loss of jobs, loss of buildings that owners cannot afford to replace, and loss of life are among these things. Coastal disasters in this country, the Ash Wednesday Storm among them, result in terrible widespread wreckage on an all too frequent basis. The 1962 Storm was a huge threat to Delaware's important tourism industry and the jobs it supports. Above, a parked car is shown awash in storm debris, and below, Funland is shown three months before the summer season was to start. (Above, courtesy *Delaware State News*; below, courtesy Lewes Historical Society.)

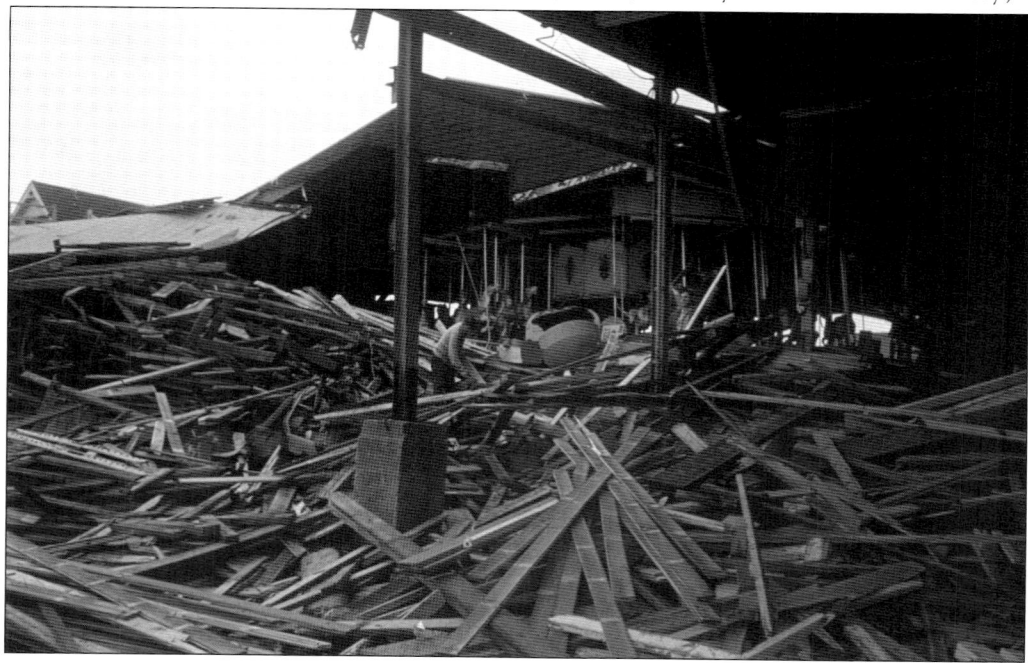

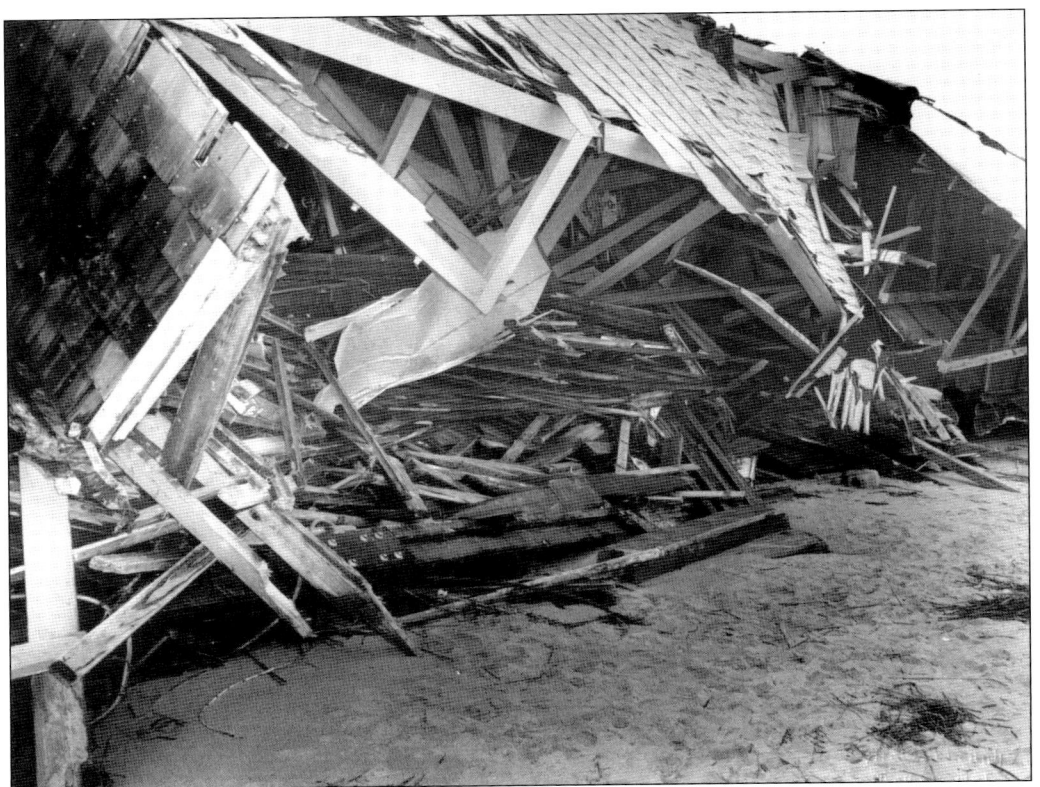

The 1962 Storm was an event that opened eyes in the affected region. Delaware learned a great deal about construction along the coast and the vulnerability of living right on the edge of the continent, with the sometimes-roaring Atlantic just a few hundred feet away. Every storm that tears apart coastal communities in this country adds to that knowledge and increases the resolve to rebuild more smartly, more resiliently, and with a far better understanding of how vulnerable residents are. The wreckage from the storm was widespread and immense, but the lessons learned were also considerable. Above is detail of an unidentified collapsed building, and below is landward of the Bethany boardwalk. (Above, courtesy Colonel McGarraugh via Marna Cupp; below, courtesy Town of Bethany Beach.)

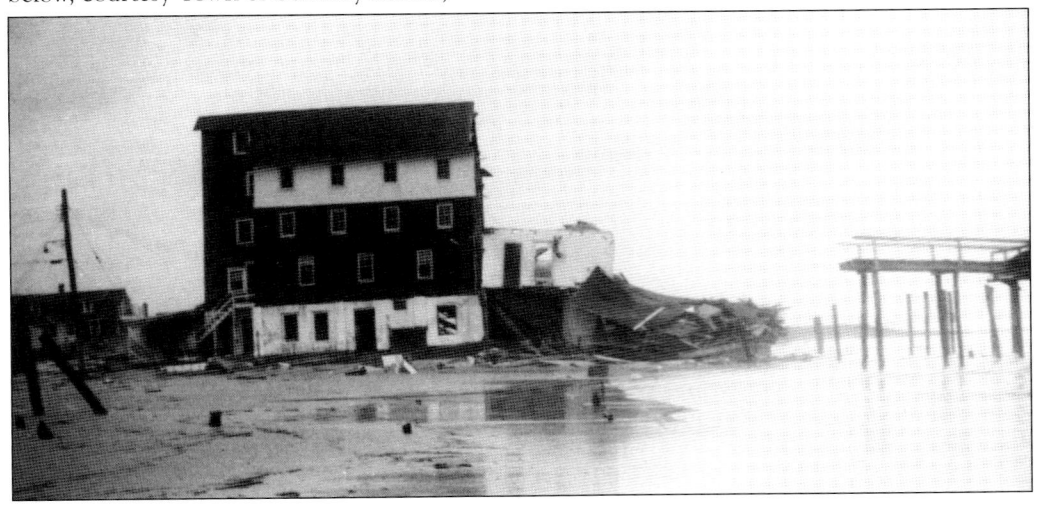

Five

Changing the Face of the Coast

Not only did this devastating storm change lives and communities, but it also transformed the face of the Delaware coast. The 1962 Storm was not a hurricane, but rather an equally impactful weather event known as a northeaster. Northeasters are also called extra-tropical storms because they develop outside of the tropics and generally result from one or more low-pressure systems off the coast. Their strong winds can blow from the northeast for days, generating large waves and higher than normal tides. Winds produced from these storms can have damaging effects on roofs, trees, and power lines, but the main influence of winds is on wave heights and wave energy. Coastal storms and associated surging water can cause extensive beach and dune erosion, which results in narrowed beaches or sand overwashed into the back barrier marshes or bays.

Flooding can be extensive—and not necessarily from excessive rainfall. Elevated water levels caused by storm surge can break through or over ocean and bay beaches and transmit huge volumes of seawater into areas that are normally dry. Breaching of the barrier beaches not only allows transport of seawater and sediments, but houses can succumb to the power of the storm surge and be carried away or obliterated altogether. The Ash Wednesday Storm significantly altered the Delaware Atlantic and bay shorelines through these very processes.

To people, the impacts from a storm can be devastating, but for coastal landscapes, these are normal processes that help shape and sustain geomorphic coastal environments. For instance, overwash is the mechanism for the barrier beach to maintain its integrity as it moves landward. Almost immediately following a storm, the natural recovery process begins. At the beach, large sandbars (formed from the sands that were transported seaward during the storm) begin to appear close to shore. As the winds and waves calm down, the sandbars are moved by waves and eventually attach to the dry beach. This is the way that a beach naturally heals. If there is enough sand, and the wind and wave conditions continue, the wide beaches and high dunes will return.

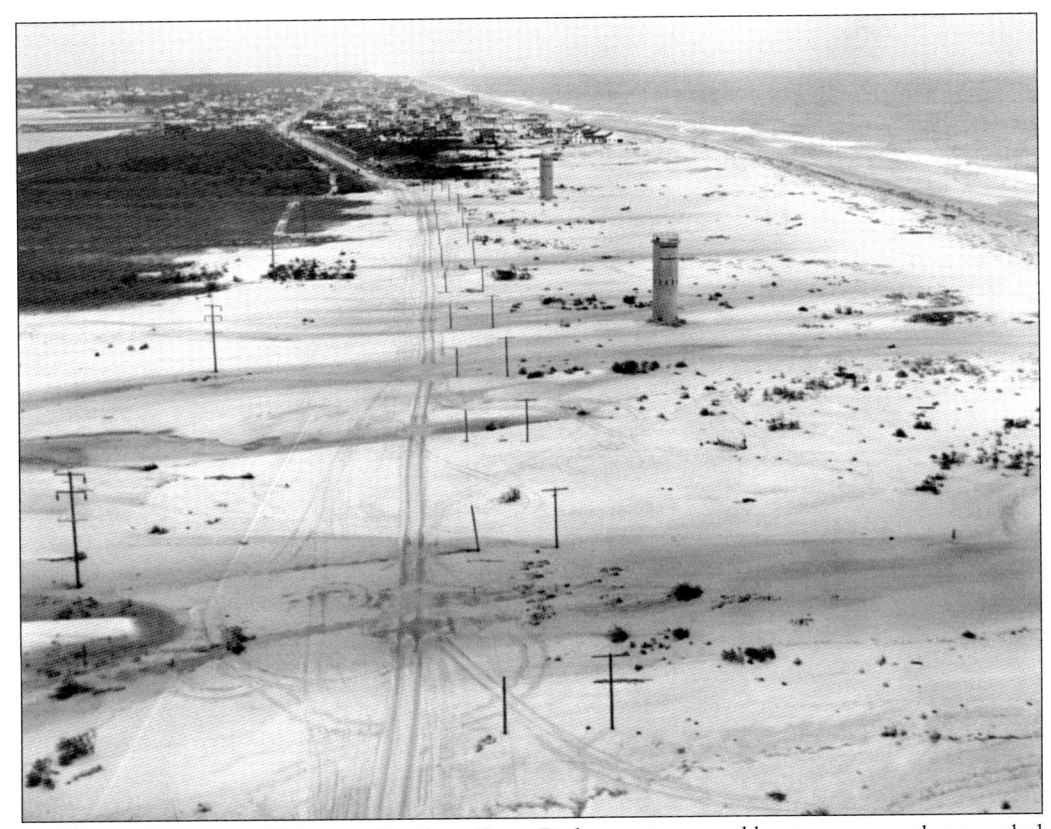

World War II towers at Delaware Seashore State Park were impacted by storm surge that toppled dunes and carried water and sand across the beach. Route 14, precursor to Route 1, was choked with sand. Spectacular overwash deposits (sandy sediments carried from beaches and dunes) were left on top of or near marshes in Rehoboth Bay. Overwash is the natural mechanism for landward barrier beach migration. (Courtesy Delaware Public Archives.)

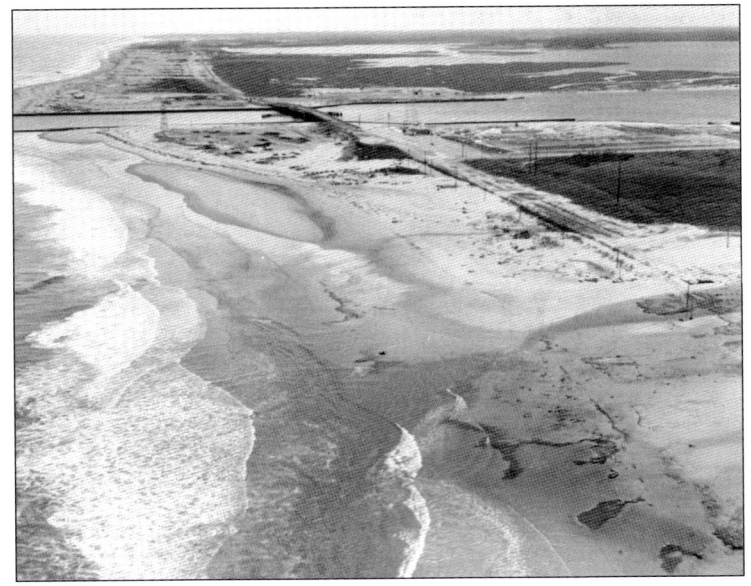

The north jetty of the Indian River Inlet may have offered some protection to the steel tower (in view just north of the jetty), but it did little to protect the nearby beaches and dunes, which were the source of overwash sands that closed Route 14. Every single dune along the Delaware coast was flattened or overtopped by the storm's waves. (Courtesy Delaware DNREC.)

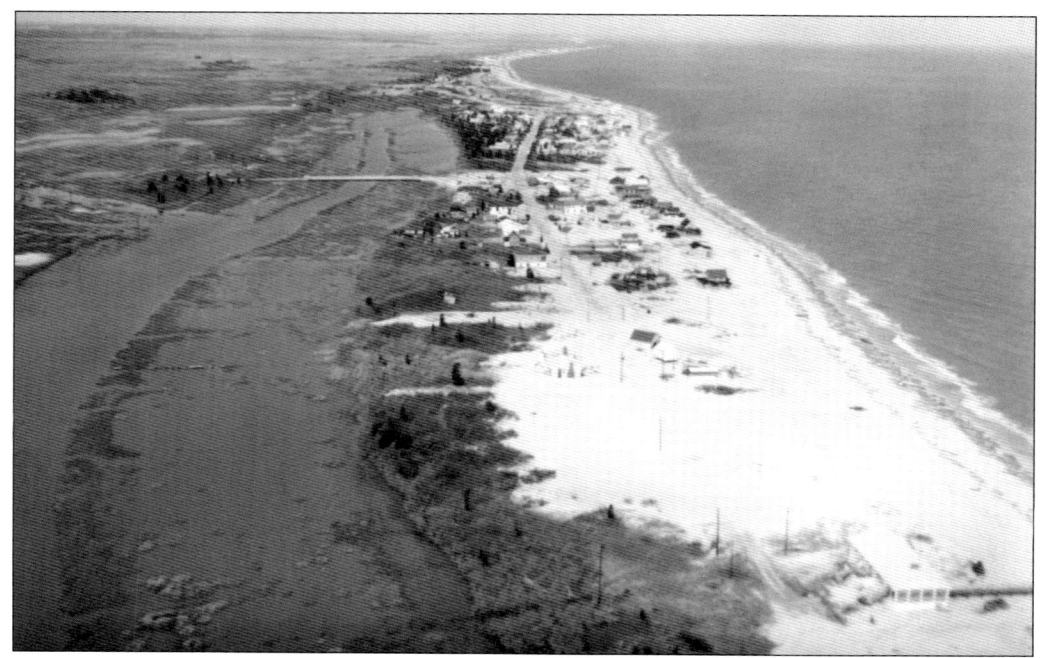

The estuarine beaches that line Delaware Bay sit on top of former marsh surfaces and consist of low dunes and thin, narrow beaches. They too were also affected by storm surge. Here, in Broadkill Beach, storm waves transported the thin layers of beach sands across the barrier and almost into the flooded Broadkill River. (Courtesy Delaware DNREC.)

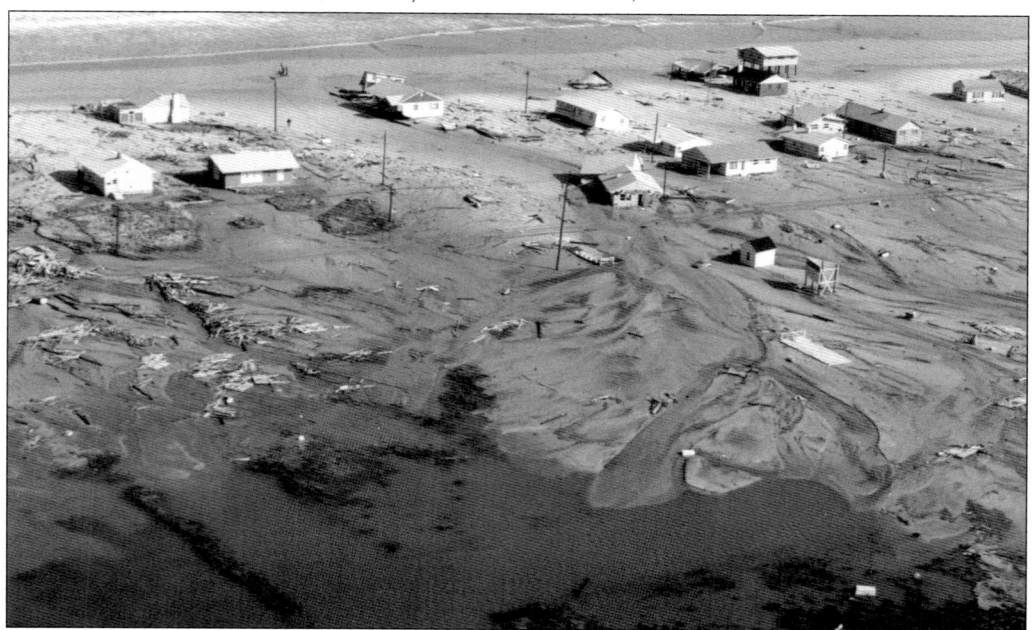

This photograph provides a closer view of the patterns created by overwashed sand deposits. When storm waves hit the shore, the low areas between dunes or low roads and pedestrian pathways are susceptible to the surge of water that is channeled through areas of least resistance. Here, the splay of sand fills a low, still flooded, area of the barrier beach system. (Courtesy Delaware Public Archives.)

89

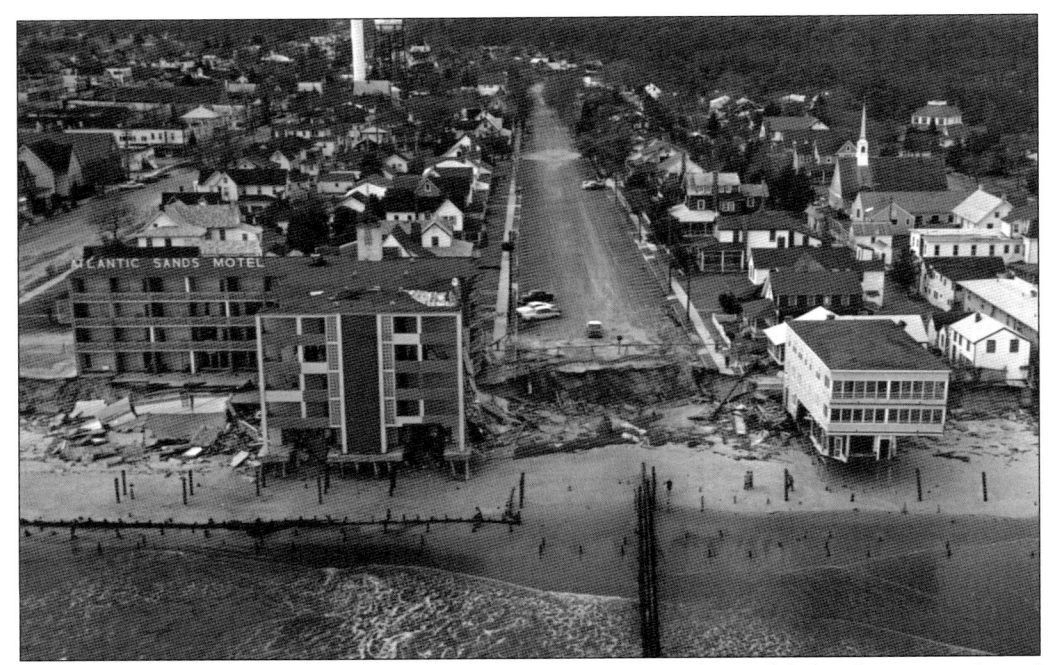

Rehoboth Beach sits on a geologic headland that was originally a tidal flat, lagoon, and sand spit formed during periods of higher sea levels over 300,000 years ago. Headlands are typically the sediment sources for beaches. Most of the storm-eroded sediments were carried by the wave-generated longshore current toward Cape Henlopen. (Courtesy Delaware Public Archives.)

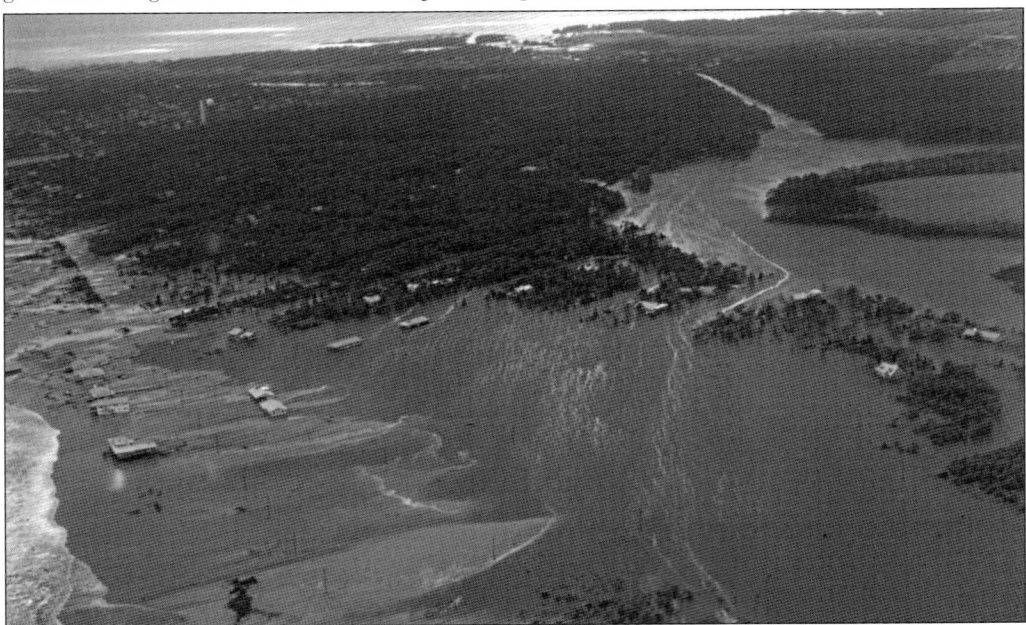

Located adjacent to the headland at Rehoboth Beach, the North Shores community (left side of photograph) on the Atlantic Ocean and the flats just south of Gordon Pond were inundated from the high tides and storm waves. The storm waters also submerged low-lying Holland Glade and Lewes-Rehoboth Canal, which carried the floodwaters into Rehoboth Bay (at the top of photograph). (Courtesy Lewes Historical Society.)

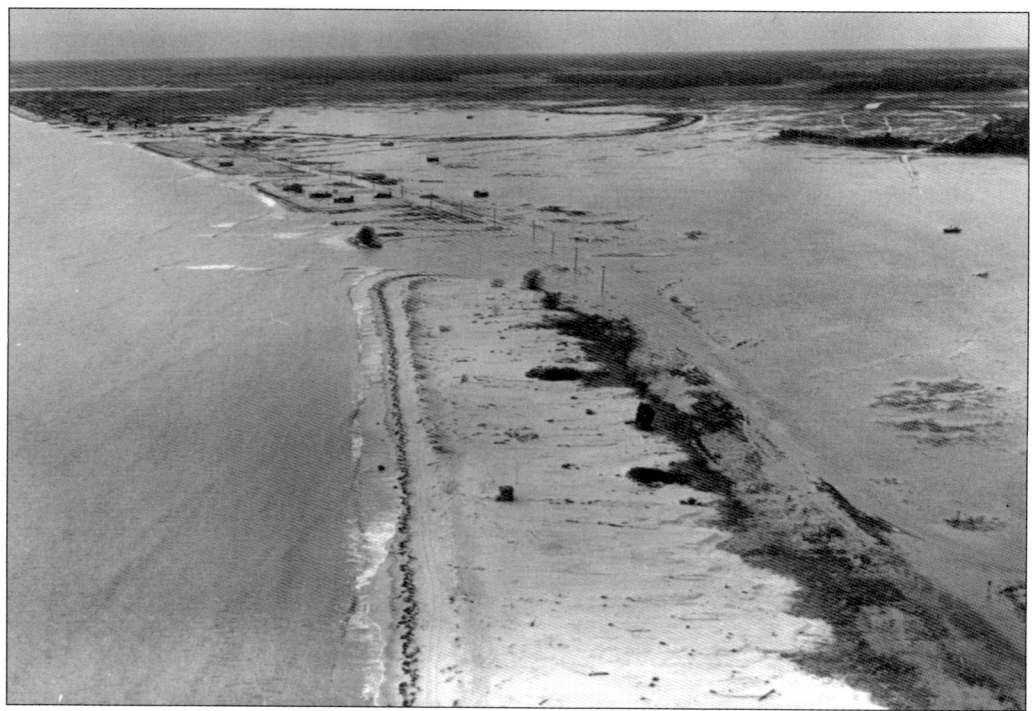

Along the low-lying Delaware Bay shoreline, storm surge created numerous channels through the coastal barrier beaches. These photographs show the northern section of Slaughter Beach, which sits on top of the ancestral Cedar Creek that later filled with compacting mud. Breaches can occur in the low-lying areas of the former creek and act as conduits for storm surge into the marshes, as well as drainage outlets from the marshes to Delaware Bay. Breaching enables large amounts of seawater to infiltrate areas that would not normally be exposed to saltwater. Agricultural lands adjacent to the marshes were also affected by the sudden intrusion of the sea. (Both, courtesy Delaware Public Archives.)

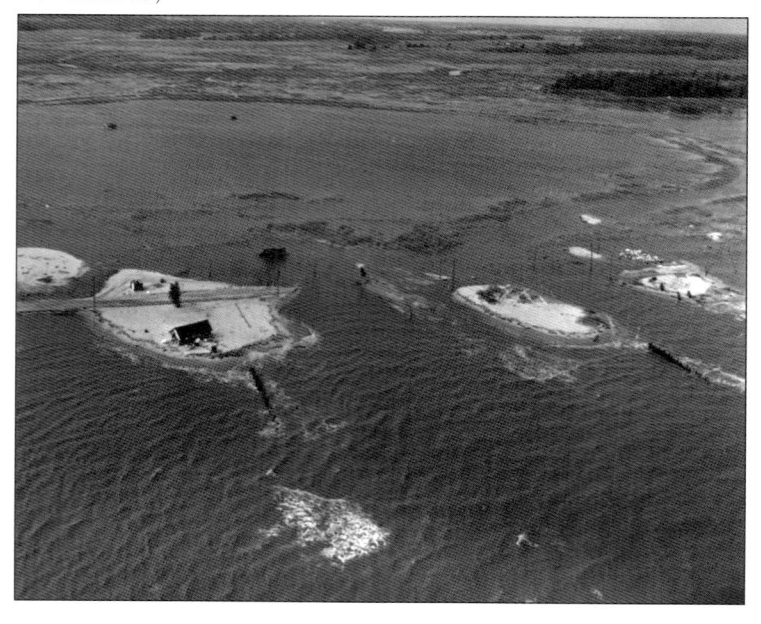

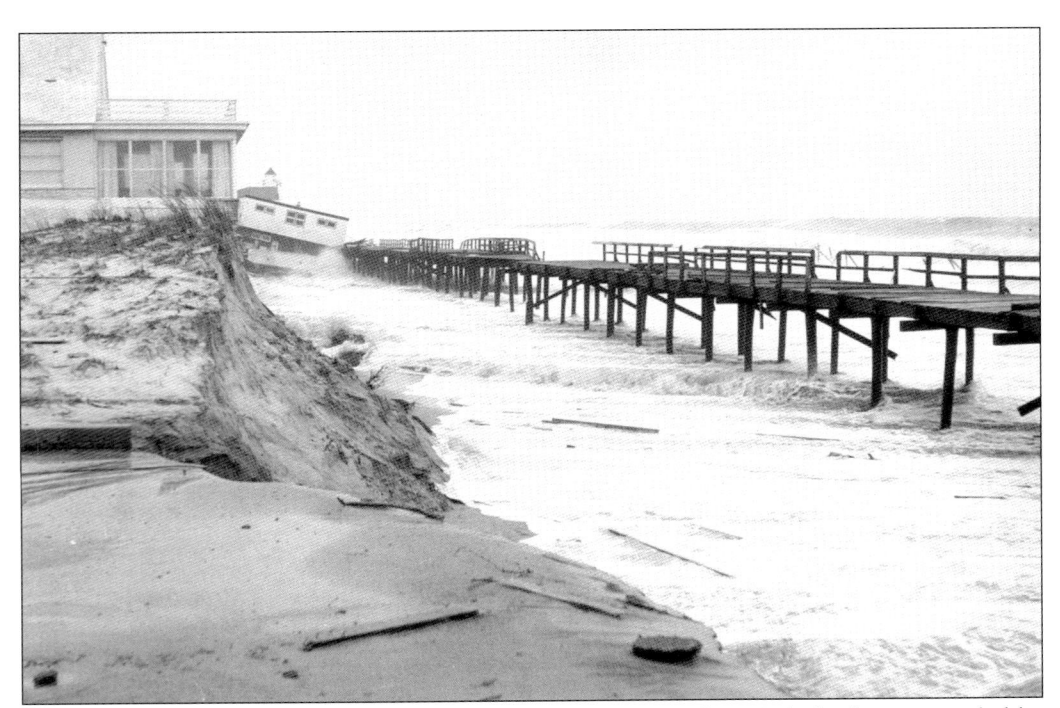

Sandy uplands that were located at the oceanfront street ends in Rehoboth were eroded by direct wave attack, creating large scarps (above). Sand that eroded from the former upland area was moved to the beach—a process that makes the beaches wider so that waves break farther offshore. Small dunes that fronted the boardwalk in the southern reach of Rehoboth Beach were not enough to protect from the damaging waves. Not only did dunes at the road ends suffer, but all dunes within all coastal communities were obliterated by the storm surge. Shown here in the vicinity of Rehoboth/Dewey (below) are the vast amounts of beach and dune sands that were transferred landward by the waves. During this process, the beach can be lowered by several feet. (Above, courtesy Lewes Historical Society; below, courtesy Delaware Public Archives.)

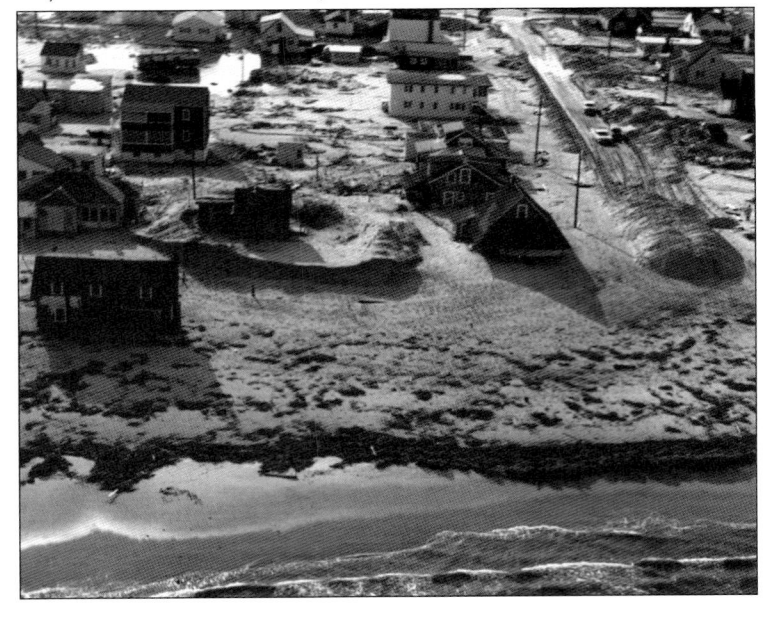

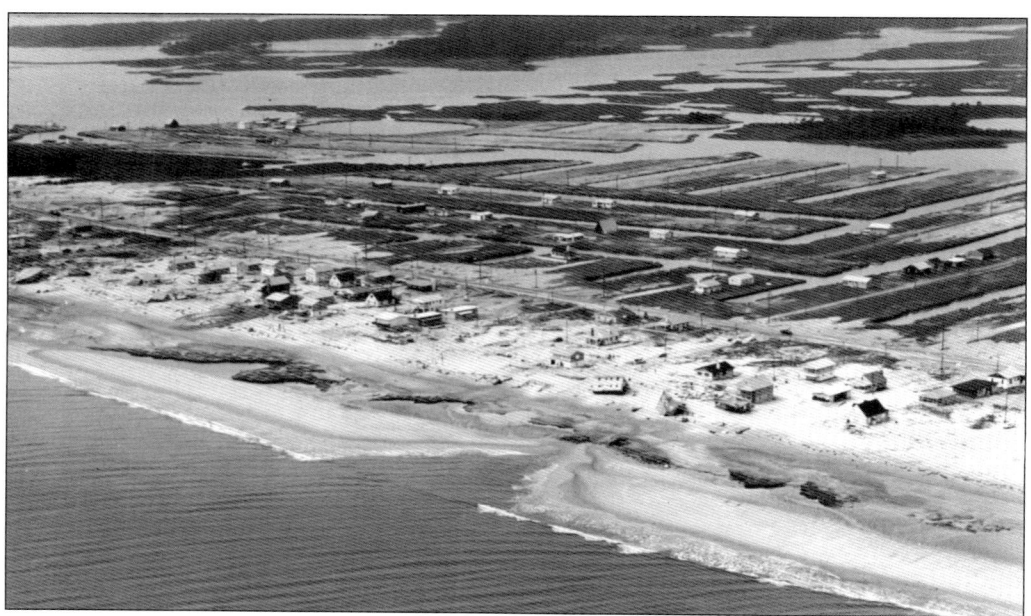

The storm waves vertically lowered the beaches in South Bethany Beach (above) and Bethany Beach (below) to the elevation of former marshes or coastal forests. Note the dark peat and organic material outcroppings in the low areas between the sandbars and the dry beach. These organic-rich marsh or remnant organic forest layers were once located landward of the shoreline and are a testament to the overall landward movement of the barrier in response to coastal storms, long-term erosion, and sea-level rise. Sometimes, tree stump remnants of coastal forests are exposed on the eroded beaches. In time, these uncovered expanses of marsh peat will be covered by newly deposited sand and may not be exposed again until another big event. (Above, courtesy Delaware Public Archives; below, courtesy Delaware DNREC.)

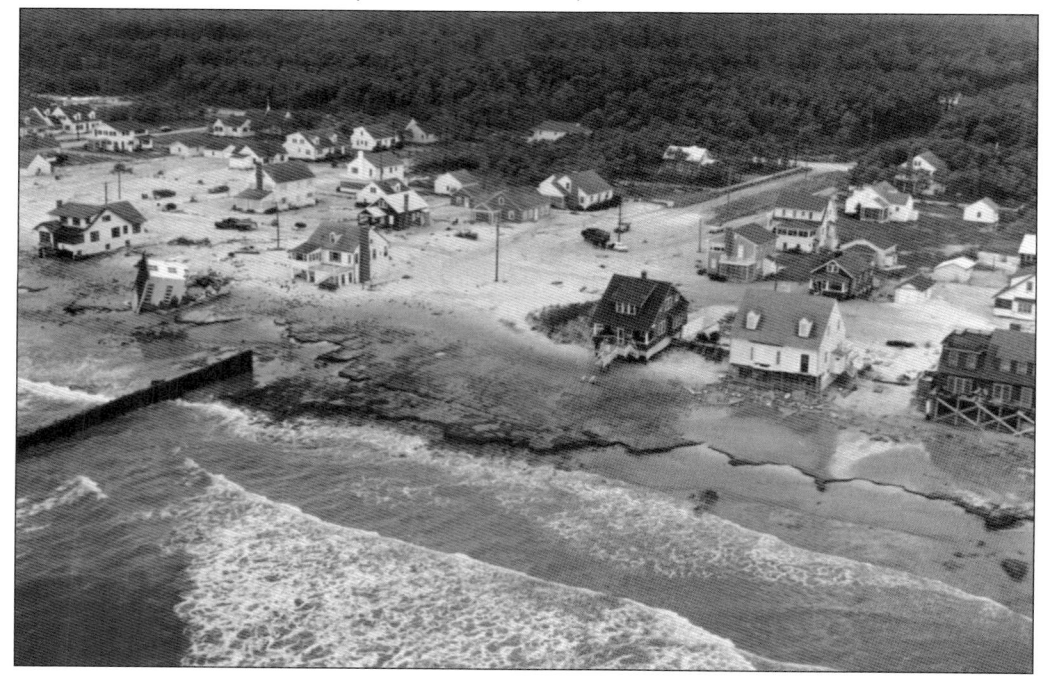

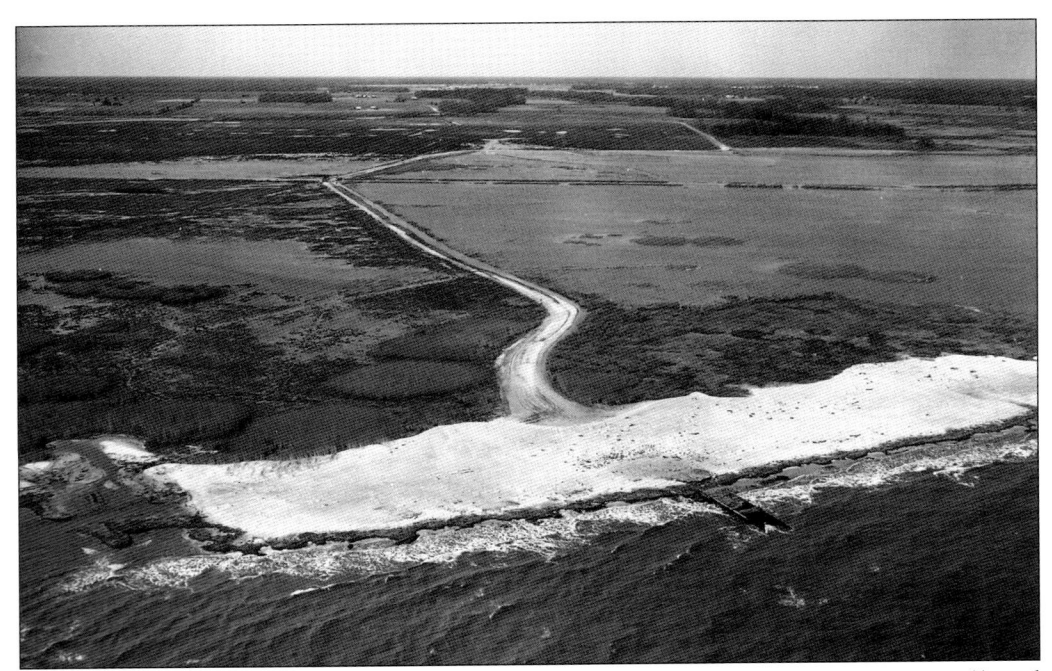

Much of the shoreline along the central and southern section of Delaware Bay consists of broad coastal marshes and sandy estuarine beaches. The photograph above shows Fowler Beach Road two weeks after the storm, where marshes and agricultural lands were still flooded from the seawater that washed in from Delaware Bay. Slaughter Creek can be recognized by the higher levee deposits and vegetation that runs roughly parallel to the shoreline. The photograph below shows overwashed sands across the Prime Hook beach community and former marsh surfaces that were exposed on the shoreline. Note that the Prime Hook National Wildlife Refuge, which includes the property behind the beach community, was established a year later as a sanctuary for migrating birds. (Both, courtesy Delaware Public Archives.)

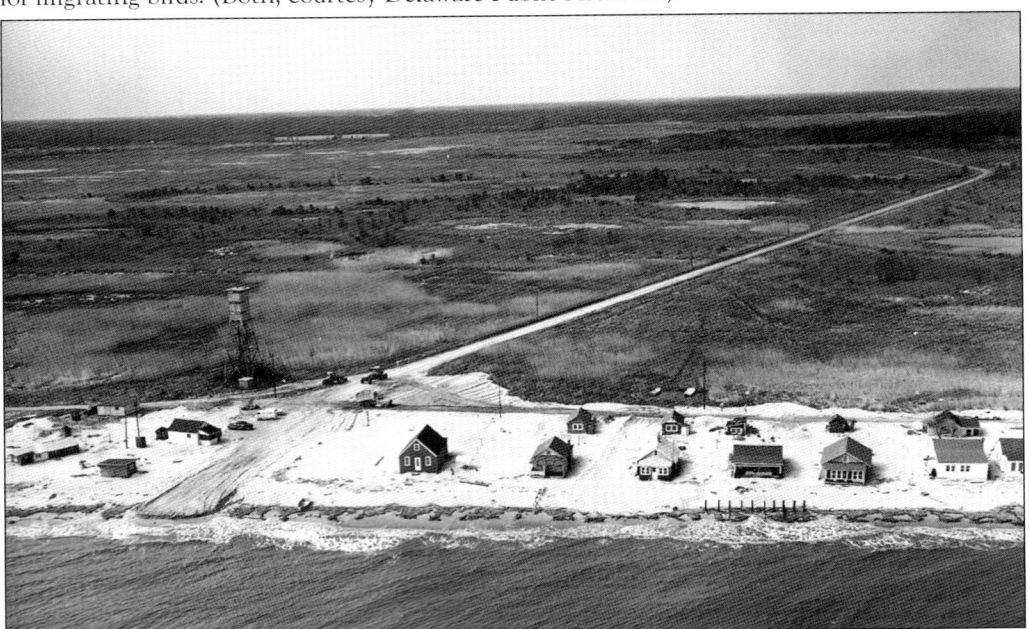

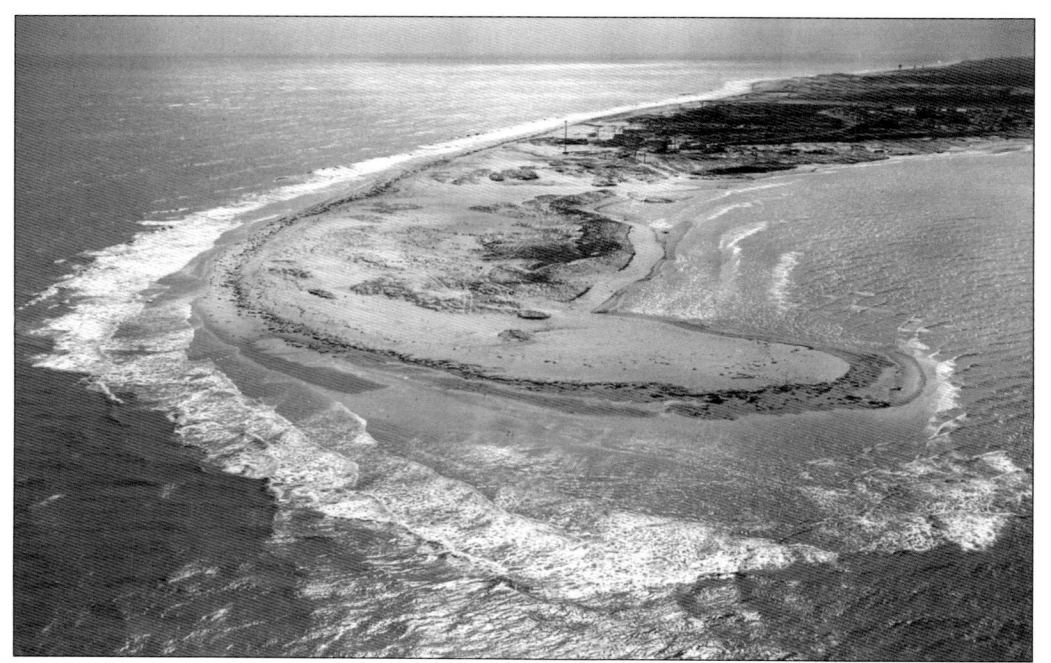

Beaches, dunes and vegetation were inundated at Cape Henlopen, though the spit (outermost stretch) managed to maintain its overall shape and orientation through the storm. Sand eroded from Atlantic beaches near southern sections of the park were quickly transported by the currents and deposited here. The cape is an active deposition zone, constantly reshaped with periodic sandbars that form and weld onto the tidal flats. (Courtesy Delaware Public Archives.)

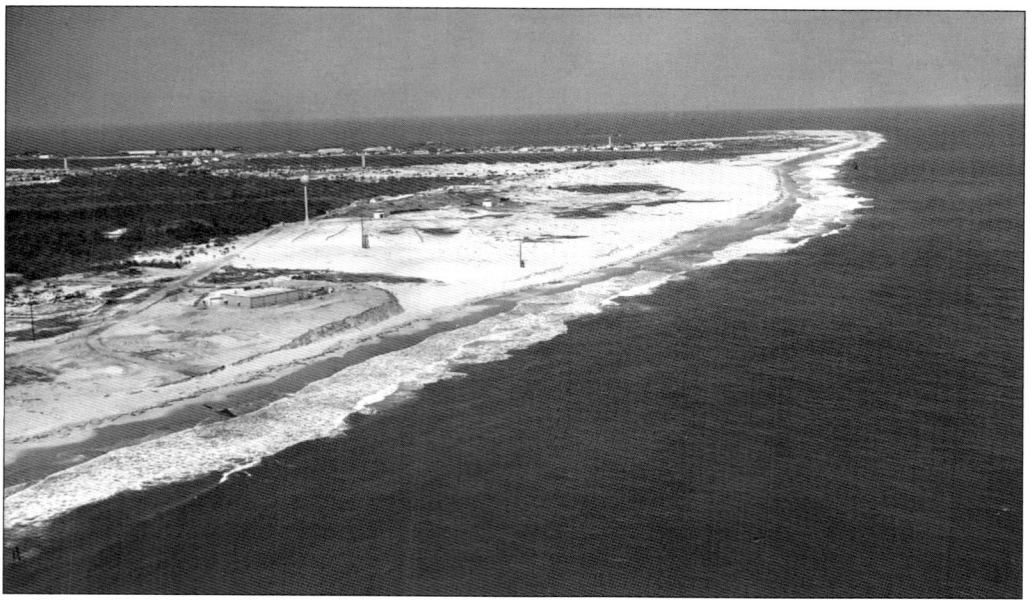

Fort Miles had occupied most of the real estate on Cape Henlopen, and fort infrastructure bore the brunt of the northeast winds and waves. Though natural coastal systems were impacted by the storm, portions of the cape with higher elevations and few structures experienced minimum storm damage. This Fort Miles property has since been dedicated to the state to become part of Cape Henlopen State Park. (Courtesy Delaware Public Archives.)

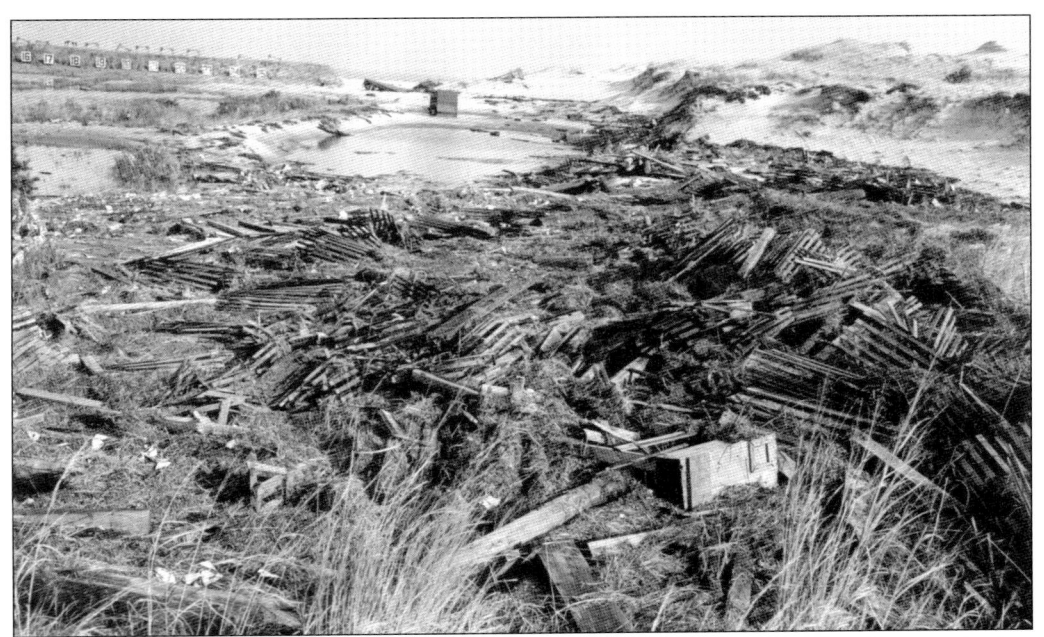

The landward limit of wave activity can be marked by the line of accumulated materials that are carried by waves and deposited when the wave has no more energy to carry them. This is known as the wrack line. Usually, this line marks the limit of the high tide line and consists of vegetation or maybe a few shells. Not so for the Ash Wednesday Storm. At Fort Miles (above), the wrack included dune fences that were washed back behind the dune into enormous drift lines of timber and trash. Below, boats and remnants of the beachfront homes in Fenwick Island were washed across Little Assawoman Bay into the western marshes. Here, the wrack line was found nearly one mile inland from the shoreline. (Above, courtesy Colonel McGarraugh via Marna Cupp; below, *Delaware State News*.)

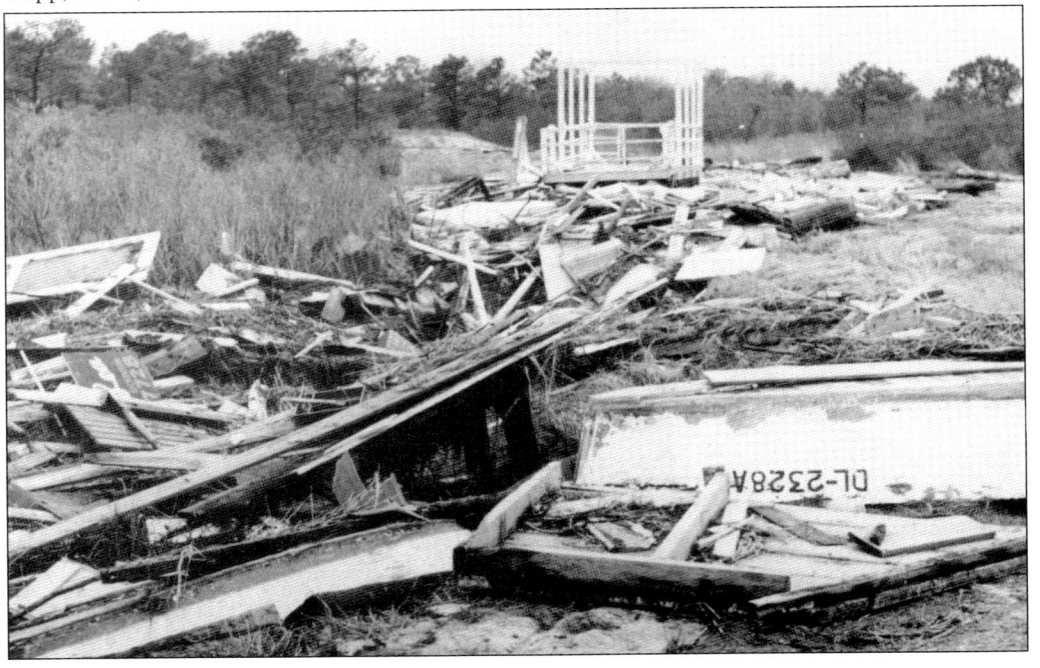

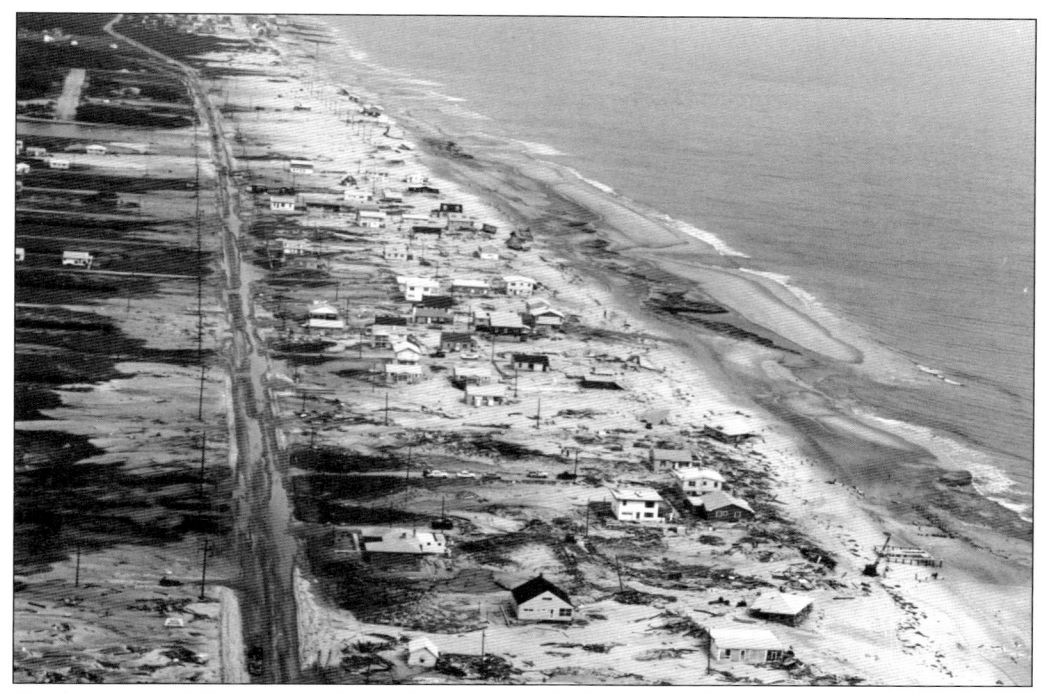

Tidal stage, wind direction, and wave height controlled the type of sediment deposition as seen in South Bethany (above)—either landward sedimentation as overwash deposits (seen in the splays west of Route 14) or seaward deposition into the surf zone. Immediately following the storm, a double-longshore sandbar system formed along nearly the entire length of Delaware's shoreline. Sandbars attached to the dry beach in the months that followed (photograph below of Delaware Seashore State Park and Dewey Beach in the distance). A low swale or runnel (shown filled with water) marks the landward extent of the merging sandbar. Only high-tide waves are able to break over the bar and carry the sands to fill the low areas. Eventually, this bar system became part of a wide, dry beach. (Both, courtesy Delaware Public Archives.)

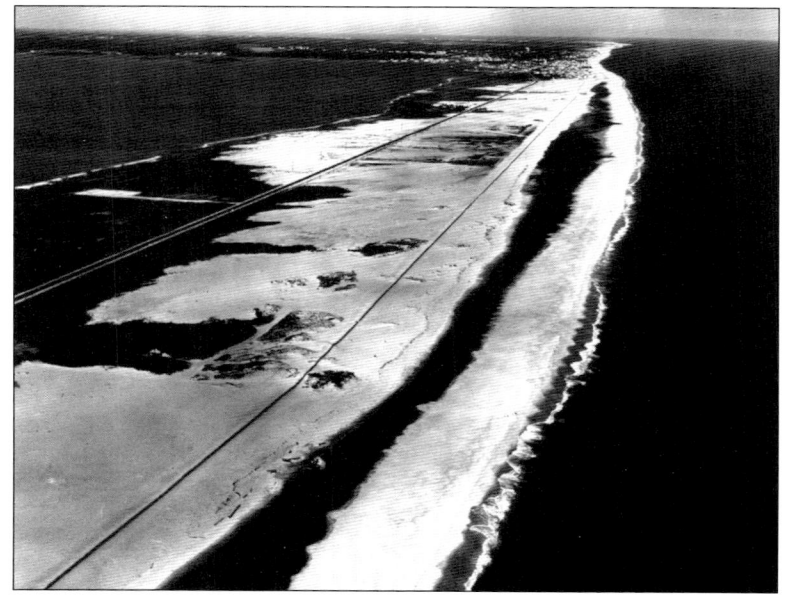

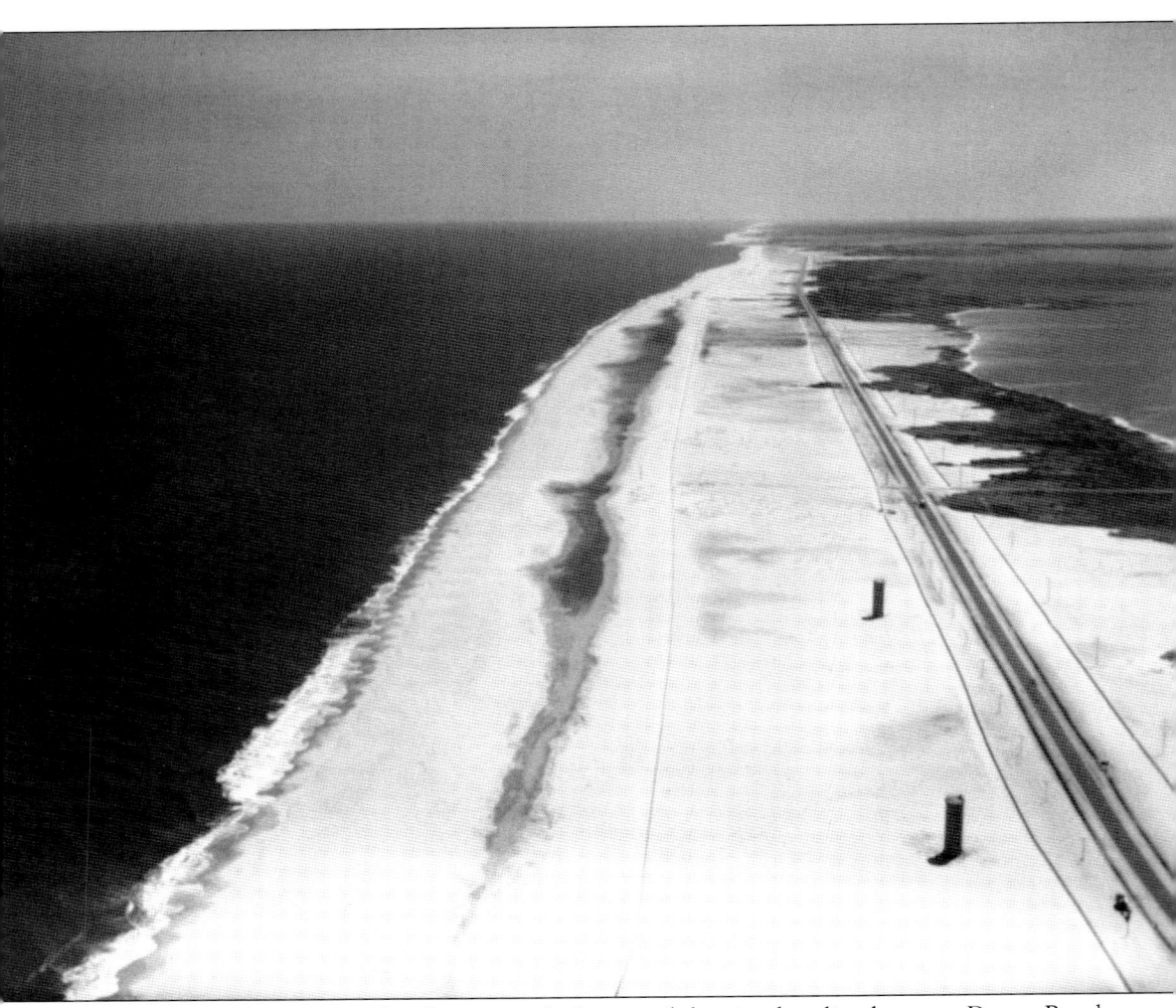

A little more than a year after the storm, the baymouth barrier shoreline between Dewey Beach and Indian River Inlet was still in a recovery phase, as shown in this May 1963 photograph of Delaware Seashore State Park. Though it did not take long to restore travel along Route 14, the natural process of barrier stabilization was continuing. Dune and overwash areas were still mostly devoid of vegetation, and dune fencing was placed along the back beach in hopes of trapping sand and creating new dunes. The sandbar that emerged immediately after the storm was still moving to fill the low areas and rebuild the beach. This is an example of coastal resiliency—the ability to bounce back after an extreme event—but also demonstrates the length of time that it can take for a beach to return back to pre-storm conditions. (Courtesy Delaware DNREC.)

Six

RESPONSE, RECOVERY, AND RESILIENCY

Damage inspections began on March 6 and continued through the follow weeks. Gov. Elbert N. Carvel toured the coast via a National Guard truck with Maj. Gen. Joseph J. Scannell, adjutant general of the state's National Guard units; Col. John P. Ferguson, head of the Delaware State Police; and William J. Miller, operating chief of the Delaware State Highway Department.

On March 8, 1962, Governor Carvel wired Pres. John F. Kennedy with an urgent request that the Delaware coast be declared a disaster area:

> For the past 14 hours I have personally been surveying the awful destruction on our Delaware coast caused by the most devastating and disastrous storm in the memory of living Delawareans. It is estimated that $50 million worth of damage has been caused to Delaware property and the end is not yet in sight. Abnormally high winds of gale velocity and high tides averaging five feet above normal continue to reap a terrible toll of destruction.
>
> Thousands of homes have been completely destroyed and many thousands more are partially under water. I urgently request that you proclaim the coastal area of Delaware, from Fenwick Island to Delaware City, for a depth of five miles westward from the coastline, as a disaster area, and subject to all the assistance which the laws of the United States provide for such a condition. We are grateful for the help being rendered to us by the Second Army and the Office of Civil Defense in this emergency.

Despite the widespread disaster and inconceivable damage, state officials spoke of resilient attitudes seen throughout devastated communities. After his tour of the storm-wrought coast, Governor Carvel said he was certain of the spirit of the people "to meet the challenge of rebuilding."

Secretary of State Elisha Dukes estimated Delaware storm-related property damage to be $42,812,650. The loss estimate included $25,411,985 to public property and $17,400,665 to private property. It did not include land lost to the sea or general business loss to merchants. Oceanfront lots that had been selling for $5,000 to $10,000 each were washed into the sea along most of the ocean coast.

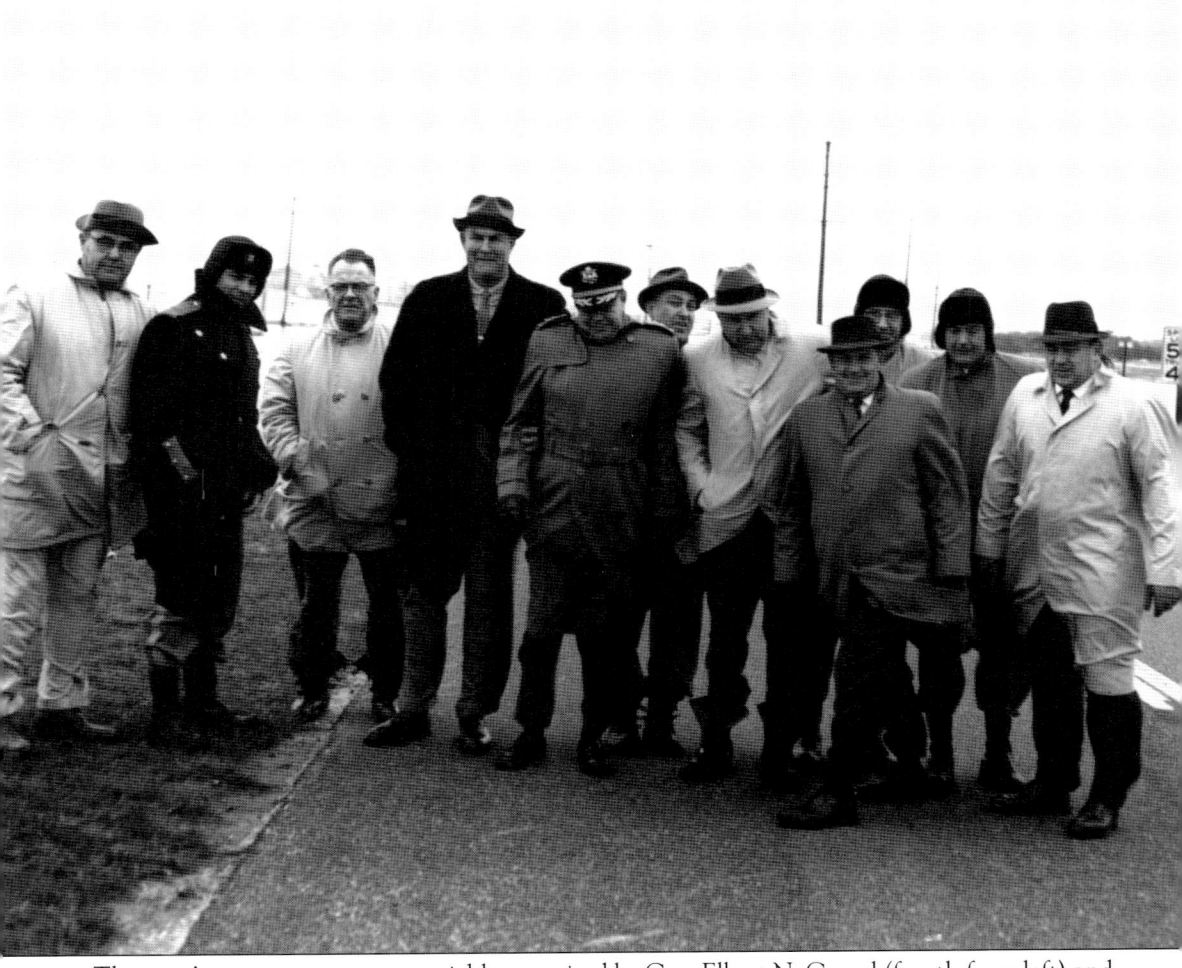

The state's storm response was quickly organized by Gov. Elbert N. Carvel (fourth from left) and Secretary of State Elisha Dukes, who was appointed coordinator of disaster relief. One of the initial assigned tasks was to obtain an accurate survey of the total damage to homes, private property, and public infrastructure. Preliminary estimates suggested that approximately 3,000 homes had been destroyed and another 7,000 suffered some sort of water damage. Original estimates of $50 million in damage seemed conservative as additional information became available. Many state agencies collaborated in surveying and documenting the damage, including the Office of Emergency Planning, the State Civil Defense Agency, the Small Business Administration, Department of Agriculture, the Department of Health, Education, and Welfare, the State Highway Department, the National Guard, and the Delaware State Police. (Courtesy Delaware Public Archives.)

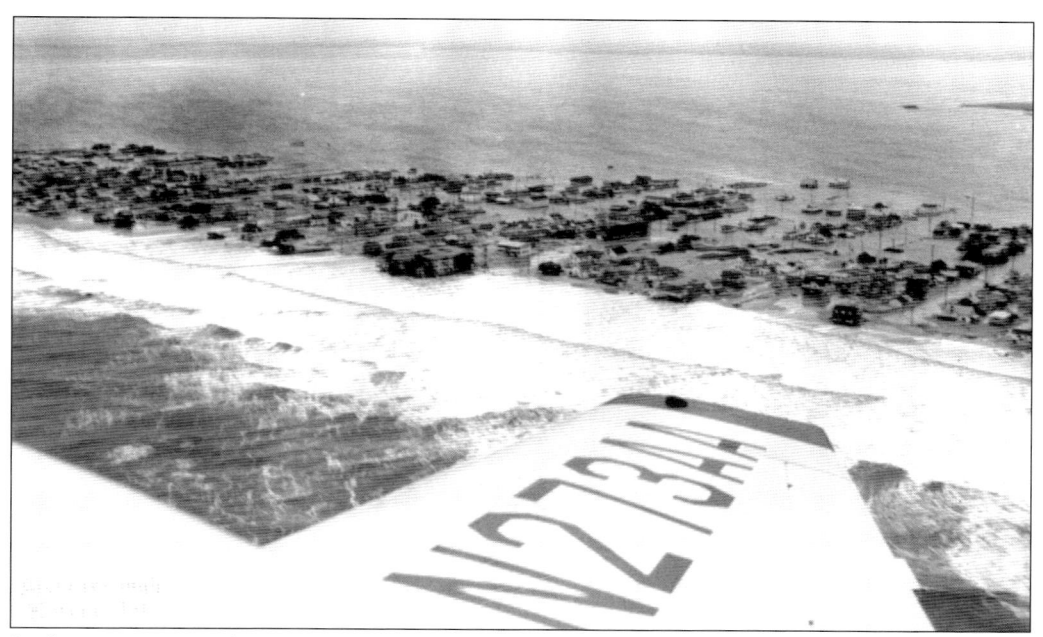

In the storm's immediate aftermath, the importance of aerial surveys of the coast and the brave men who piloted the aircraft cannot be overstated. The roads that would have provided access to the damaged areas were flooded and impassable for weeks. Top Delaware officials flew the area in planes or helicopters to see the destruction firsthand. The *Wilmington Morning News* reported that "even though many had read stories of the damage and had seen pictures, the sights they saw still stunned them." Colonel Ferguson spoke of his plane trip over the area: "You cannot imagine the tremendous damage and destruction until you can see it from the air. You get a pretty good picture of conditions on the ground, but when you are above it the sight is fearful." (Above, courtesy Colonel McGarraugh via Marna Cupp; below, courtesy Lewes Historical Society.)

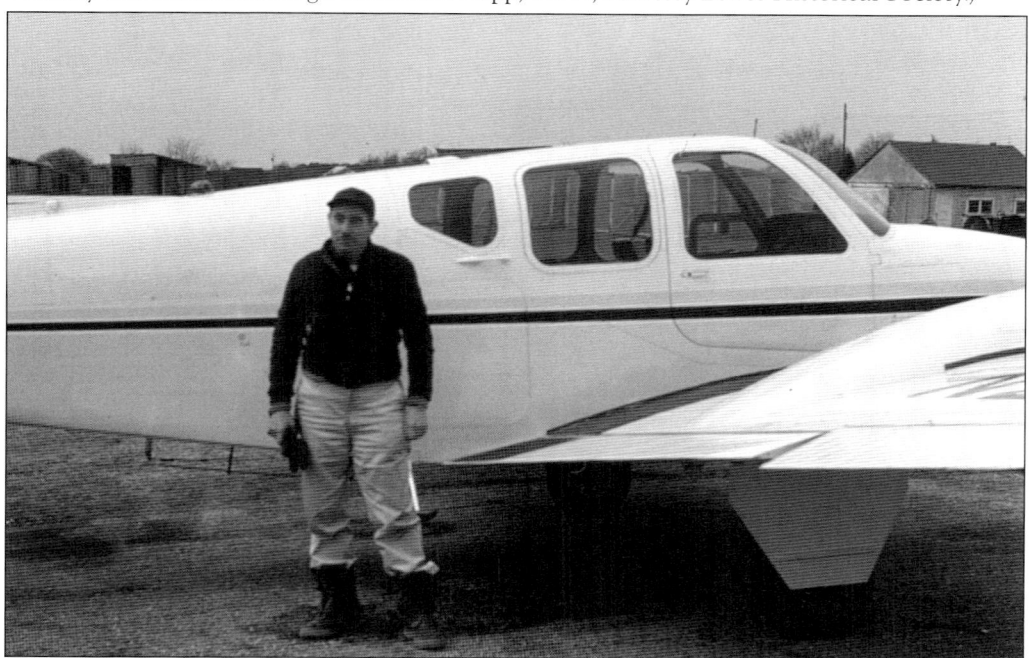

101

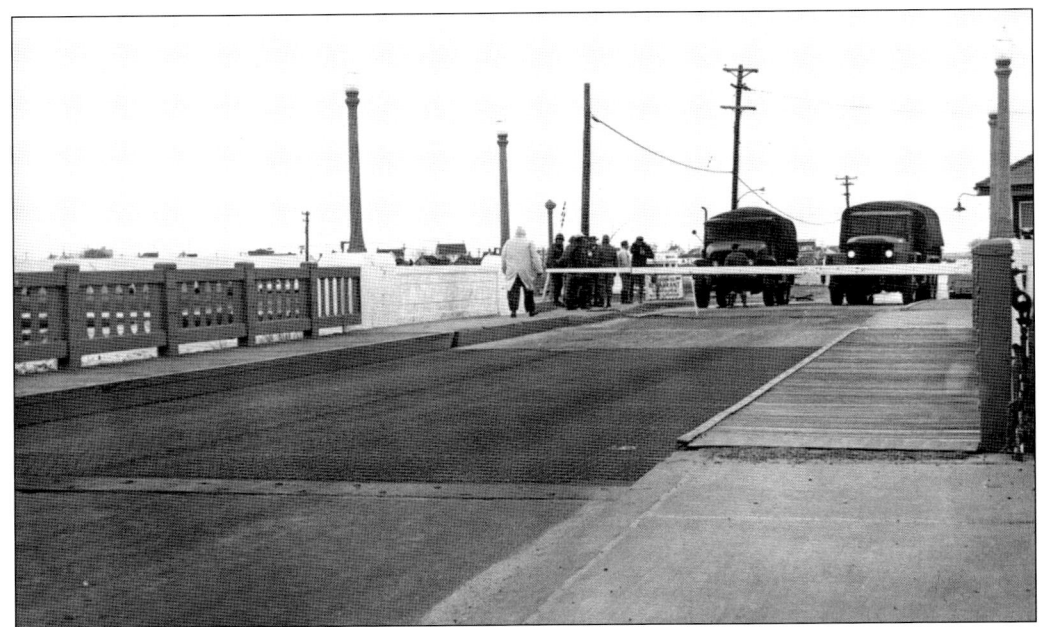

Governor Carvel called the National Guard to duty on the afternoon of March 6. By March 7, there were 86 officers and 634 enlisted men on emergency duty, armed and patrolling Delaware's vulnerable coast under the command of Maj. Gen. Joseph J. Scannell. From March 6 to 15, approximately 1,200 men were called to active duty in response to the storm. Three primary duties were assigned: 1) assist in evacuating persons still endangered by high tides; 2) set up road blocks to keep auto and pedestrian traffic out of emergency areas; and 3) protect property and prevent looting. For evacuations, the National Guard used heavy trucks and dusters—tanklike vehicles that operate on tracks and were able to reach flooded areas in which trucks could not operate. (Above, courtesy Lewes Historical Society; below, courtesy Town of Bethany Beach.)

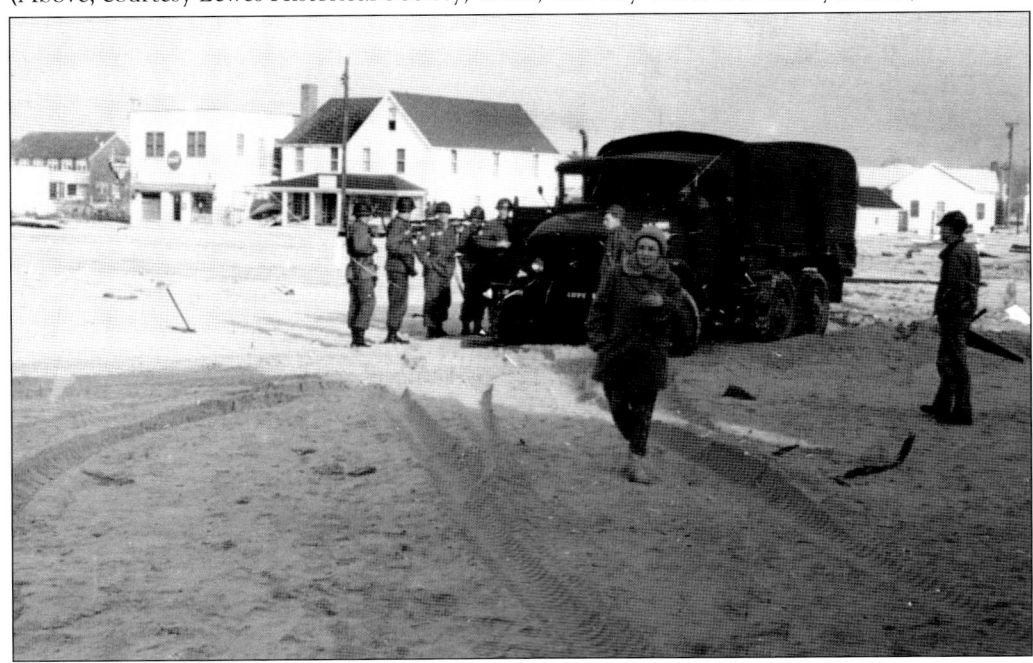

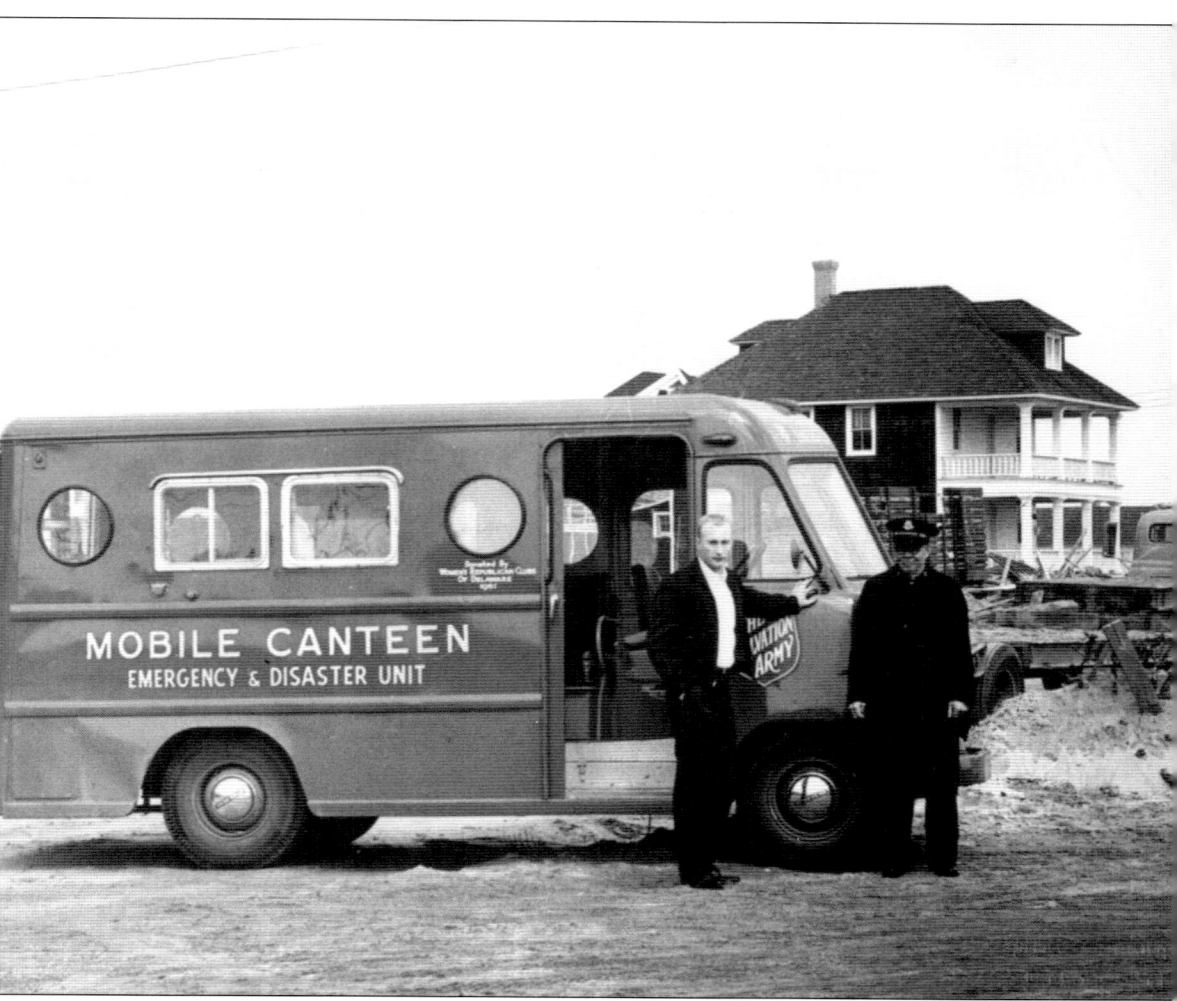

Response from local, state, and federal organizations and agencies was rapid, efficient, and effective. Volunteer firemen throughout the state worked around the clock to provide assistance and aid with evacuation work. In parts of New Castle County and Bridgeville, state police assigned to the normal 8:00 a.m. to 4:00 p.m. shifts were working 12-hour shifts, thus relieving the 4:00 p.m. to midnight shifts for assignment in Georgetown. All leaves and days off were canceled for the duration of the emergency. The Delaware chapter of the American Red Cross estimated it was caring for 300 evacuees from beachfront areas in Georgetown, Milford, Lewes, and Ocean View. When the storm struck, the 11 branch areas under the Delaware chapter went into action with carefully prepared disaster plans. Red Cross shelters were opened in Lewes, Georgetown, Milford, Dover, and Ocean View, and one in Millsboro was opened on a standby basis. As seen in the photograph above, Salvation Army mobile canteens provided hot coffee and sandwiches to those assisting in the enormous cleanup task. (Courtesy Colonel McGarraugh via Marna Cupp.)

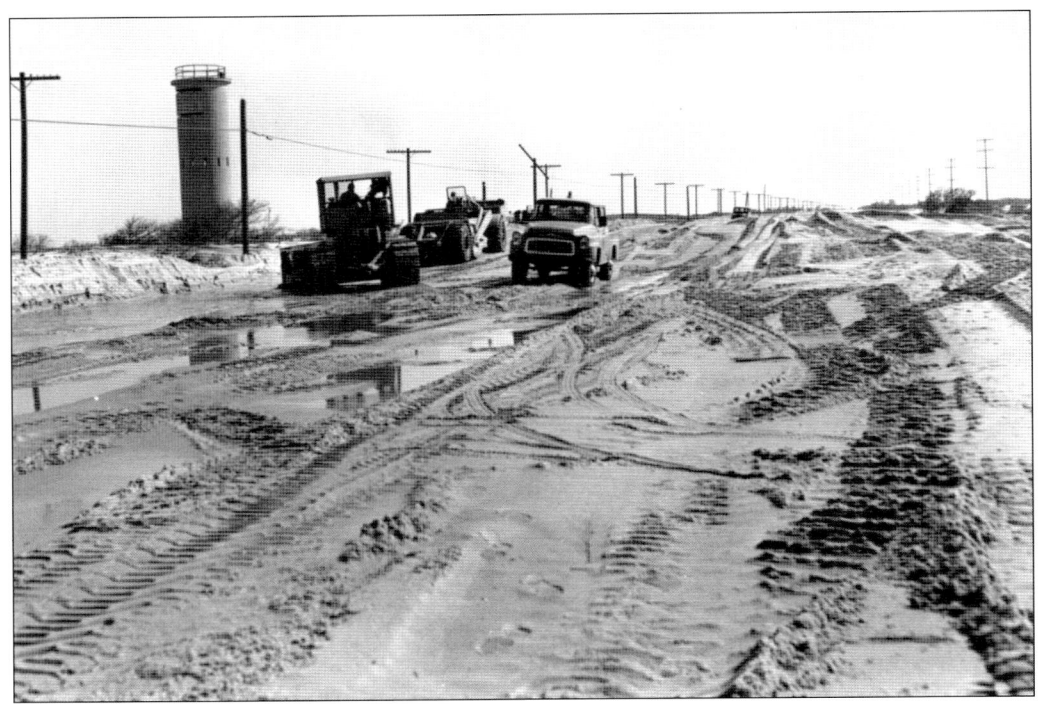

The Delaware State Highway Department faced a monumental task as they evaluated the condition of Route 14 from Dewey to Fenwick Island. Bulldozers worked day and night to clear sand off the roads and move it back to the beach. Additionally, highway crews had to seal up several inlet channels where the ocean flowed right across and through Route 14 to Rehoboth Bay. As seen below in Dewey Beach, four to five feet of sand had to be cleared from the roads in most oceanfront communities. (Both, courtesy Delaware Public Archives.)

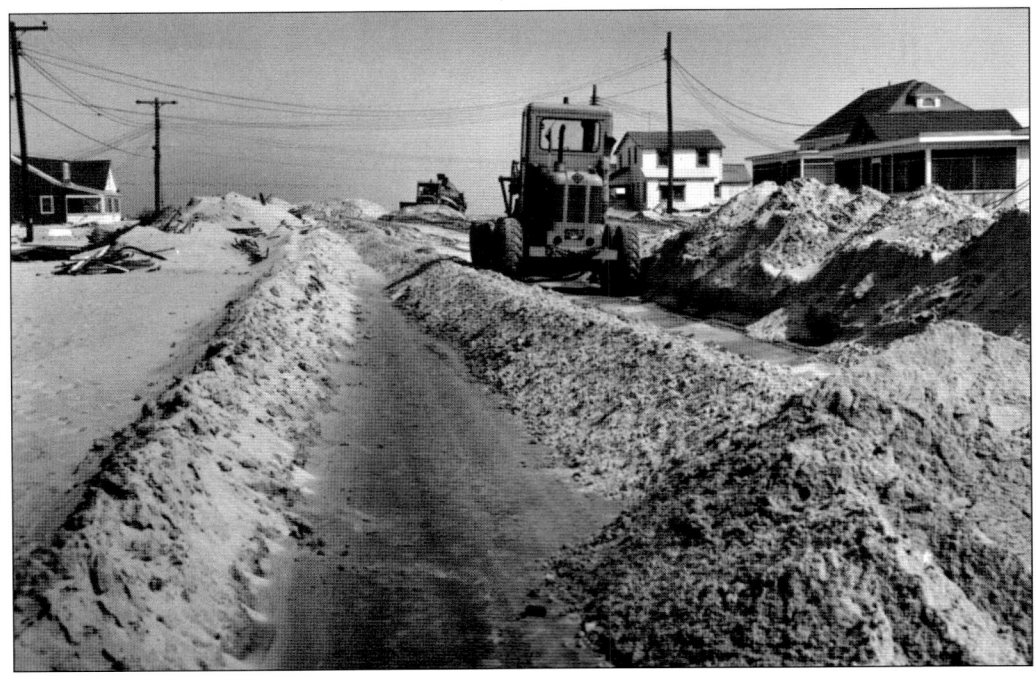

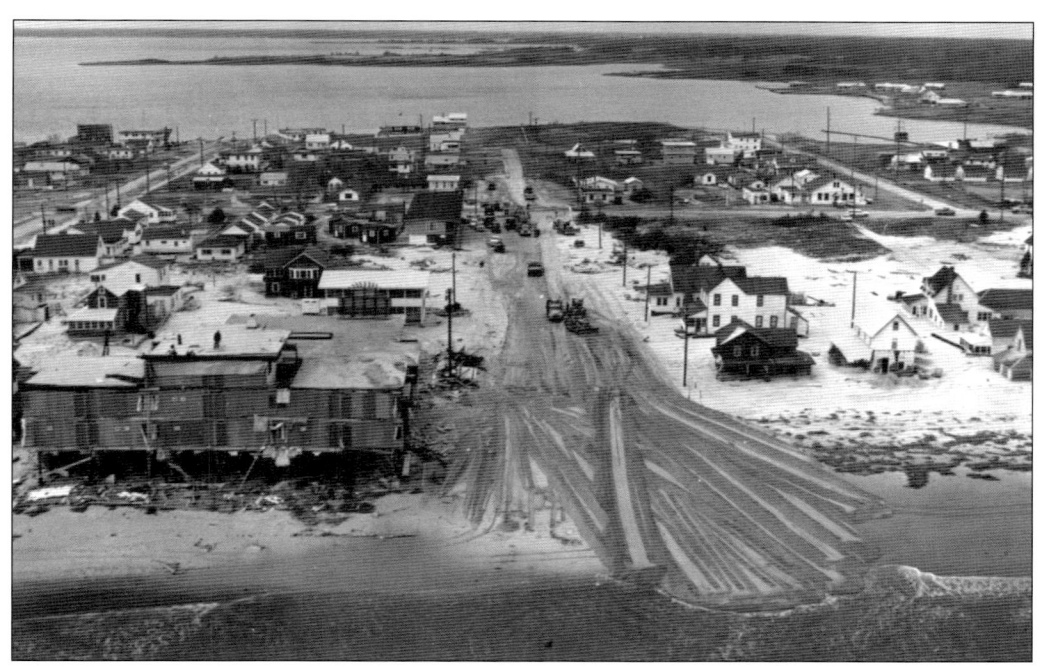

These aerial views of Dewey Beach show the magnitude of the task facing those charged with response and recovery efforts throughout the state. The first order of business was to clear primary roadways to provide access for local, state, and federal officials. Damage estimates had to be prepared before federal aid could become available. The painstaking and dangerous process of bulldozing through sand and debris began as early as March 10, or when floodwater receded from roadways. Contamination from toxic substances was a concern, as was drinking water safety. The Board of Public Health recommended that water be boiled before drinking, and typhoid shots were available and recommended but not required. (Both, courtesy Delaware DNREC.)

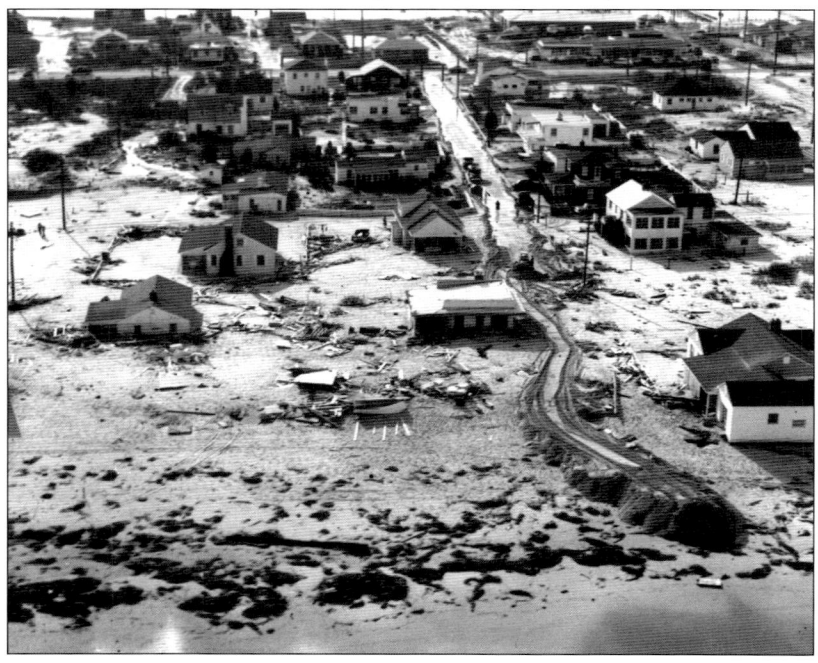

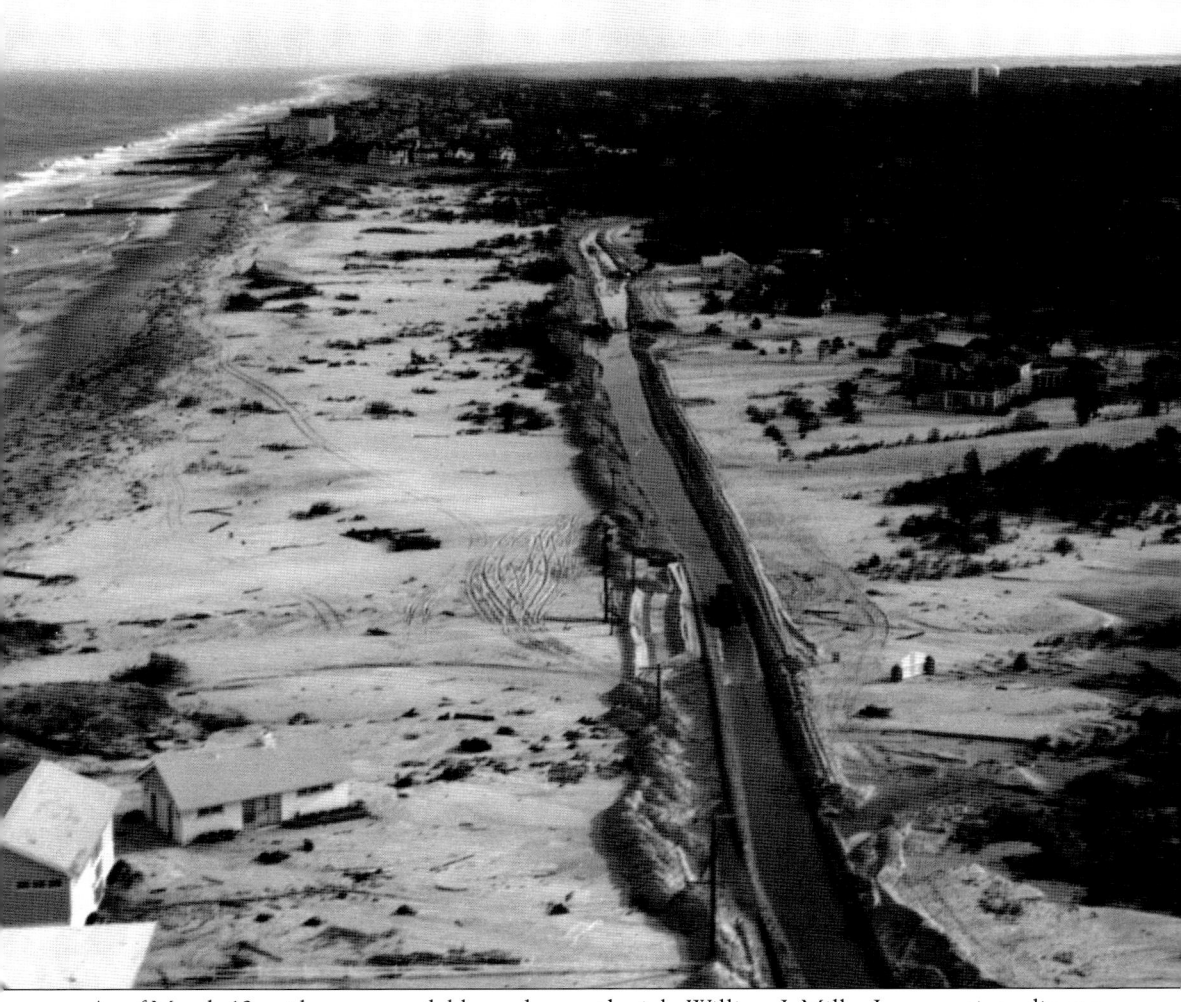

As of March 13, with every available worker on the job, William J. Miller Jr., operations director for the State Highway Department, reported to the *Evening Journal* that "Route 14 remains closed most of the way between Dewey Beach and the inlet. It is the only major road still closed for an appreciable distance." Although clearing and maintenance of primary roads were obvious priorities for the State Highway Department, many secondary roads were also sand-covered and impassable, as shown in this area just north of Rehoboth Beach. Highway department vehicles labored to improve sand-clogged streets, paving the way for property owners to inspect storm-related damage. Continued recovery efforts were impeded on March 12 when additional rain and high tides impacted the ravaged coast as east-northeasterly winds blew along the coast. Once again, tides flooded sections of Route 14, delaying work in storm-flattened areas. The *Evening Journal* reported that in the Slaughter Beach area, bulldozer crews gouged a roadway through three to four feet of sand-covered roads. (Courtesy Delaware Public Archives.)

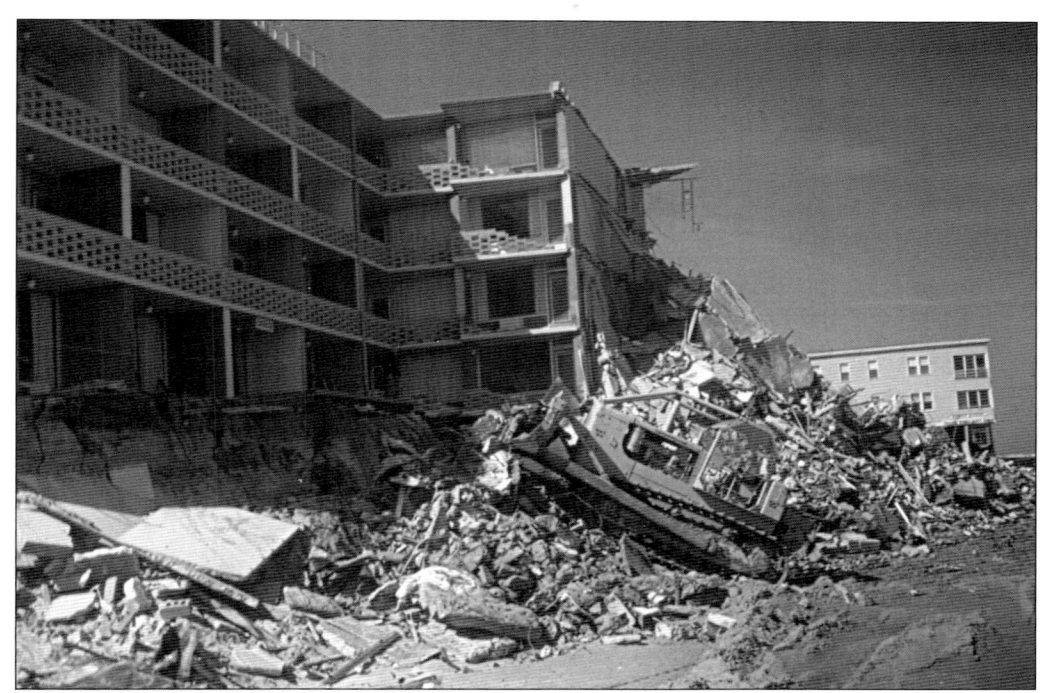

Debris removal required an enormous effort of manpower, equipment, and money. Beachfront communities faced months of work in debris removal and reconstruction. The photograph above shows demolition work beginning on the Atlantic Sands Hotel, while at right a crane works to remove the damaged face of the Henlopen Hotel. For scale, note the man standing on the hotel's third floor even as the crane works to pull debris from the beach. (Above, courtesy Lewes Historical Society; right, courtesy Colonel McGarraugh via Marna Cupp.)

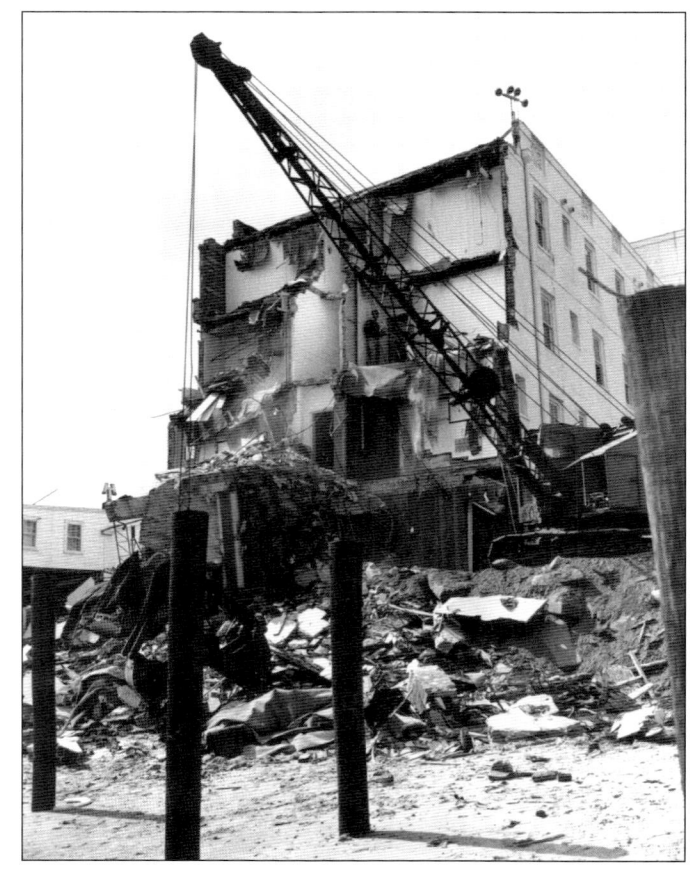

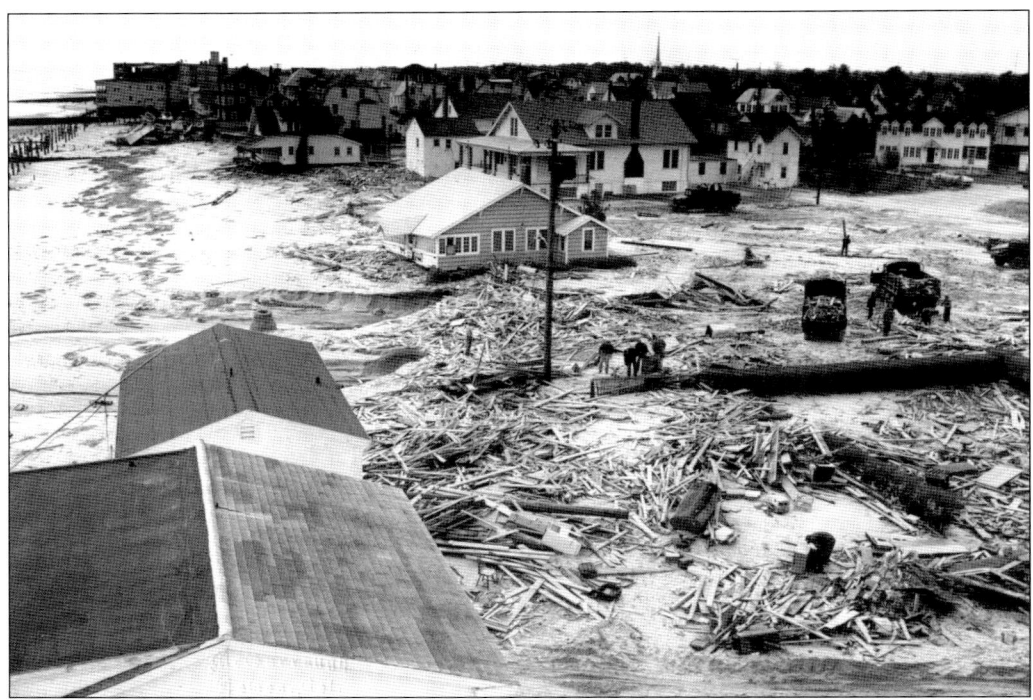

Many volunteered to help with the overwhelming task of getting the devastated coast back to a state of near normalcy. Included as part of the cleanup corps were volunteering prisoners. Rehoboth officials made a statewide appeal for food to provide 200 lunches daily for prisoners over a two-week period. Three Wilmington-area businesses quickly offered to provide bread, rolls, meats, and cheeses. Among the workers who assisted Bethany Beach residents with cleanup operations was a group of approximately 100 Mennonites from Pennsylvania. Red Cross canteens continued to provide coffee and sandwiches for volunteers. Local fire departments hosed out houses to wash out sand, muck, and salt. Debris management posed a special challenge throughout the state. The photograph below shows a pile of burning debris in South Bethany. (Above, courtesy Colonel McGarraugh via Marna Cupp; below, courtesy South Bethany Historical Society.)

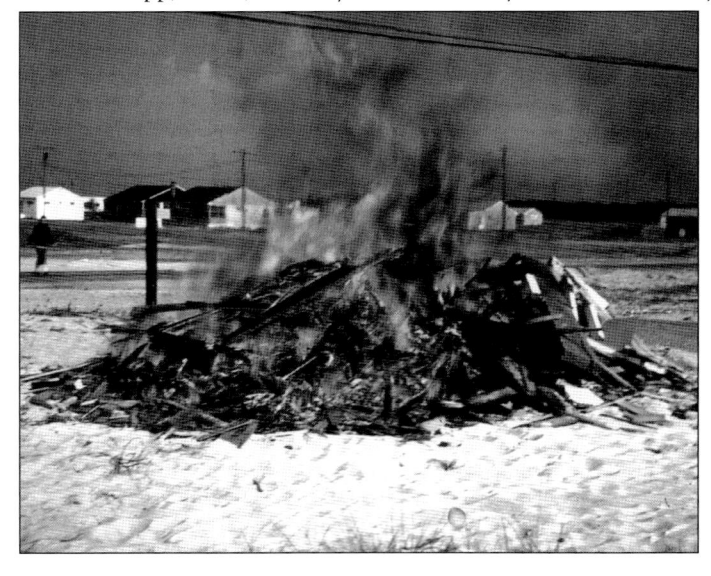

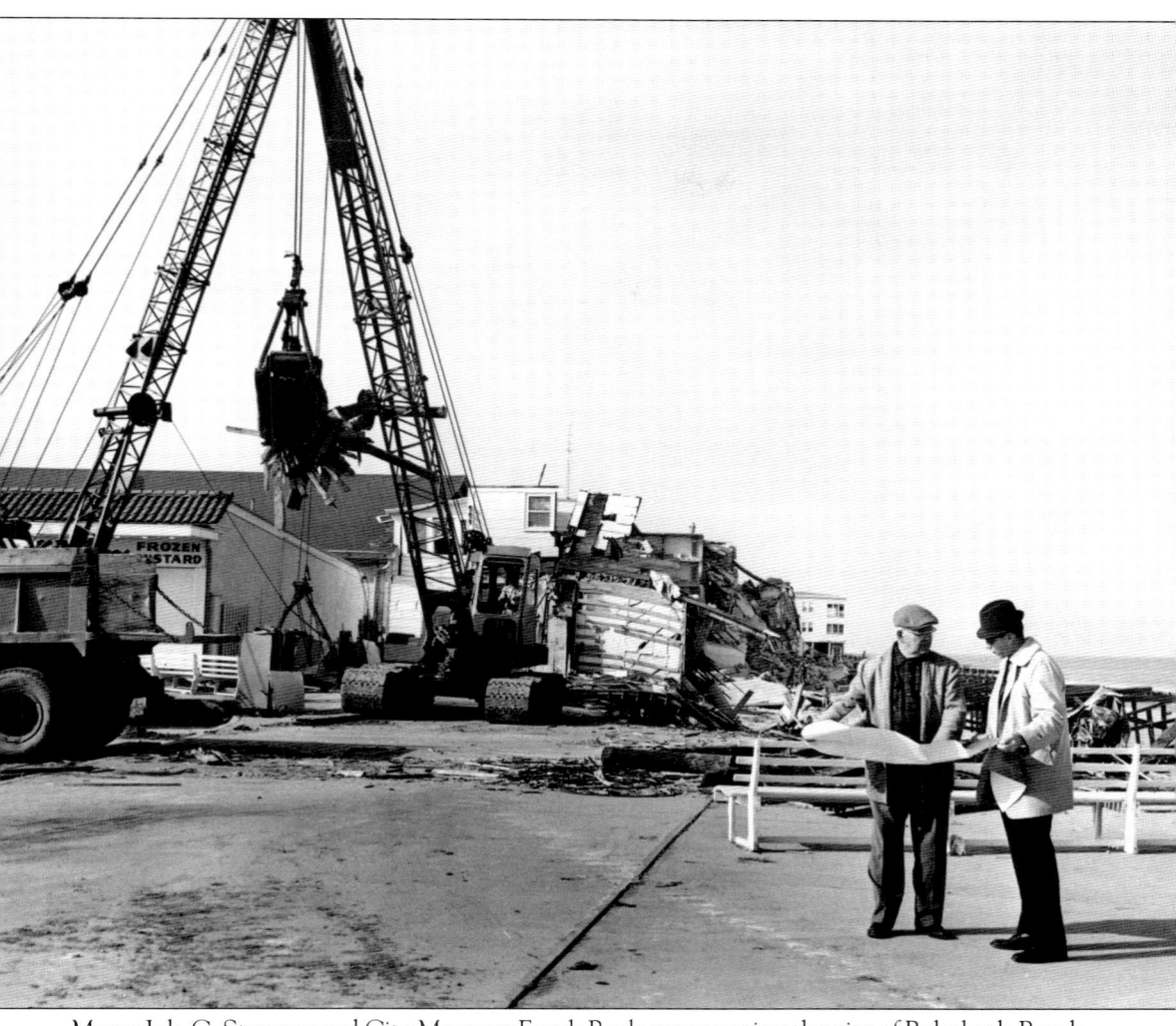

Mayor Jule C. Stamper and City Manager Frank Buck, representing the city of Rehoboth Beach, discuss reconstruction plans as they stand on what remains of the boardwalk at the end of Rehoboth Avenue. The working crane is removing what remains of the Dolle's building. Storm-ravaged businesses collapsed onto the beach. As early as March 10, Mayor Stamper had coordinated several planning meetings regarding boardwalk reconstruction. Beachfront property owners discussed the advisability of relinquishing acreage so the boardwalk could be moved farther landward. Stamper also coordinated with the US Army Corps of Engineers. As of March 12, he reported that the Army Corps thought it was "remotely possible" to restore the beach to its original condition. The estimated cost of pumping sand to fill Rehoboth Beach was more than $1 million. (Courtesy Delaware DNREC.)

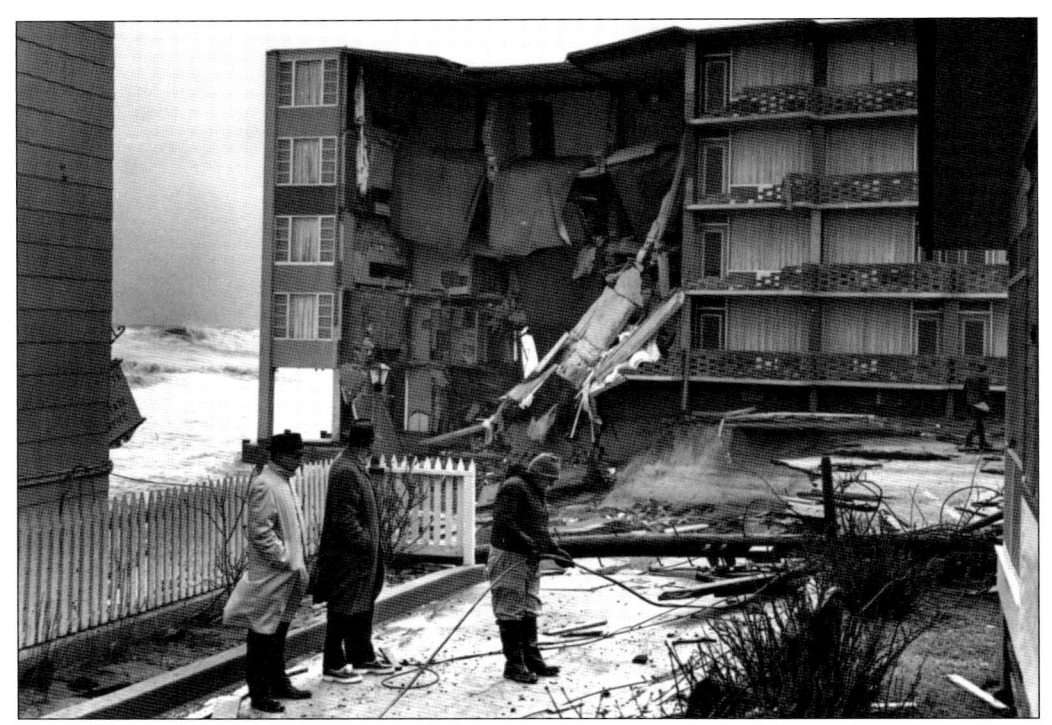

Like most oceanfront structures, the Atlantic Sands Hotel suffered extensive damage. In fact, the front 20 rooms collapsed just minutes after the above photograph was taken. Business owners, city officials, and local contractors wasted no time in getting communities back on their feet. Immediate inspection of property provided insight into which buildings had not yet fallen but might soon collapse. As early as March 15, a Thoro-good's Concrete Company truck was pouring concrete in all likelihood to shore up the foundation of Rehoboth's Shirl Ann Motel. (Both, courtesy Delaware Public Archives.)

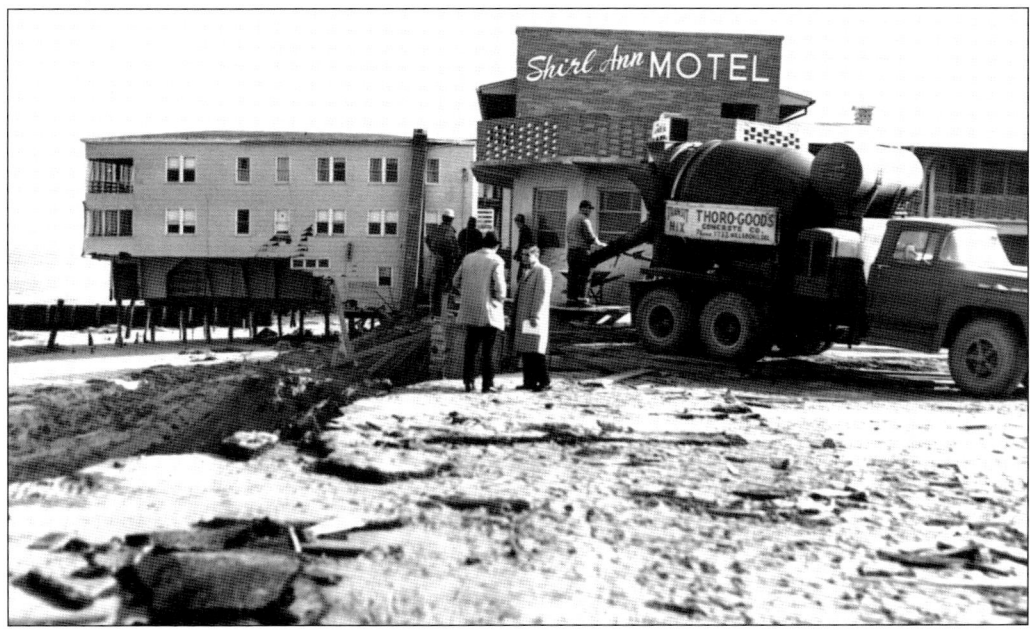

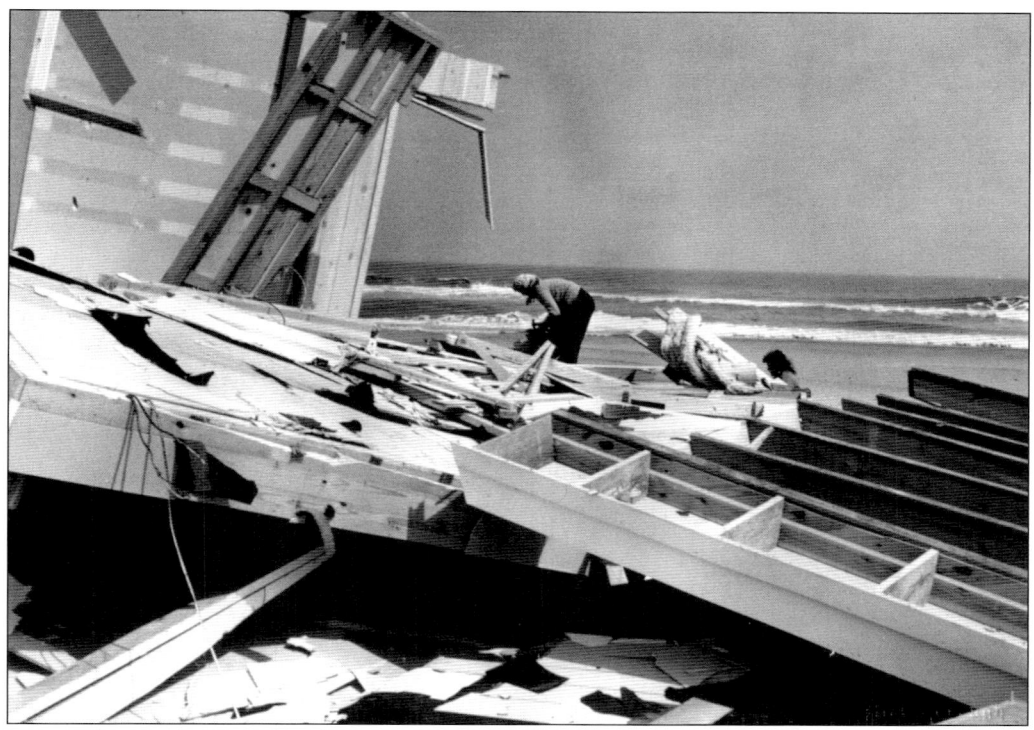

As conditions permitted and after required passes were obtained from local police, property owners were eventually allowed into communities to assess damage to homes and property. In many instances, they returned to scenes of wreckage and ruin, and could only look over what was left of their homes and lives as they knew them at the beach. In many cases, they found total devastation; nothing was salvageable, and property owners realized that entire life savings had been swept away. (Above, courtesy Colonel McGarraugh via Marna Cupp; below, courtesy Delaware Public Archives.)

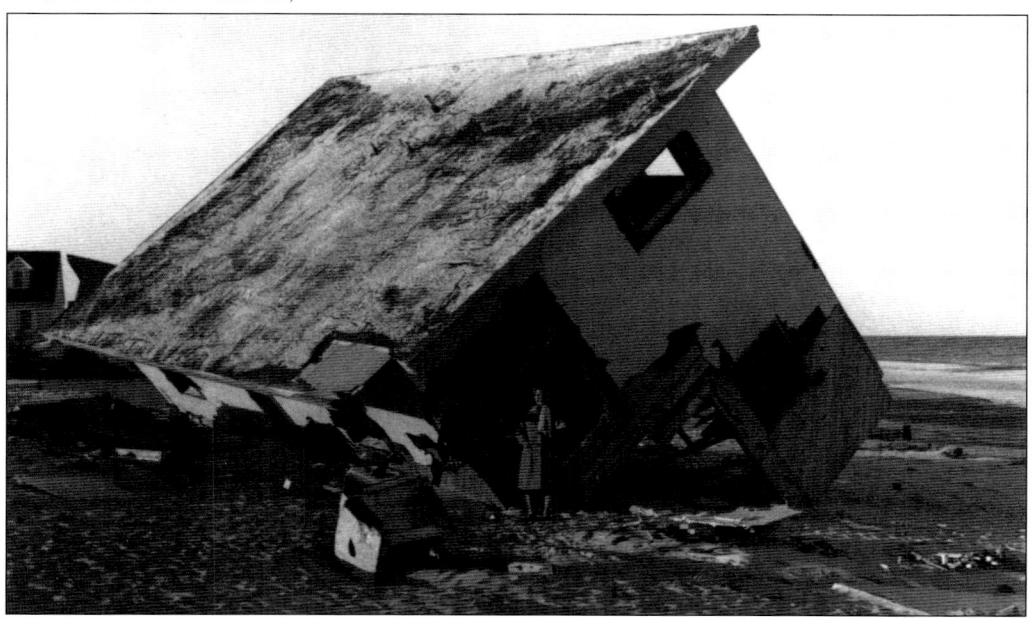

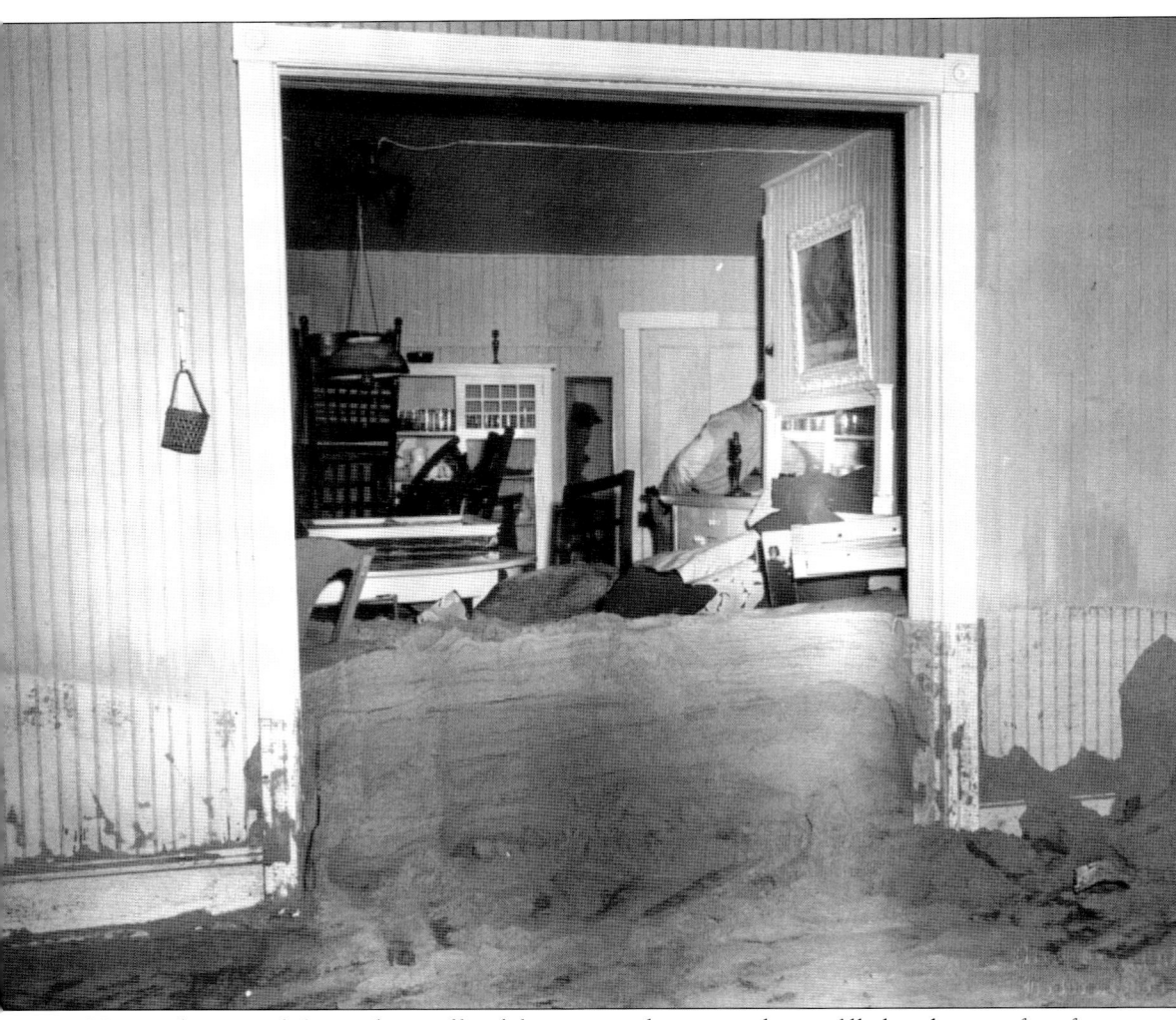

Homes that were left standing suffered from water damage and were filled with up to four feet of sand. Many returning homeowners who found only piles of sand considered themselves lucky. The *Wilmington Morning News* quoted Eugene Bookhammer as he described owners of sand-filled homes in Dewey Beach: "I expected tears, but they were delighted. Everybody pitched in to start digging out the sand." In many areas adjacent to the Delaware Bay and inland bays, houses were filled and covered with mud. Homeowners were advised to wait until their houses dried out before beginning repair work. According to the *Evening Journal*, University of Delaware extension specialists recommended that "all woodwork be scrubbed with a stiff brush and plenty of water to remove mud and silt from corners and cracks before the house dries out." At the time, it was advised to remove mold from the wood surfaces with "a cloth dipped in water to which a small amount of kerosene has been added, or with a solution of borax dissolved in hot water." (Courtesy Colonel McGarraugh via Marna Cupp.)

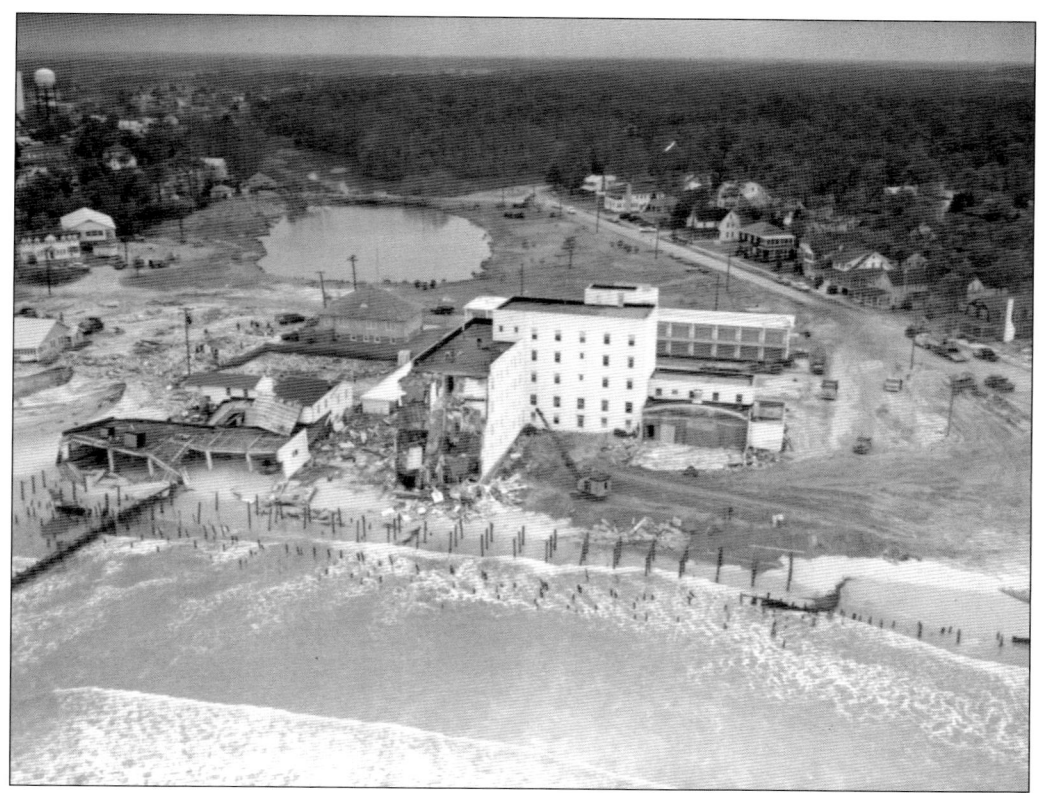

The rate at which recovery was implemented in Rehoboth Beach was nothing short of amazing—a true demonstration of human spirit and determination. Reconstruction of the Henlopen Hotel was rushed with the hopes of opening for the summer season. As early as March 9, Ashley Jenkins, owner of the badly damaged business, had crews working to clear away sand and remove damaged parts of the structure. As reported in the *Evening Journal* newspaper, Jenkins was determined to be open for the summer season, stating, "We're going to be open in May and we intend to meet all our convention commitments." The goal was met, and the Henlopen Hotel was open for Memorial Day business. Shown above is the condition of the Henlopen Hotel on March 13, 1962 and at right on October 15, 1962. (Both, courtesy Delaware DNREC.)

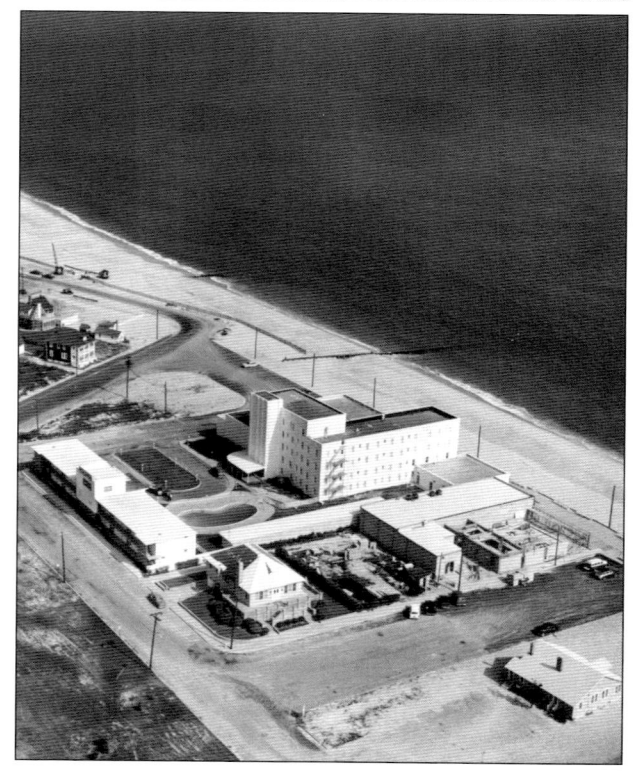

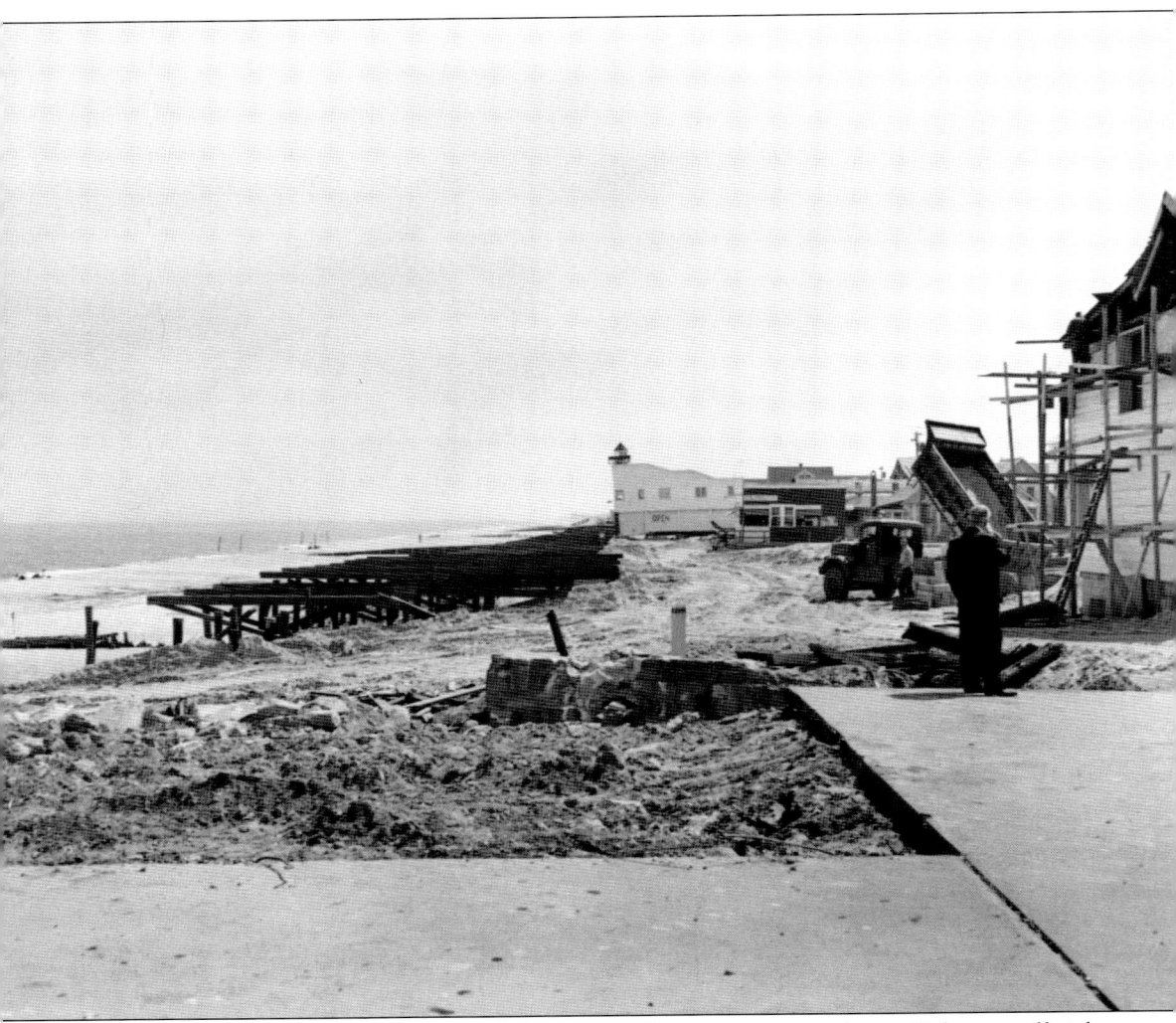

In the storm's aftermath, one of the most urgent and expensive issues facing Delaware officials was that of preserving the beaches—not only for their recreational value, but more importantly for the protection they would provide during the next storm. Although preliminary storm damage estimates were developed in March, cleanup and recovery tasks were so monumental that statewide progress was necessarily slow. Federal financial aid was expected to be secured by mid-April. The US Army Corps of Engineers completed initial damage surveys in mid-March, and estimated that emergency work to make the inlet to Fenwick Island beaches immediately storm-safe would cost $5.5 million. This estimate includes repair of seawalls, dunes, bulkheads, and boardwalks. The photograph above shows the condition of Rehoboth Beach on May 3, 1962. It is difficult to imagine that the beach and boardwalk would be ready for summer visitors. (Courtesy Delaware DNREC.)

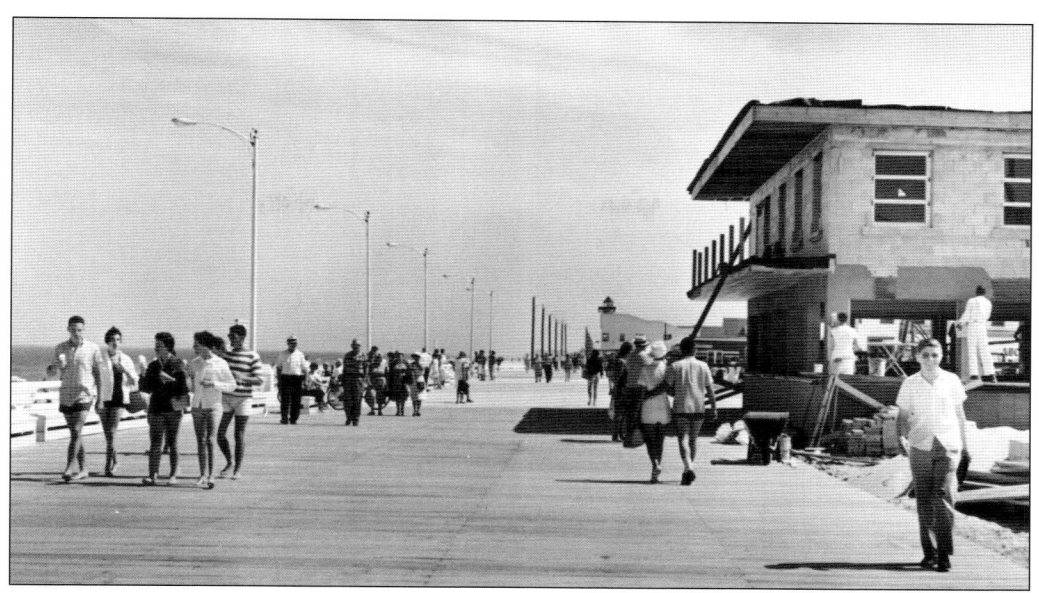

Almost unbelievably, Rehoboth Beach and boardwalk were ready for the 1962 summer season, even as cleanup and rebuilding efforts continued. The photograph above shows a scene of summer visitors as they strolled the boardwalk on June 27. Note that while much of the boardwalk had been repaired and replaced, not all boardwalk businesses were ready to open. The photograph below shows that a business clearly displays an open sign to encourage patrons to stop by. The beach, while wide enough for sunbathing visitors, is still marked by heavy equipment tracks. (Above, courtesy Delaware DNREC; below, courtesy Delaware Public Archives.)

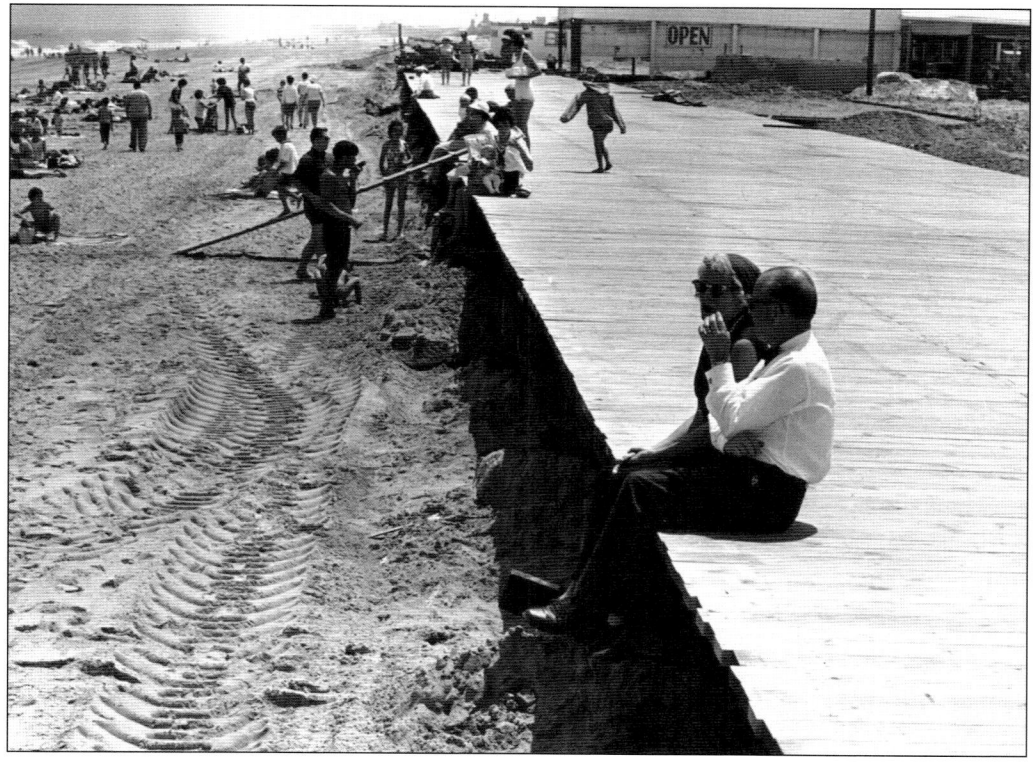

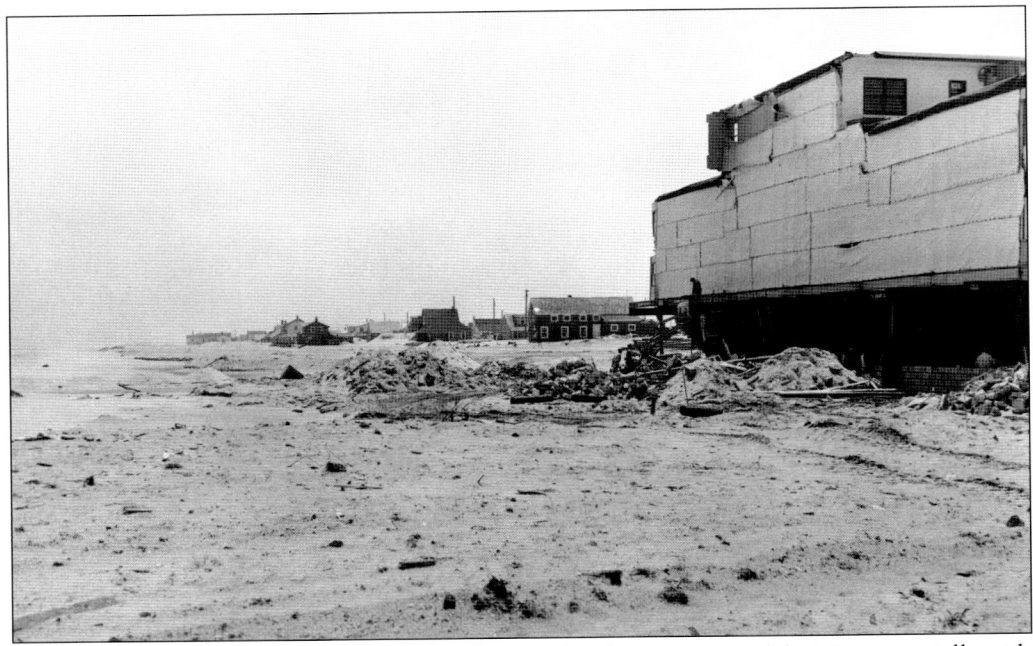

Beach recovery was an expensive process. The state faced a monumental decision, especially with an estimated cost of $20–$30 million to restore state-owned beach lands. Secretary Dukes said, "We must decide first whether to attempt to save the beaches between the ocean and the bay or to move our shoreline back to the bayfront and forget about our beaches." This photograph of Dewey Beach (seen above on May 3, 1962) shows that there was still much work to be done. Large pieces of debris had been cleared from the beach, but smaller pieces of rubble remained, and there was not much room between the ocean and the front row of houses. The photograph below shows bulldozers working to rebuild dunes between the ocean and Route 14 along an undeveloped stretch of Delaware coast. (Both, courtesy Delaware DNREC.)

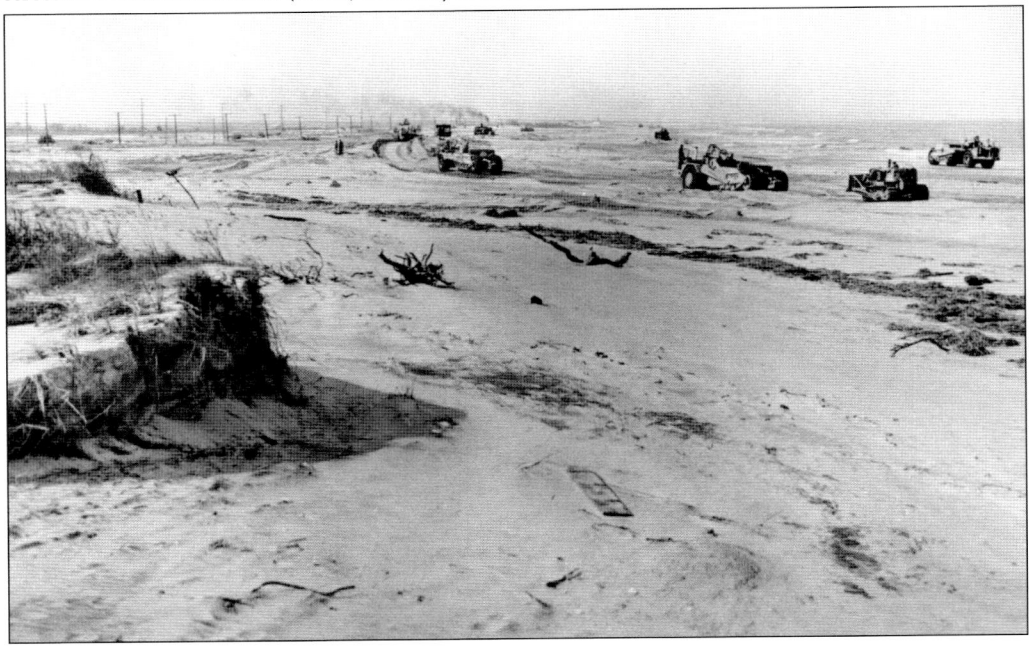

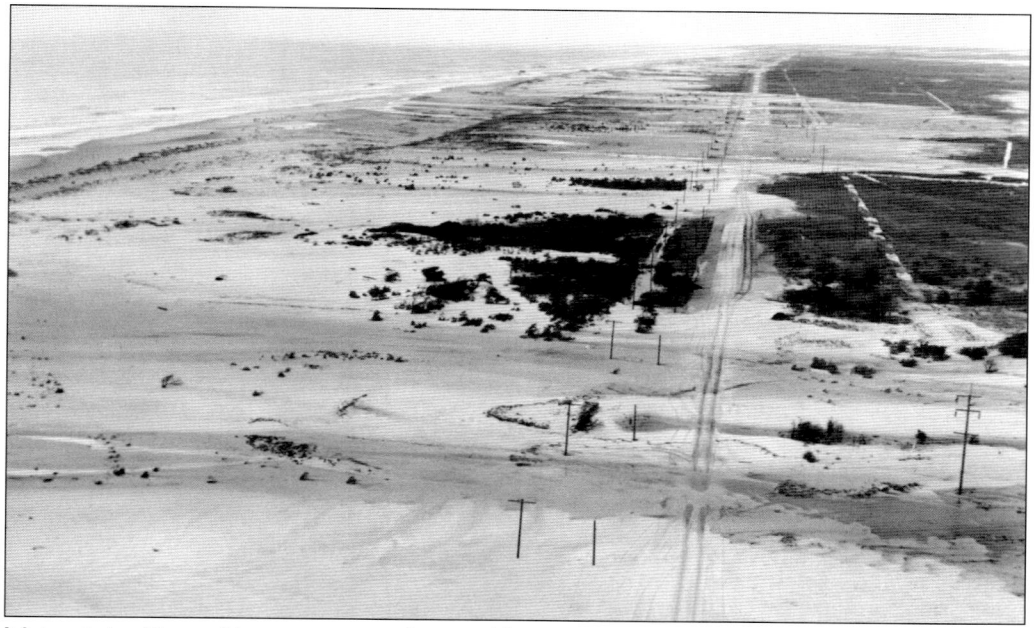

Maintaining Route 14 as an open and accessible transportation corridor was a priority in 1962. The photograph above, taken March 13, 1962, shows vehicle tracks in sand on what had been Route 14 before the storm. A narrow channel, or inlet breach, can be seen with water still flowing from the ocean to Rehoboth Bay. It was reported that at least six inlets had been opened in this area, with one large enough to permit small craft to travel back and forth. The Delaware State Highway Department made it a priority to evaluate costs to repair this critical thoroughfare. The photograph below shows the same stretch of road on November 11, 1962. Although the two-lane road had been cleared, it remained extremely vulnerable to overwashing by sand and surf from the next big storm. (Both, courtesy Delaware DNREC.)

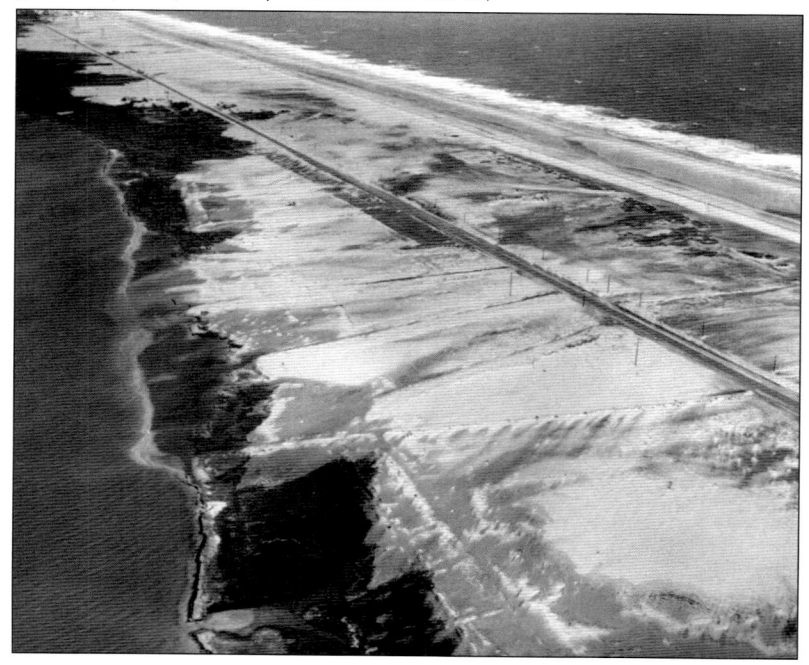

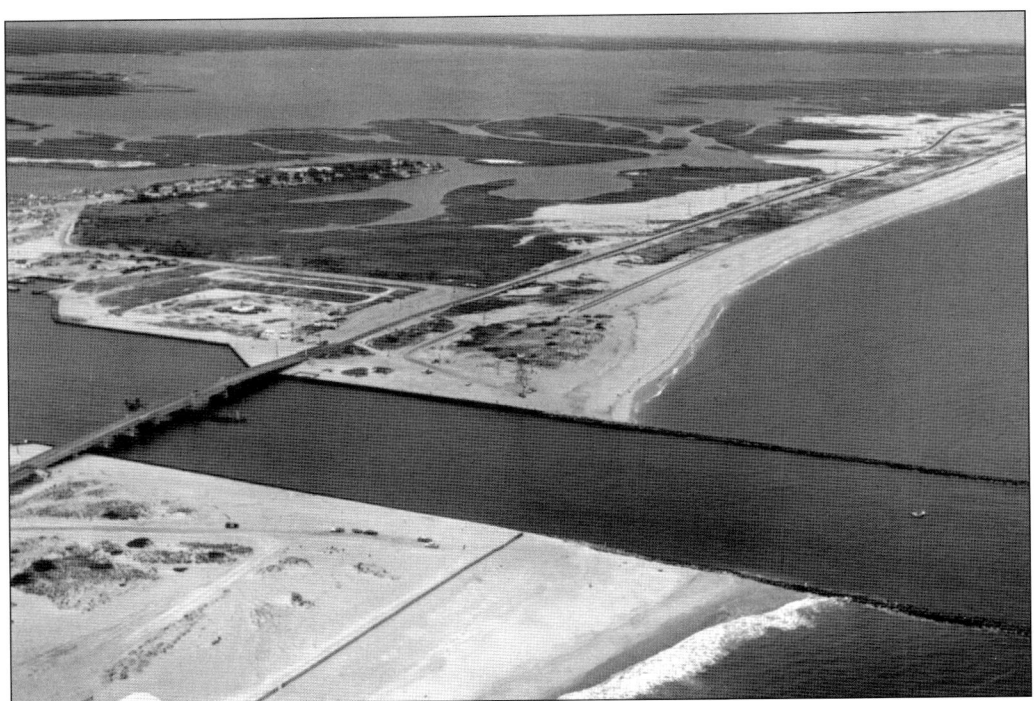

Natural recovery of beach and bar systems occurred over the months following the storm. In photograph above, dated October 15, 1962, the Indian River Inlet Bridge and Route 14 are open to vehicles and pedestrians alike. Note the extensive sand deposits on the marsh adjacent to the highway. The photograph below shows a view along the Atlantic coast northward from Bethany Beach on October 15, 1962. Although oceanfront homes are absent, the boardwalk and beaches have been built back—the boardwalk by people and the beach by nature with assistance from the State of Delaware and the US Army Corps of Engineers. (Both, courtesy Delaware DNREC.)

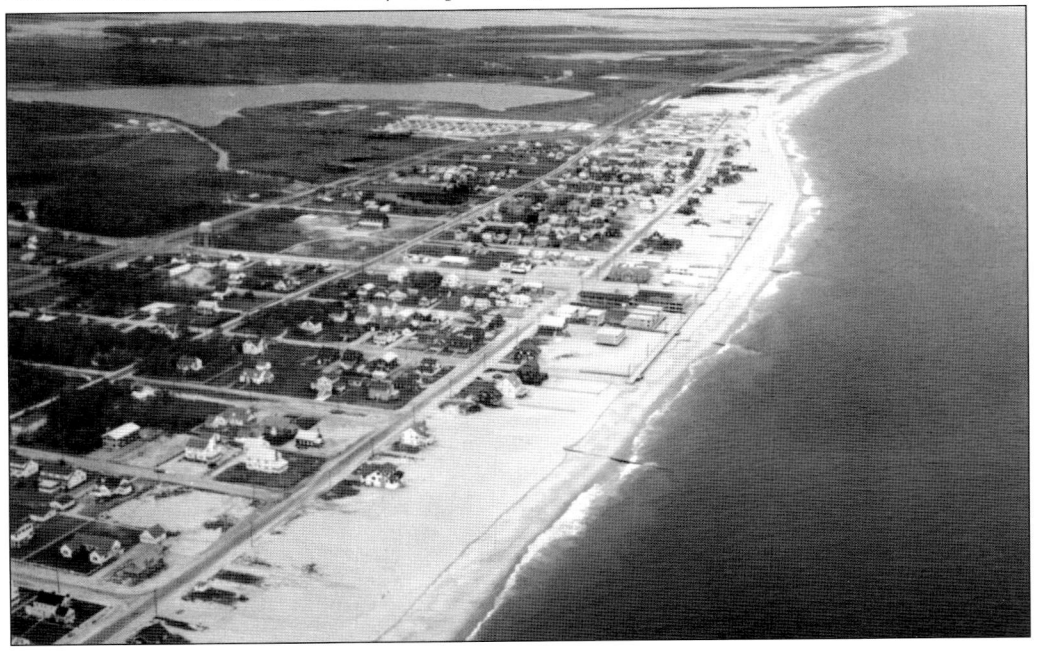

Seven

LASTING RISKS AND VULNERABILITIES

The Great Storm of March 1962 and most recently Hurricane Sandy are brutal and expensive reminders that severe coastal storms are a very real part of the natural cycle of the coast. Storms and the high tides that they bring are necessary tools in helping to redistribute sand along the shore and are aids in keeping barrier beaches elevated above the rising sea. Barrier beaches and dunes are impermanent landforms over the long term, but people place structures and infrastructure expected to be permanent on these land features. Throughout the first half of the 20th century, construction of buildings and roads on barrier beaches was conducted with little attention paid to the stability of the underlying or supporting land. There are coastal storms with higher-than-normal tides virtually every year on the Delaware coast, but the big, truly memorable storms have occurred decades apart. The 1933 hurricane, the 1962 northeaster, and the very scary near hit of Hurricane Sandy in 2012 are in the class of Delaware coastal events that change the way people do things for decades to come. For all the unfortunate and too often tragic things that storms bring, there are valuable lessons learned as well.

Building foundation failures resulting from the 1962 Storm were compelling examples of why buildings need to be elevated above expected floodwaters with a foundation that will not give way if water and waves flow around it. Use of pilings to support and elevate buildings in the decades following the storm has become so commonly expected that rarely is there a second thought about it. But perhaps the biggest lesson learned from storms and other natural disasters is that the investment in resiliency is far less expensive than going through the storm, suffering the losses, cleaning up the mess, and then rebuilding communities. By looking at whole communities and by using the accumulated knowledge of construction standards and the protection provided by a wide beach and dune, people can better withstand the next big storm.

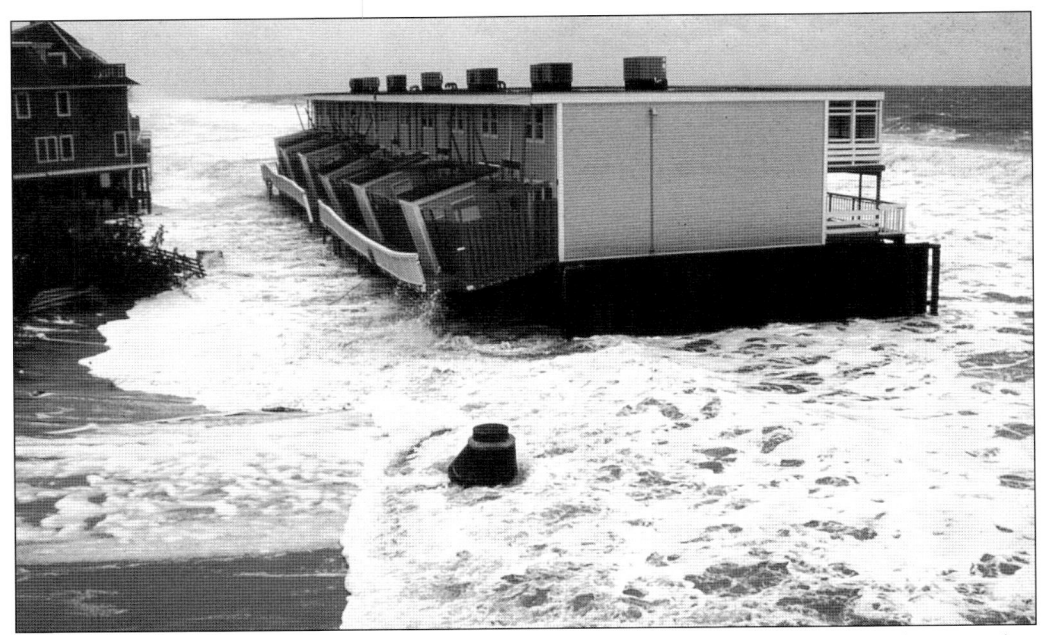

Many notable storms have impacted the Delaware coast since 1962. In 1974, an early December storm severely impacted the dunes, and again in January and December 1992 as well as two storms about a week apart in 1998, causing widespread damage and loss of dunes. These two photographs, taken in 1992 and 1998, are illustrative of the type of damage wrought by these storms. The photograph above is of McKinley Street in Dewey. Note the exposed manhole with the road all gone, so similar to 1962. The photograph below is Ocean Drive in South Bethany. In both locations, the building survived because piling foundations supported them and water washed around the piles without them failing. (Both, courtesy Delaware DNREC.)

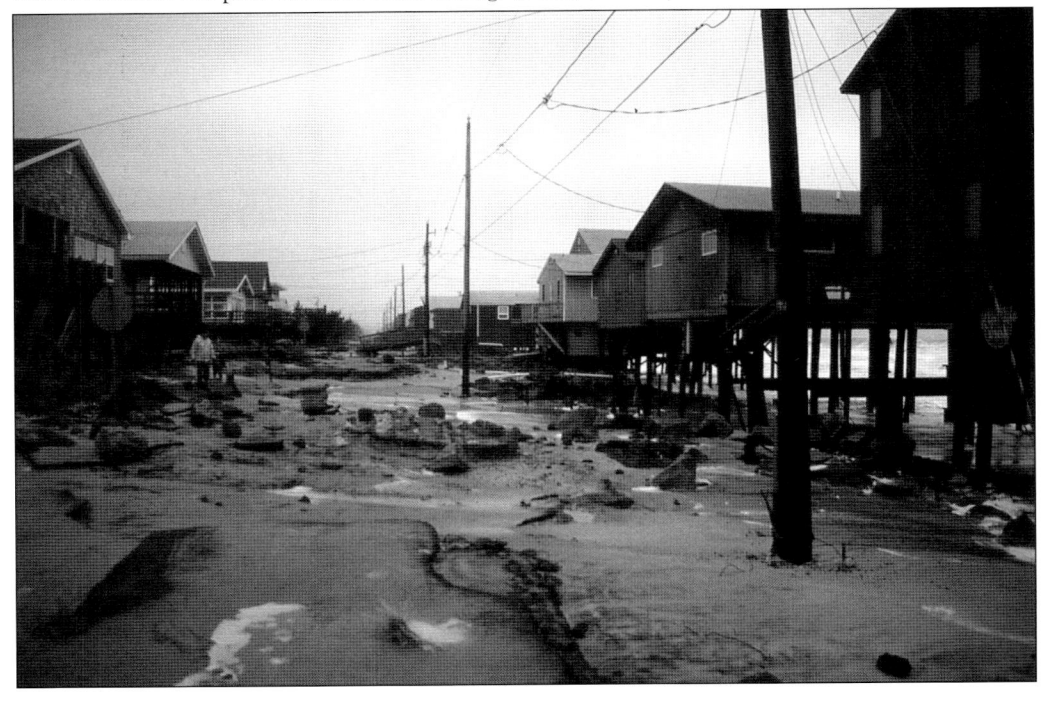

In 2012, Hurricane Sandy made landfall on the coast about 60 miles north of Delaware. While the effects in Delaware were severe, as seen in these photographs, damages were devastating in New Jersey and New York, closer to where the storm center struck the coast. For many hours, forecasters predicted that Sandy would make a direct hit on the coast between Ocean City, Maryland, and Lewes, Delaware. The devastation that effected New Jersey and Long Island with regards to severity of flooding and wave damage could all too easily have been right on the Delaware/Maryland coast. Although they may be uncommon, very severe storms will definitely hit again. (Both, courtesy Delaware DNREC.)

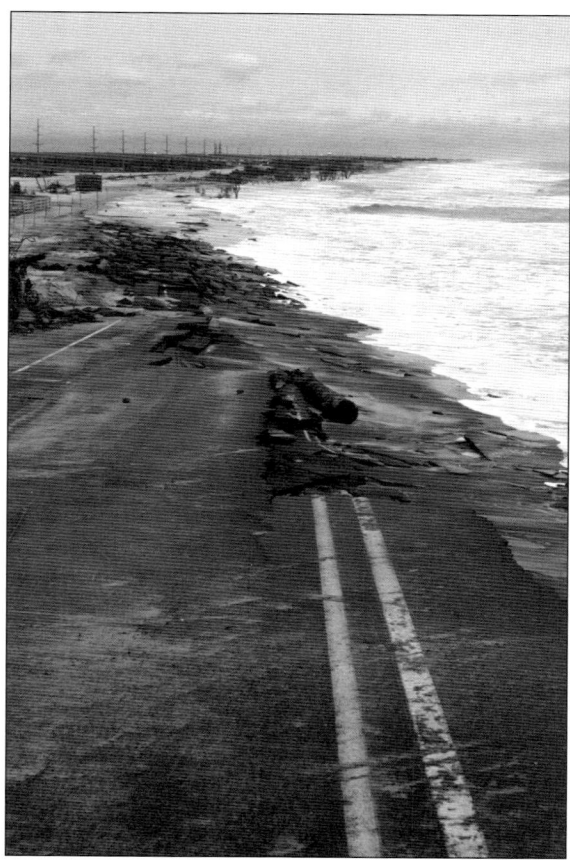

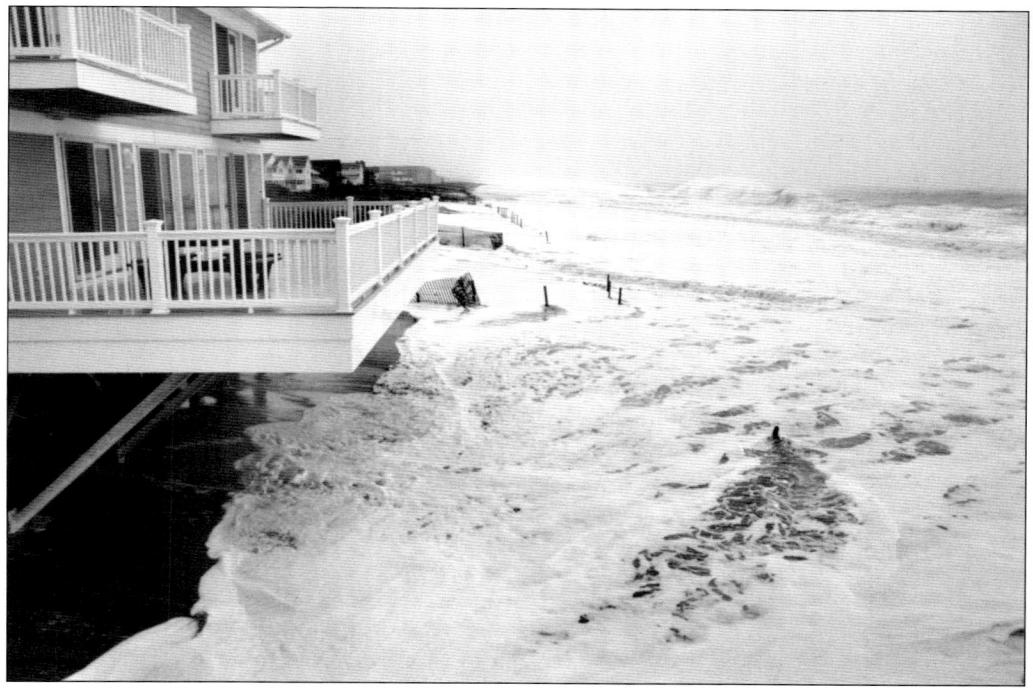

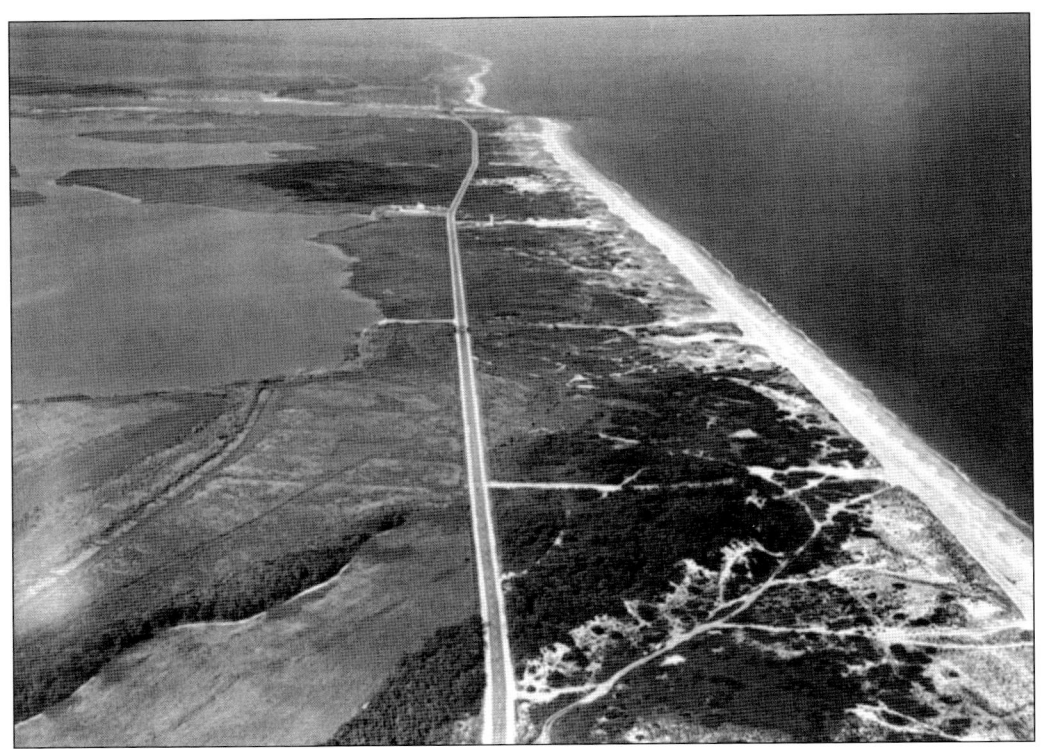

The uptick in development along the coast that began in the 1950s continues today. The nation as a whole is experiencing increasing development along the shore that outpaces other locations. Certainly the mid-Atlantic, including Delaware, continues to experience development growth that exceeds inland locations, particularly as the baby boomer generation reaches retirement age and more and more people choose the coast as their retirement destination. These photographs illustrate extensive development and growth in the coastal area south of Indian River Inlet from the 1950s (above) and early 2000s (below). This is the trend all along the coast, and the very real concern is that this intensity of development on land that is susceptible to severe storm damage and intense flooding is building potential disaster in the future. (Both, courtesy Delaware DNREC.)

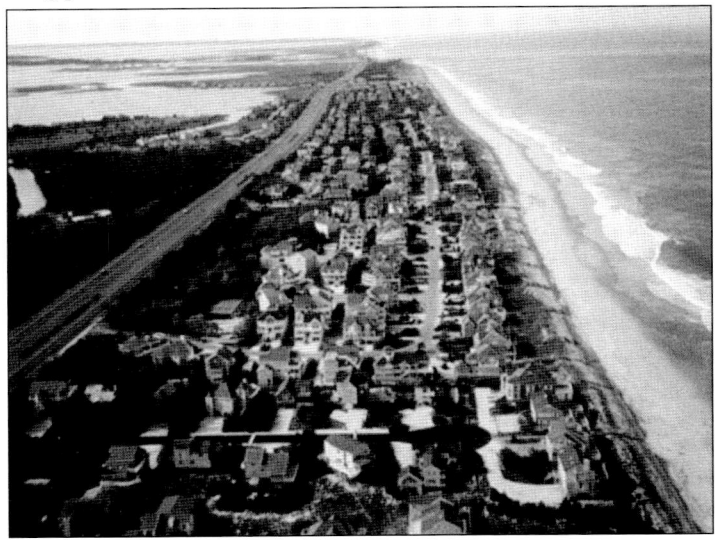

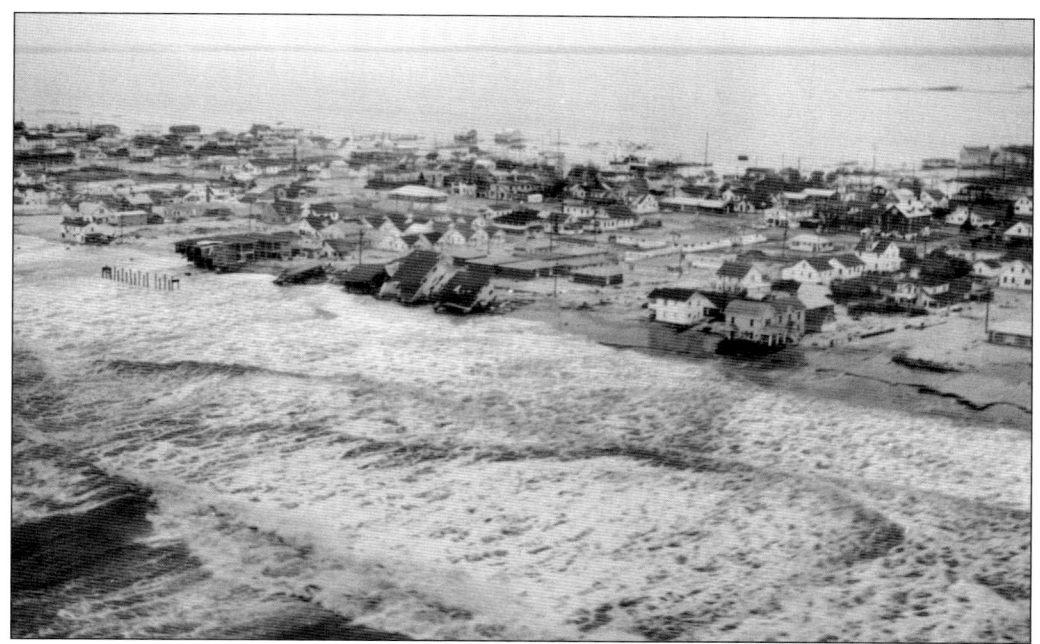

Fortunately many improvements on several fronts have better prepared the area for major coastal storms. Weather forecasting is light years ahead of where it was in the early 1960s. Aided by satellite images and robust computer model capabilities, forecasters today can give accurate details of impending weather events usually several days before they happen. Buildings are far more resistant to the wind, wave, and flood forces they will be exposed to. As seen in these photographs of Dewey Beach, water levels in a 1992 northeaster (below) were nearly as high as in 1962 (above), but there was very little damage to buildings and no loss of life due to better warnings of the storm and more resilient construction. (Above, courtesy Norman Rossiter; below, courtesy Delaware DNREC.)

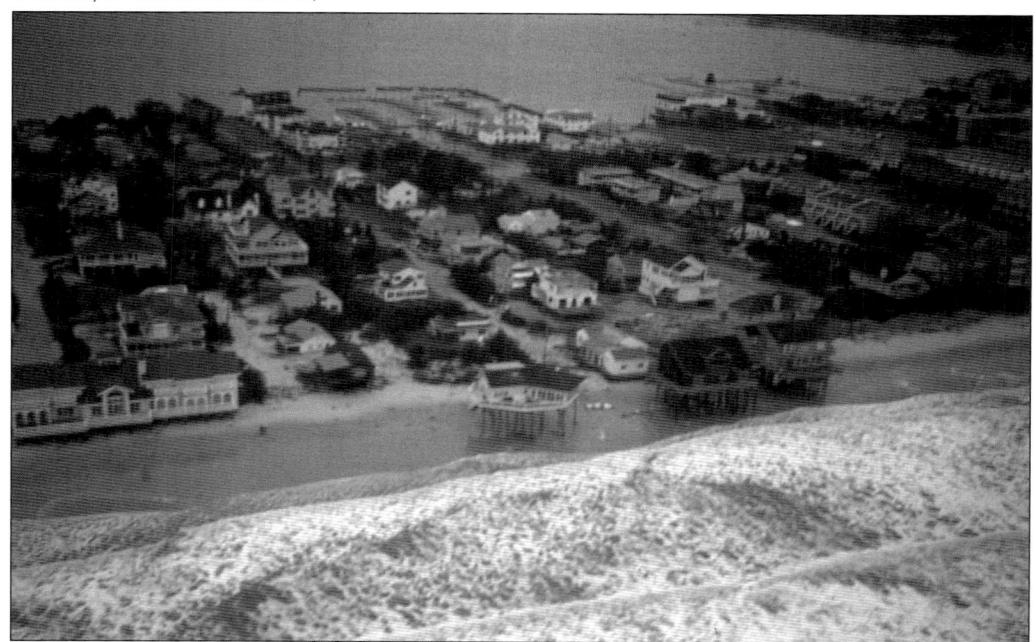

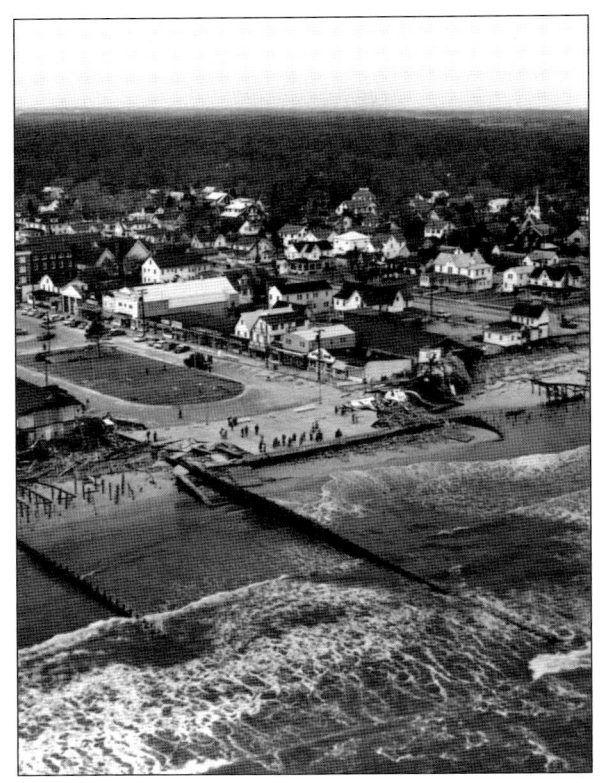

In response to the 1962 Ash Wednesday Storm and the fresh memories of associated damage, heartache, and costs, Delaware passed a 1971 law that required construction along the state's beaches to be landward of the dune to allow that storm protection feature to protect communities. The law also established funding for the Department of Natural Resources and Environmental Control (DNREC) to proactively manage beaches and dunes to enhance their storm protection values. Shown here are two photographs of Rehoboth in 1962 (left) and 2009 (below), illustrating just how similar the storm damage was to the beach. The 2009 photograph shows Rehoboth Beach after a November northeaster; the dune scarp line does not quite reach the boardwalk. (Left, courtesy Delaware Public Archives; below, courtesy Delaware DNREC.)

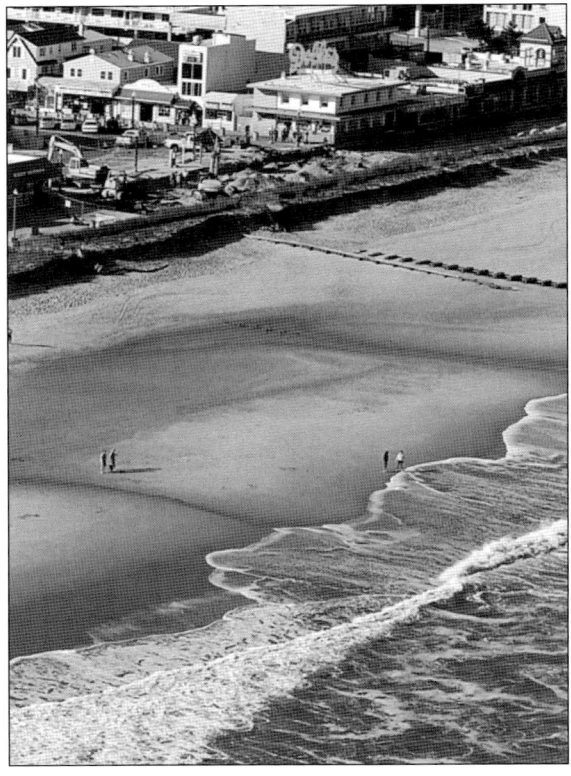

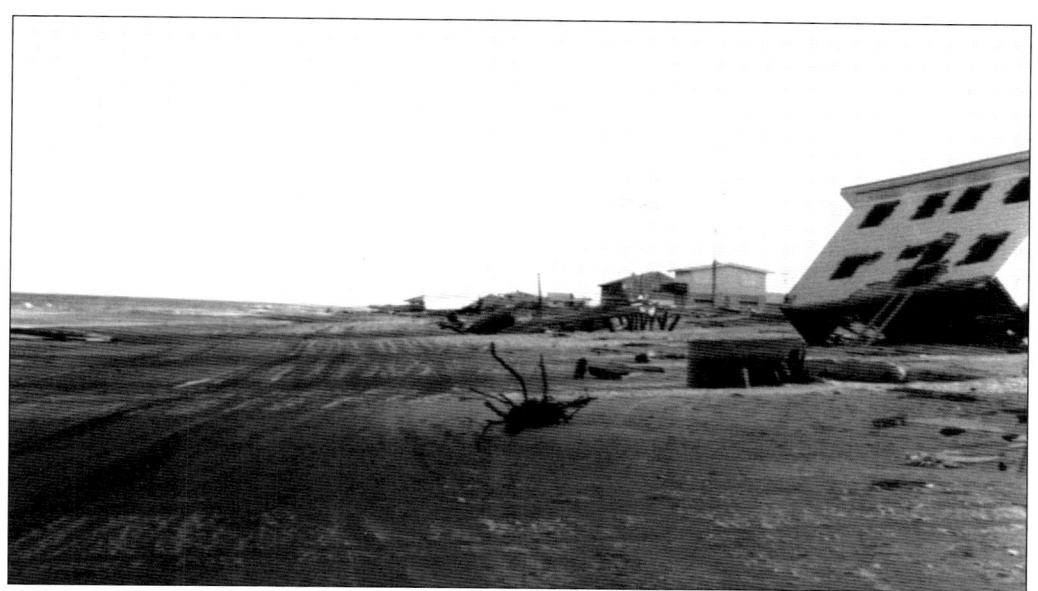

Funding provided to Delaware DNREC has gone towards maintaining the dune defense system for the state and towards pumping sand onto beaches to widen both the beaches and the dunes for greatly improved storm resistance. These two photographs of South Bethany illustrate the resulting improved condition of the protective beach. In 1962, houses were built where the dunes had once been and they had inadequate foundations (above). In 2012, Hurricane Sandy hit, but there was a wide beach and dune in place because of beach nourishment projects conducted by the US Army Corps of Engineers and Delaware DNREC. Because of this, storm damage from Hurricane Sandy was confined to the dunes (below). Note the piles supporting the houses in the 2012 photograph, keeping homes above floodwaters and damaging waves. (Above, courtesy Delaware Public Archives; below, courtesy Delaware Sea Grant.)

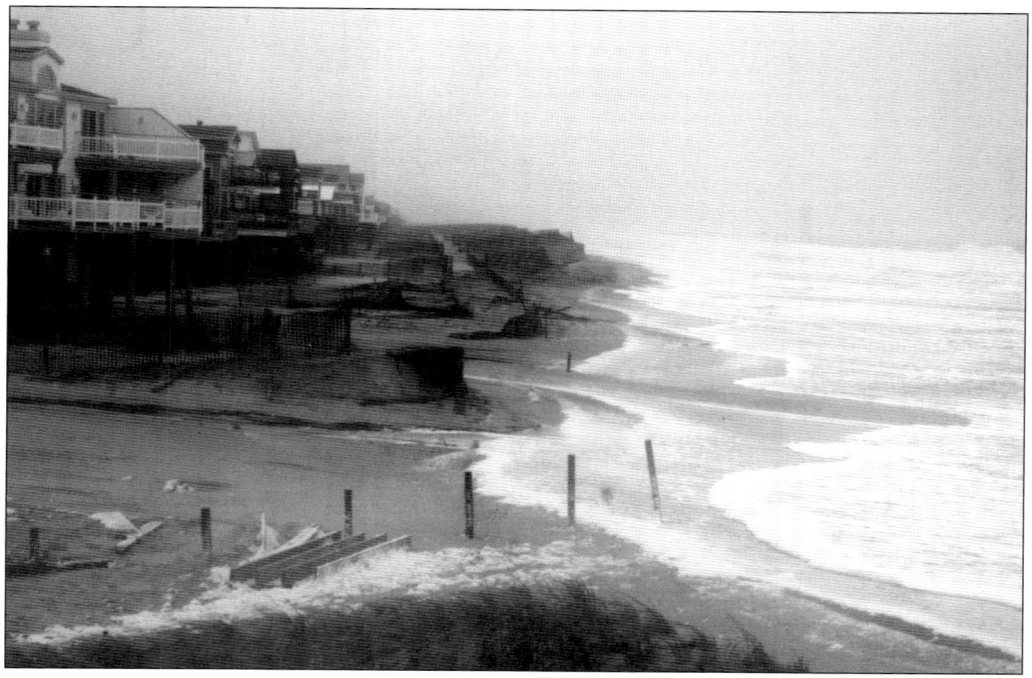

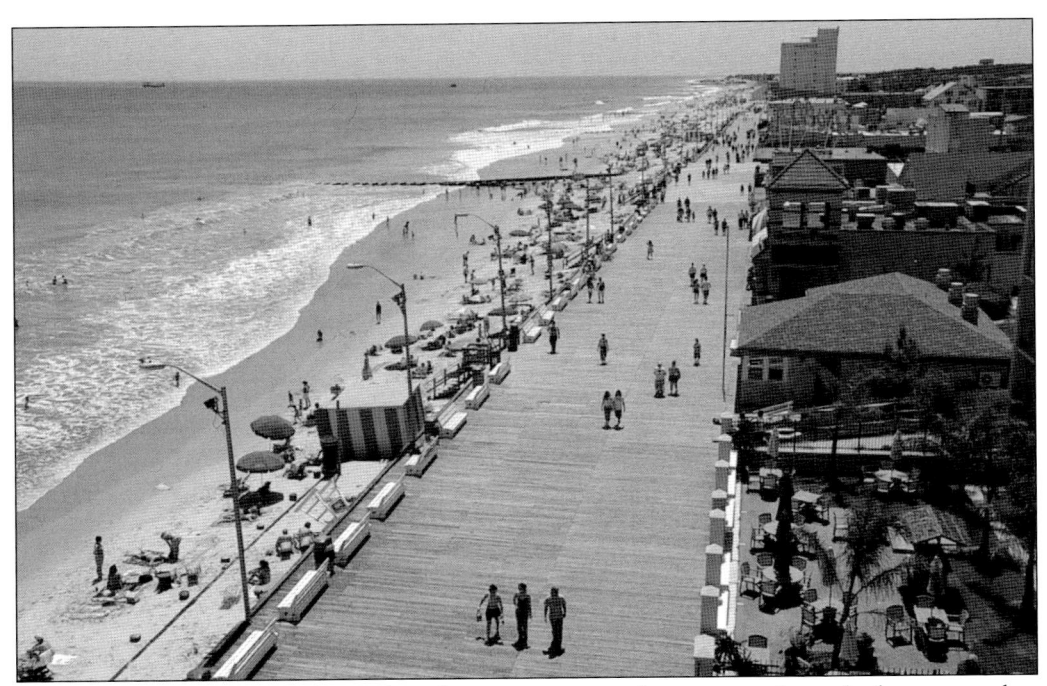

The status of the coast today is that the community is fortunate to have far better weather forecasting capabilities, which are constantly improving with better weather data and modeling. People know more about the forces to be expected in severe coastal storms and can therefore design more resilient buildings and infrastructure. They also now have a much better appreciation for the value of wide beaches and dunes in their ability to absorb the energy of large storms before the waves reach buildings and roads. These photographs show Rehoboth's narrow beach without a dune in 2004 (before nourishment, above) and the same section of Rehoboth with a wider and protective beach/dune system after the 2005 nourishment project (below). The work toward more resilient coastal communities is far from done, as indicated by the recent impact of Sandy. But the coast is far better off than it was in 1962. (Both, courtesy Delaware DNREC.)

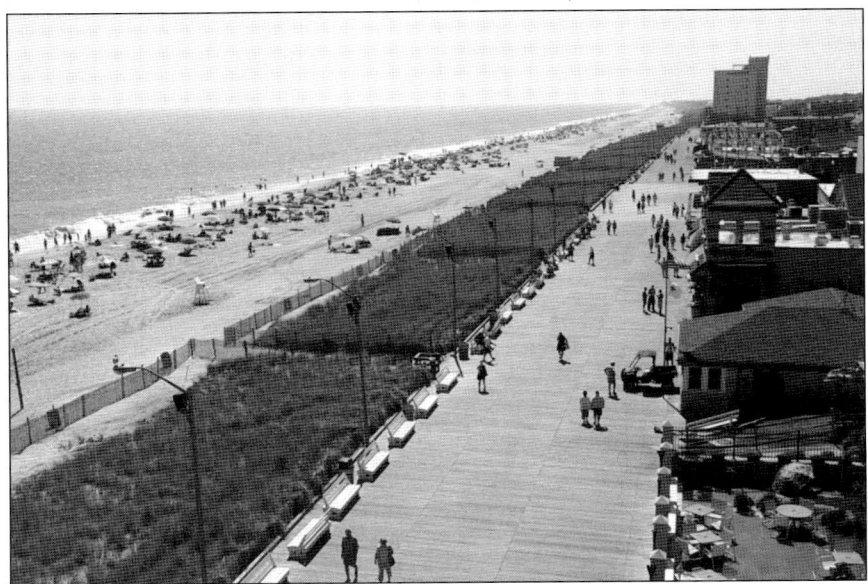

BIBLIOGRAPHY

Carey, Wendy, Evelyn Maurmeyer, and Tony Pratt. *Striking a Balance—A Guide to Coastal Dynamics and Beach Management in Delaware*. Dover, DE: Delaware Department of Natural Resources and Environmental Control, Document No. 40-07-01/04/08/06, 2004.

Climatological Data, Maryland and Delaware—March 1962. Volume 66, No. 3, National Oceanic and Atmospheric Administration, Environmental Data and Information Service. Asheville, NC: National Climatic Data Center, U.S. Department of Commerce, 1962.

Delaware Coastal Storm Damage Report, 1923–1974. Technical Report No. 4, Delaware Coastal Management Program, Document No. 1003-78-01-05. Newark, DE: Department of Geography, University of Delaware, 1977.

Delaware State News. Dover, DE: March 8 and March 12, 1962.

Evening Journal. Wilmington, DE: March 6–March 16, 1962.

Kraft, John C., Elizabeth A. Allen, Daniel F. Belknap, Chacko J. John, and Evelyn M. Maurmeyer. *Delaware's Changing Shoreline*. Newark, DE: Department of Geology, University of Delaware, 1976.

Pictorial Report of Delaware's Great Storm of March 1962. Dover, DE: *Delaware State News*, 1962.

Ramsey, Kelvin W., John H. Talley, and Darlene V. Wells. *Summary Report: The Coastal Storm of December 10–14, 1992, Delaware and Maryland*. Newark, DE: Open File Report No. 37, Delaware Geological Survey, University of Delaware, 1993.

Ramsey, Kelvin W., Daniel J. Leathers, Darlene V. Wells, and John H. Talley. *Summary Report: The Coastal Storms of January 27–29 and February 4–6, 1998, Delaware and Maryland*. Newark, Delaware: Open File Report No. 40, Delaware Geological Survey, University of Delaware, 1998.

The Great Atlantic Coast Storm—March, 1962. Rehoboth Beach, DE: Atlantic Printing Company, 1962.

The Great Northeaster of 1962: Delaware's Coastal Storm of the Century. Dover, DE: Delaware Department of Natural Resources and Environmental Control and Delaware Sea Grant, 2002.

The Storm of '62—From Ruin to Recovery. Seaford, DE: Sussex Printing Corporation, April 1962.

US Army Corps of Engineers, Philadelphia District. *Operation Five-High, March 1962 Storm*. Philadelphia, PA: Civil Works Branch, Construction-Operations Division, North Atlantic Division, 1963.

US Army Corps of Engineers, Philadelphia District. *Post flood Report; Coastal Storm of 6–7 March 1962, Southern New Jersey and Delaware*. Philadelphia, PA: Office of the District Engineer, North Atlantic Division, 1962.

Wilmington Morning News. Wilmington, DE: March 6–March 16, 1962.

Discover Thousands of Local History Books
Featuring Millions of Vintage Images

Arcadia Publishing, the leading local history publisher in the United States, is committed to making history accessible and meaningful through publishing books that celebrate and preserve the heritage of America's people and places.

Find more books like this at
www.arcadiapublishing.com

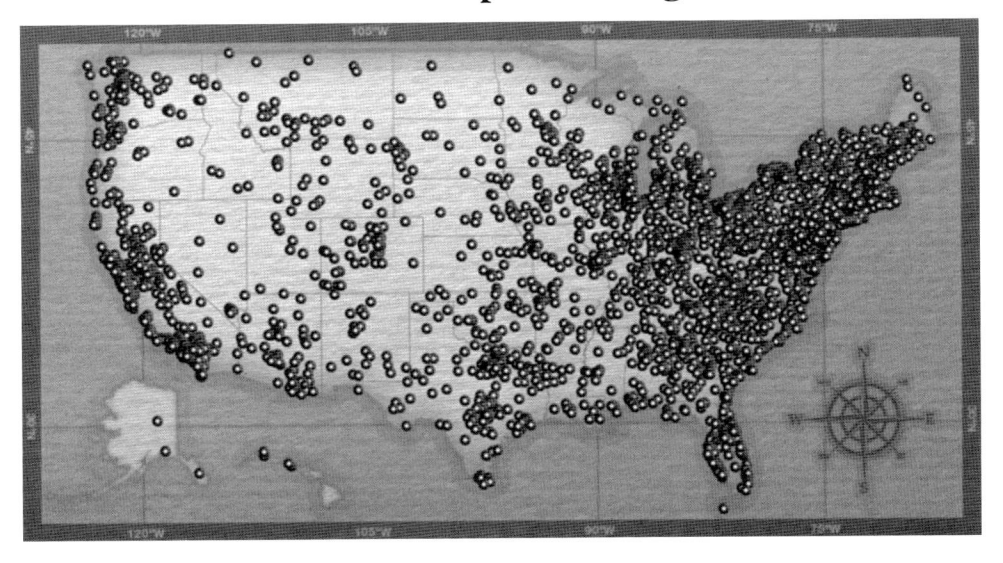

Search for your hometown history, your old stomping grounds, and even your favorite sports team.

Consistent with our mission to preserve history on a local level, this book was printed in South Carolina on American-made paper and manufactured entirely in the United States. Products carrying the accredited Forest Stewardship Council (FSC) label are printed on 100 percent FSC-certified paper.

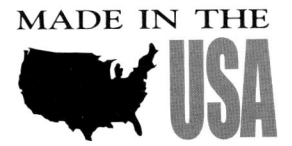

MADE IN THE USA